Patricia Wells at Home in Provence

ALSO BY PATRICIA WELLS

Patricia Wells' Trattoria
Simply French
Bistro Cooking
The Food Lover's Guide to France
The Food Lover's Guide to Paris

Patricia Wells at Home in Provence

RECIPES INSPIRED BY HER FARMHOUSE IN FRANCE

Patricia Wells

PHOTOGRAPHS BY ROBERT FRÉSON

KYLE CATHIE LIMITED

First published in Great Britain in 1997
by Kyle Cathie Limited
20 Vauxhall Bridge Road, London SW1V 2SA

ISBN 1 85626 192 1

Designed by Margery Cantor
Set in Adobe Garamond and Poetica

Clos Chanteduc label and oak tree linoleum cut by Melanie Reim

Patricia Wells is hereby identified as the author of this work in accordance with Section 77 of the Copyright, Designs and Patents Act, 1988

A Cataloguing in Publication record for this title is available from the British Library

Printed in Hong Kong through Worldprint Ltd.

For my editor Maria Guarnaschelli:
With respect and gratitude
for her immense talents,
true friendship,
and certain touch of genius.

ACKNOWLEDGMENTS

IN ESSENCE, THIS BOOK FORMS A SCRAPBOOK OF THE PLEASURABLE YEARS WE HAVE spent in Provence. The days and nights have been greatly enhanced by the presence of friends, family, neighbours, and merchants who have shared our table and helped create a joyous background for life.

I am most grateful to our friends Rita and Yale Kramer, who discovered Chanteduc for us, and to Maggie and Al Shapiro who for more than ten years have helped turn many ordinary days into extraordinary fêtes. Thank you Johanne Killeen and George Germon, Devon Fredericks and Eli Zabar, Sheila and Julian More, for always being willing to shop, cook, and 'faire la fête' at the drop of hat.

Winemakers have played a large role in our lives, beginning with our very own patient and dedicated winemaker, Daniel Combe, and his wife, Chantal. Many restaurateurs have helped expand our knowledge of the region and enhance our enjoyment at the Provençal table: Special thanks to Tina and Guy Julien of La Beaugravière in Mondragon, and to Mireille and Jean-Louis Pons of Le Bistrot du Paradou in Le Paradou.

But most of all, to those who were always present in spirit, our friends in Vaison-la-Romaine. Special thanks to Colette and Jean-Claude Viviani and Colette and Jean-Claude Tricart, who have been with us every step of the way. To our merchant friends: Roland Henny, butcher par excellence, Josiane and Christian Deal of Lou Canestéou, Josiane and Corine Meliani of Les Gourmandines, Giuseppino and Serre Giacomo of La Maison des Pâtes Fraîches, Eliane and Aymar Berenger of the Poissonnerie des Voconces, Hervé Poron, our truffle expert from Plantin in Puymeras, and Laurence and Jean-Marc Avias, who have shared much of their knowledge of Provençal lore.

I feel particularly honoured and humbled to have had the good fortune to work with photographer Robert Fréson, and thank him not only for his stunning photographs but his friendship as well. Thank you also to his assistant, Vicki Moriarity, who enlivened every photo session.

I want to thank my able assistant, Alexandra Guarnaschelli, for her careful editing and invaluable recipe testing, and to Judy Jones for all her careful recipe attention.

At Scribner, I am most grateful to Carolyn Reidy for her support, Pat Eisemann for her publicity ideas, Susan Moldow, Roz Lippel, Olga Leonardo, fantastic designers Margery Cantor and Jenny Dossin, and John Fontana for the beautiful cover.

My greatest respect and admiration go to my editor, Maria Guarnaschelli, who steered me through yet another opus. And of course, to my dear husband Walter Newton Wells: His talents as all-purpose handyman are second only to his ability to keep us on that golden path to true happiness.

CONTENTS

Patricia in her ochre-toned kitchen.

PATRICIA WELLS AT HOME IN PROVENCE

I often wish that Chanteduc could speak, and tell tales of centuries of the labor, love, storms, renovations, celebrations, and happiness it has witnessed over the centuries.

1

PALATE OPENERS
& APPETIZERS

A T CHANTEDUC, THE APERITIF HOUR SIGNALS the end of the work day, the beginning of the play day. Whether it's a lively session with the mason to work out the design on a new bread oven, a social gathering with the winemaker and his wife, or simply a time to catch up on events with neighbours or visiting guests, the end of the day is synonymous with the cocktail hour, the sunset hour. It's then that bottles of anise-flavored pastis and homemade liqueurs, bowls of home-cured olives, thin slices of local black-olive-stuffed sausages, tapenade, and varied cheese spreads are brought out to the sunset terrace, to begin the evening's relaxation in earnest. The following are some of my favourite palate openers, ranging from the simple Smoked Trout Tartare to the elegant Curried Courgette Flowers, food designed to assuage hunger as well as stimulate the appetite for what's to come.

ANNE'S GOATS' CHEESE GRATIN

Anne McCrae is a Scottish neighbour in Provence, who shares my love of simple big tastes. She served this luscious gratin one spring evening and explained that she devised the recipe when she and her husband, John, lived in an isolated part of northern Provence, in the Drôme. There were no fresh produce markets nearby, but thanks to neighbouring farmers she always had plenty of fresh goats'-milk cheese – known as *tomme.* Her larder was always filled with the meaty black olives from nearby Nyons, and wild herbs were as near as the back door. In summer months, Anne prepares the sizzling, fragrant first course with fresh tomatoes, and in the winter months she uses canned tomatoes. That evening, she served the gratin in individual gratin dishes, but I suggested it might be easier to just make one huge gratin and pass it around. 'I used to do that,' she countered, 'but people got greedy and never left enough for the other guests!' So controlled portions it is! This dish lends itself to endless variations: Think of it simply as a pizza without the crust. Add julienned bits of prosciutto, a bit of cooked sausage, sautéed mushrooms, or marinated artichokes. It's also a convenient dish when you're alone and want something warm and quick. I always add fresh hyssop, for the Provençal herb's pungent, mint-like flavour blends well with the tomato-cheese-olive trinity.

EQUIPMENT: Six shallow 15-cm (6-in) round gratin dishes or one 27-cm (10½-in) round baking dish

About 300 g (10 oz) soft goats' cheese, or a mix of rindless soft goats'-, cows'- or sheep's-milk cheese, cubed
2 teaspoons finely chopped fresh hyssop leaves (optional)
2 teaspoons finely chopped fresh rosemary leaves
2 teaspoons finely chopped fresh oregano leaves or a pinch of dried leaf oregano
350-500 ml (12-16 fl oz) thick Tomato Sauce (page 325), at room temperature
About 24 best-quality black olives (such as French Nyons), stoned and halved

1. Preheat the grill.
2. Scatter the cheese on the bottom of the baking dish or dishes. Sprinkle with half of the herbs. Spoon on just enough tomato sauce to coat the cheese evenly. Sprinkle with olives and the remaining herbs.
3. Place the baking dish or dishes under the grill, about 8 cm (3 in) from the heat. Grill until the cheese is melted and fragrant, the tomato sauce sizzling, 2 to 3 minutes.

SERVES 6

WINE SUGGESTION: Think of what you'd normally serve with pizza, a pleasant vigorous red, such as a young French Corbières from the Roussillon, a dry Italian red such as a Barbera d'Alba, an Australian Shiraz or a Californian Zinfandel.

SMOKED TROUT TARTARE

Not far from our village in Provence, there's a trout farm begun centuries ago in the town of Suze-la-Rousse. The farm smokes its own salmon trout, curing it lightly with the local olive oil. I always have the delicacy on hand and love to serve it plain on rounds of homemade toast topped with nothing but snippets of dill from my garden. I also prepare it 'tartare-style', that is hand-chopped bits tossed with crème fraîche and dill. The dish is easy to prepare, and requires nothing more than a sharp knife and clean cutting board. (Do not attempt it in the food processor: even if you are careful, the mixture turns mushy. Hand-chopping brings out the quality and flavour of the fish that tends to be masked by the food processor.) If top-quality salmon trout is not available, substitute smoked trout or smoked salmon. Usually no salt is necessary, since the smoking process imparts a pungency of its own.

This makes a great appetizer served either with drinks in the living room or individually plated and served before the first course. Accompany with slices of toasted bread or with Provençal Olive Oil Brioche (page 167) prepared with added fennel.

> About 125 g (4 oz) thinly sliced smoked trout or smoked salmon
> 2 tablespoons double cream or crème fraîche
> 2 tablespoons fresh dill or fennel fronds, snipped with scissors

1. Trim any unwanted bits and ends from the fish. Lay each slice flat on a cutting board and cut into thin matchstick-sized strips, keeping the strips evenly aligned. Cut these across into tiny cubes of fish about the size of the fat end of a pencil. (You want a kind of elegantly chunky, not a mashed, tartare.)
2. In a bowl, lightly mix the fish with the cream and herbs.
3. Serve on chilled salad plates with tiny mounds of dressed herbs or lettuce alongside. If desired, garnish with additional fennel or dill. Or, serve atop slices of freshly toasted bread, such as the variation of Provençal Olive Oil Brioche (page 168) prepared with added fennel seeds.

MAKES ABOUT 250 ML (8 FL OZ), TO SERVE 4

WINE SUGGESTIONS: A dry white wine goes nicely with this smoked tartare: Try a fresh and fragrant French Sancerre, an oak-aged Californian or New Zealand Fumé Blanc, or a Californian or French Riesling.

HERB-CURED FILLET OF BEEF: CARPACCIO

This is a fabulous preparation, ideal for those who love the qualities of a classic carpaccio, but look for more herbal flavours in their food. Quite simply, a fillet of beef is marinated for 48 hours in a mixture of sea salt, tarragon, parsley, basil and thyme, then sliced very thinly, carpaccio-style. The herbs permeate the beef, making for a lively delicious warm-weather appetizer. Serve as you would any carpaccio, with thin slices overlapping on a chilled salad plate, drizzled with olive oil and plenty of coarsely ground black pepper. For a wholesome salad, drape slices of cured beef over dressed rocket, then continue with the oil and the Parmesan shavings. (I find that the beef stays perky and fresh for 3 days more. If any is leftover, chop it finely, form into patties and fry it up as a luxury hamburger.) Note that the herbs need not be stalked here, since they are used simply to flavour the beef and will not be consumed.

500 g (1 lb) fillet of beef, rinsed and patted dry
8 sprigs of fresh tarragon, rinsed and dried
8 sprigs of fresh parsley, rinsed and dried
8 sprigs of fresh basil, rinsed and dried
10 sprigs of fresh thyme, rinsed and dried
1½ tablespoons coarse sea salt

1. On a piece of foil large enough to wrap the beef, place half the herbs in a single bed. Sprinkle with half the salt. Place the beef on top of the herbs. Add the rest of the herbs and the salt on top of the beef. Wrap securely in the foil and place on a large plate to catch any juices that might run from the beef. Refrigerate for 48 hours.
2. Two hours before serving the beef, transfer to the freezer to firm it up and to facilitate slicing.
3. Unwrap the beef. With the tip of a knife, brush aside the herbs and salt. With a very sharp knife or an electric slicer, cut the beef as thinly as possible.

SERVES 20

WINE SUGGESTIONS: A good choice here would be a red Sancerre, a Tavel rosé or – if you can find a bottle – a Ladoix-Serrigny from northern Burgundy, a wine that marries remarkably well with the flavours of rare or raw meat.

LOU CANESTÉOU'S CHEESE CHIPS

These cheese chips make an ideal appetizer – the richness and the saltiness stimulate the palate, as all good appetizers must. I prepare these with the firm Provençal sheep's milk cheese I buy at the our village cheese shop, Lou Canesteou. The earthy, buttery cheese (which resembles sheep's milk cheese from the Basque region of France) melts beautifully, and rewards the palate with a tangy richness. You will have greater success if the cheese is grated while cold, so the cheese doesn't clump up or stick to the bowl.

125 g (4 oz) sheep's milk cheese or Dutch Gouda, rind removed

1. Preheat the grill.
2. With a hand grater, grate the cheese into a small bowl.
3. With your fingers, sprinkle 1 tablespoon of grated cheese into a 5-cm (2-in) round (like a small cookie), on a cold non-stick baking sheet. Take care to spread the cheese out as thinly as possible, so it cooks evenly. Leave enough space between rounds to allow the cheese to spread out as it cooks.
4. Place the baking sheet under the grill, about 8 cm (3 in) from the heat. Watch the cheese very carefully as it bubbles, turns lacy and browns slightly, 1 to 2 minutes. When the bubbling subsides, the chips can be removed from the grill. If some of the chips are not fully cooked at the edges, rotate the pan and hold them under the heat until they are done. (If making chips in batches, take care that the baking sheet is cooled before continuing the next batch.)
5. Allow the chips to cool and firm up, 1 to 2 minutes. Using a spatula, carefully transfer the chips to a cooling rack. Serve as appetizers. (The chips can be stored in an airtight container for up to 1 week.)

MAKES 25-30 CHIPS

WINE SUGGESTIONS: The ideal wine here, is of course a few sips of bubbling pink champagne. Short of that, try for a Clairette de Die from the Drôme, or a white wine that likes cheese, such as an Alsatian Riesling or Pinot Gris, or a Swiss Fondant.

FACING PHOTOGRAPH: *A selection of local goat and sheep's milk cheese from our fromagerie, Lou Canestéou. Top left box:* Square *mascaré, prepared from a mix of half goat and half sheep's milk and enveloped in dried chestnut leaves; tiny* chèvre au poivre, *pure goat's milk cheese flavoured with black peppercorns; the larger* chèvre à la sarriette, *goat's milk cheese flavoured with a sprig of fresh summer savory; Banon, made with 95 percent goat's milk and 5 percent sheep's milk, wrapped in dried chestnut leaves. To the right is a jar of* chèvre à l'huile, *young goat's milk cheese preserved in olive oil with fresh herbs. Top right box: A selection of local goat's milk cheese flavoured with* poivre d'âne, *the Provençal name for peppery summer savory. Middle left box: An assortment of local goat's milk cheese from a farm in nearby Buis-les-Baronnies – one natural and one aged and covered with ash. Middle right box: An assortment of* Picodon de Dieulefit, *goat's milk cheese ripened with a washing of brine and wine and aged in earthenware pots, giving the cheese a sharp edge. Bottom box: An assortment of goat's milk cheese curds (*chèvre caillé*), draining in antique earthenware moulds.*

JR'S PRAWNS WITH BASIL

When I first offered cooking classes at Chanteduc, French chef Joël Robuchon volunteered to inaugurate the school. I would have been a fool to turn him down! He came with an entourage and prepared a feast to remember. I was up at 5 a.m. to fire up the bread oven for his homemade sourdough rolls and begin work on guinea fowl stuffed with foie gras and set on a bed of potatoes, a recipe we worked on together for our book *Simply French*. The lunch began with sips of cool, bubbly champagne and the following delicacies: Golden, deep-fried Mediterranean pastry twisted around sea-fresh langoustines, and dipped in a vibrant green basil sauce.

At home, fresh giant prawns are a worthy substitute. For a festive and elegant winter touch, the basil leaves wrapped around the prawns can be replaced by thin slices of fresh black truffles. The truffles do a remarkable job of bringing out the iodine-rich flavour of the sea.

2 bunches of fresh basil, leaves only, washed and dried

1 tablespoon coarse sea salt

3 tablespoons extra-virgin olive oil

2 spring onions, peeled and finely chopped

Several tablespoons chicken stock (if necessary)

Fine sea salt and freshly ground white pepper to taste

12 large prawns, peeled and deveined

About 3 sheets of filo pastry

12 small toothpicks

Vegetable oil (peanut or safflower) for deep-frying

1. Set aside about 12 leaves of basil for decoration. In a large saucepan, bring 1 litre (1¾ pints) of water to a rolling boil over high heat. Add the coarse sea salt and the remaining leaves of basil. Blanch for 2 minutes. Transfer to a fine-mesh sieve and refresh under cold running water to stop further cooking and maintain the rich green colour. Drain again. Transfer the leaves to the bowl of a food processor and purée. Set aside.

2. In a medium-size frying pan, combine the olive oil and spring onions and cook gently over low heat until just softened, 3 to 4 minutes. Add the onions to the basil purée and stir to blend. Set aside. (This can be done several hours in advance.)

3. At serving time, warm the basil purée in the top of a double boiler set over lightly simmering water. If the basil purée is too thick, add a bit of warmed chicken stock to thin it.

4. Season the prawns with salt and pepper. Cut the filo into pieces about 15 cm (6 in) square. Place a prawn at the corner of each piece of pastry. Place a basil leaf on top of the prawn and roll tightly in the paper. Twist each end in opposite directions to form a bow. Secure by piercing the prawn in the centre of the roll with a toothpick. Repeat for the remaining prawns. The prawns should not be rolled in advance.

5. Place the oil in a heavy 3-litre (5-pint) saucepan, or use a deep-fat fryer. The oil should be at least 5 cm (2 in) deep. Place a deep-frying thermometer and a wire skimmer in the oil and heat the oil to 160°C (325°F). Add the reserved basil leaves and fry until crisp, 1 to 2 minutes. Remove and transfer to paper towels to drain. Season each side of each leaf with fine sea salt. Set aside.

6. Bring the oil to 190°C (375°F). Fry the prawns in batches, three to four at a time, until the pastry is crisp and lightly browned, about 1 minute. Remove and transfer to paper towels to drain.

7. To serve as appetizers, place the prawns and the basil leaves on a large warmed platter. Place the warmed basil purée in a small bowl for dipping. To serve as a first course, place a prawns on a small warm plate. Place a bit of warmed basil purée around the prawns and add a few fried basil leaves for decoration. Serve additional sauce on the side.

SERVES 12

WINE SUGGESTION: Champagne is the ideal accompaniment here. For a very festive occasion, try a vintage pink champagne, from the house of Veuve Clicquot.

TIP: Ever have a problem with fried food sticking to the skimmer when you attempt to retrieve fried food? It won't happen if you warm the skimmer as you heat the oil.

CURRIED COURGETTE FLOWERS

Everyone who has a garden in Provence grows courgettes, and with that versatile green vegetable (which grows from the female portion of the plant) you have the advantage of the showy golden flowers, which sprout from the male portion. The flowers – which grow in Provence from June to early September – are always picked in the early morning, while they are still firm and closed. At our local farmers' market, farmers sell the home-grown flowers in neat bundles. One Saturday a farmer offered me a baker's dozen, making it 13. Then he asked if I was superstitious, and I said, 'No.' He responded that he was, so he upped the number to 14 flowers for the evening's appetizer!

The flowers are extremely delicate and fragile and should be cooked the day they are picked. Place the stems in a vase of water as soon as possible, to keep them fresh and unwilted. If courgette flowers are not readily at hand, the same deep-fried delicacies can be prepared with fresh courgette slices.

This batter is much lighter than a classic fritter, or beignet, batter prepared with eggs. The idea was inspired by chef Joël Robuchon, who has a great love for curry powder and its magical ability to stimulate the appetite. The resulting flavour of these deep-fried flowers is quite haunting, almost a spicy caramelized candy-like treat. I usually prepare these with guests in the kitchen, so they can eat the flowers as soon as they are cooked.

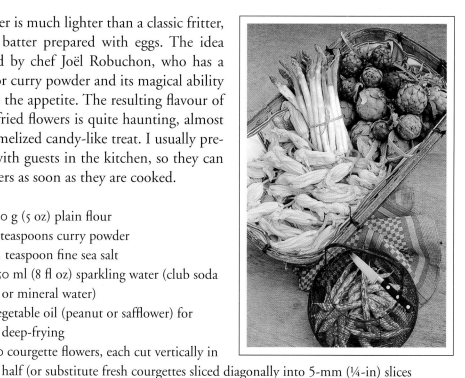

150 g (5 oz) plain flour
2 teaspoons curry powder
¼ teaspoon fine sea salt
250 ml (8 fl oz) sparkling water (club soda or mineral water)
vegetable oil (peanut or safflower) for deep-frying
20 courgette flowers, each cut vertically in half (or substitute fresh courgettes sliced diagonally into 5-mm (¼-in) slices

1. In a large shallow bowl, whisk together the flour, curry powder, and salt. Add the sparkling water and whisk only until the batter is smooth. (Overbeating will build up the gluten in the flour and make the batter rubbery). Set aside for at least 10 minutes, to allow the gluten to relax. (The batter can be prepared a day in advance and refrigerated, covered, until needed.)
2. Place the oil in a heavy 3-litre (5-pint) saucepan, or use a deep-fat fryer. The oil should be at least 5 cm (2 in) deep. Place a deep-frying thermometer and a wire skimmer in the oil and heat the oil to 190°C (375°F).
3. With tongs or your fingers, dip each section of the flowers (or courgette slice) into the batter, rolling them to coat evenly. Shake off any excess batter.
4. Carefully lower the flowers, a few at a time, into the oil. Fry until golden on all sides, turning once, for a total cooking time of about 2 to 3 minutes. Fry only about 6 pieces per batch. (Make sure that the oil returns to 190°C/375°F before adding each new batch.)
5. With the wire skimmer, lift the flowers from the oil, drain and transfer to paper towels. Immediately season each side of each petal or courgette slice with sea salt and serve.

MAKES ABOUT 40

WINE SUGGESTIONS: I enjoy this with champagne (who wouldn't?), a glass of sparkling white Vouvray from the Loire Valley, or a Clairette de Die from the Drôme.

PORQUEROLLES ISLAND TOASTED ALMONDS

One summer while dining on the French Mediterranean island of Porquerolles, we were served a glass of the easy-going local white wine along with a small bowl of these fragrant almonds, toasted with fresh thyme, coarse salt and a touch of olive oil. I instantly added the almonds to my repertoire at Chanteduc, anticipating the day I can make them with a crop from my newly planted almond trees. In the winter time, I prepare these just as guests are arriving: The toasted thyme fills the house with a heady aroma that shouts Provence! loud and clear.

125 g (4 oz) unblanched almonds
2 teaspoons extra-virgin olive oil
2 teaspoons fresh thyme, leaves only
2 teaspoons coarse sea salt

1. Preheat the oven to 200°C/400°F/gas mark 6.
2. In a large, shallow bowl, combine all the ingredients and toss with your hands thoroughly to coat the nuts with salt, oil and thyme. Transfer to a non-stick baking sheet, spreading the nuts out in a single layer.
3. Place in the centre of the oven and toast until the nuts are lightly browned and a fragrant aroma of thyme wafts from the oven, about 4 minutes. Remove the baking sheet from the oven. Serve warm or at room temperature. The almonds can be stored, well sealed, for up to 2 weeks.

MAKES ABOUT 125 G (4 OZ) NUTS

Everything ends this way in France—everything.
Weddings, christenings, duels, burials, swindlings,
diplomatic affairs—everything is a
pretext for a good dinner.

JEAN ANOUILH

SCRUBBED TOAST

So what's the big deal about 'scrubbed toast'? Try it, and you'll see. This is my favourite version of this Catalan classic, one that depends heavily upon superb hearth bread with a thick appealing crust, really ripe red tomatoes and best-quality anchovies. Be sure to begin by rubbing the garlic along the crusty edge, to enhance the aroma and flavour.

6 thick slices of country bread, preferably homemade
1 plump fresh garlic clove, peeled and halved
1 large ripe tomato, halved crosswise
12 anchovy fillets in salt (page 330) or 12 canned anchovy fillets in olive oil, drained

1. Grill the bread – preferably – over an open fire. Alternatively, toast under a grill or in a toaster. While the bread is still hot, rub one side of each slice with the halved garlic, beginning at the crusty edge, then moving over the rest of the toast. Literally 'scrub' the toast with the tomato – cut side toward the bread – rubbing until each slice fully absorbs the tomato juice and the seeds coat the bread.
2. Place 2 anchovy fillets on each slice and serve immediately. And don't forget the napkins, for at its best, the bread should be dripping with the juicy ripeness of tomatoes. Serve as an appetizer, or as a quick snack.

SERVES 6

WINE SUGGESTION: This lusty dish calls for your favourite 'daily-drinking red'. Ours is a Côtes-du-Rhône.

The whole Mediterranean, the sculpture, the palms, the gold beads,
the bearded heroes, the wine, the ideas, the ships, the moonlight,
the winged gorgons, the bronze men, the philosophers – all of it
seems to rise in the sour, pungent taste of these black olives between
the teeth. A taste older than meat, older than wine.
A taste as old as cold water.

LAWRENCE DURRELL

SHEILA & JULIAN'S QUICK FOIE GRAS

Sheila and Julian More are good friends and neighbours in Provence, and we've spent many a happy hour together on their lamp-lit terrace with its panoramic view of the mountains and vineyards that dot their village of Visan. In winter months, we move indoors near the fire, where one Christmas night they served an instant version of foie gras cured in salt. The preparation demands much less work than a classic terrine, and the resulting foie gras is uniquely unctuous, smooth, and distinctly elegant. This festive dish should be served as a first course with plenty of freshly grilled toast.

1 fresh duck foie gras (about 500-750 g/1-1½ lb)
About 1 kg (2 lb) coarse sea salt
Freshly cracked black and white peppercorns to taste

1. Prepare the foie gras: With a small sharp knife, gently scrape away any traces of green bile on the exterior of the foie gras. Place the lobe on a large clean towel. With a small sharp knife, scrape off and lift away the clear membrane that covers the outside of the duck liver. Use the point of a knife to guide your fingers into the underside of the lobe, in search of the large blood vessel that runs down the inside. Wherever sinews or vessels are visible, pull gently but firmly to remove them, using your fingers and the point of a knife to go into the foie gras. You may have to poke around a bit to find the vessel, but work slowly and methodically, handling the liver as little as possible. Trim off and discard any visible blood spots or any greenish parts, which would turn the foie gras bitter. Slice the foie gras lengthwise into 2 or 3 equal portions, each weighing approximately 250 g (8 oz).
2. Pour half the sea salt into a deep rectangular vessel (such as a roasting pan). Place the pieces of foie gras on the bed of salt, side by side in a single layer. Cover with the remaining salt (reserving a little for serving). Set aside at room temperature to cure for 2 hours.
3. Remove the pieces of foie gras from the salt. Gently brush away any excess salt with your fingers. Rinse the pieces quickly under cold running water and pat dry with a clean

kitchen towel. (The foie gras will take on a mottled colour as the salt draws blood out of the liver.)

4. To assemble: Place a piece of plastic wrap larger than each piece of foie gras on a flat work surface. Place one of the pieces of foie on the plastic wrap. Using the plastic wrap to help you push, roll the foie up lengthwise, cigar-style, to enclose the foie gras. Gently twist the ends of the plastic to secure and remove any air pockets in the roll. Repeat for remaining foie gras. Refrigerate until firm, at least 2 hours and up to 6 hours, depending upon your schedule.

5. To serve: Place the chilled roll of foie gras on a flat work surface. Remove and discard the plastic. With a sharp knife, slice into 2-cm (¾-in) thick rounds, counting two per serving. Place the slices of foie gras on a chilled salad plate and season generously with freshly crushed black and white peppercorns, and a fine sprinkling of coarse sea salt, if desired. Serve accompanied by a small version of The True Salad's Fan Salad (page 57), a few spoonfuls of Mostarda: Fig & Prune Chutney (page 331) and freshly grilled bread.

SERVES 8-10

Not only are olives and oil omnipresent in Provence, but so are the diverse utensils made from the wood of olive trees: salad tongs, olive picks, salad bowls, and mortar and pestles.

Happy is the family which can eat onions together.
They are, for the time being, separate from the world
and have a harmony of aspiration.

CHARLES DUDLEY WARNER

CRUSTLESS ONION QUICHE

This beautifully golden crustless quiche makes a great Sunday night supper in front of the fire, served with a zesty tossed green salad. I've also served it as a sit-down appetizer at a cocktail party, with a glass of chilled white wine.

EQUIPMENT: One 27-cm (10½-in) round baking dish.

45 g (1½ oz) unsalted butter
500 g (1 lb) onions, peeled
1 tablespoon fresh thyme leaves, carefully stemmed
Sea salt and freshly ground black pepper to taste
Freshly grated nutmeg to taste
4 large eggs
4 tablespoons whole milk
3 tablespoons double cream

1. Preheat the oven to 220°C/425°F/gas mark 7.
2. Generously butter the bottom and sides of a 27-cm (10½-in) round baking dish. Set aside.
3. Slice an onion in half lengthwise. Place the halves cut side down on a cutting board and slice across into very thin slices. Slice the remaining onions in this manner.
4. In a large unheated frying pan, combine the onions, butter, thyme, salt, pepper and nutmeg. Sweat over moderate heat, covered, until the onions are soft, about 8 minutes. They should not caramelize or turn brown. Taste for seasoning. Set aside.
5. Crack the eggs into a medium-size bowl and whisk just to blend. Whisk in the milk and cream.
6. Transfer the onions to the prepared baking dish, using the back of a spoon to even them out. Pour the egg mixture over the onions. Season with additional pepper and nutmeg. Place in the centre of the oven and bake until the top is a deep golden brown and the custard is firm, about 30 minutes. To test for doneness, insert the tip of a knife in the centre of the tart: The tart is done when the knife comes out clean. Do not under-bake, or the tart will be mushy, not firm.

7. Let sit for about 5 minutes to firm up. Serve warm, cut into thin wedges.

SERVES 8

WINE SUGGESTION: I love a light young Viognier with this, but any good drinkable white will do.

VARIATION: To give the tart a Provençal accent: Just before baking, arrange 8 rinsed and soaked anchovy fillets in a pinwheel over the tart. Place a stoned black olive between each anchovy.

∿ **NUTMEG AND DAIRY, A PERFECT MARRIAGE** ∿ Nutmeg is marvellous in savoury dishes as well as desserts. A fruit of the *mystica fragrans*, nutmeg is so perky that a touch of it showered on stir-fried spinach or a hearty braised daube imparts a sweet spiciness as well as whole new layer of flavour. The best marriage, however, is between nutmeg and dairy products. The nutty bite of the nutmeg works magic in cutting through the fat of milk, cream, eggs or cheese. The highest calibre of nutmeg reputedly grows on the island of Grenada in the southern Caribbean. The flavour of nutmeg is richest when it is grated whole as you need it. The same heady, perfumed aroma, and rich oily flavour cannot be achieved with nutmeg that is purchased ready-ground.

HERB CHEESE LYONNAIS

Ever since my first journey to the food-loving city of Lyons nearly 20 years ago, this has been a dish I look forward to sampling each time. The French names for the dish include *claqueret* and *cervelle de canut*, which translate as silkworker's brains. The name echoes back to the days when Lyons was a silk-making capital, and the workers ate this zesty cheese at the everyday bistros called 'machons'. Generally prepared with a blend of *fromage blanc* (a smooth French version of cottage cheese), shallots, garlic, and herbs (chives are essential), the spread is also animated by a bit of white wine, vinegar, and oil.

500 ml (16 fl oz) cottage cheese (full-fat or low-fat)
2 shallots, peeled and finely chopped
1 plump fresh garlic clove, peeled and finely chopped
3 tablespoons fresh chives, snipped with scissors
3 tablespoons fresh tarragon leaves, finely chopped with scissors
3 tablespoons fresh parsley leaves, snipped with scissors
½ teaspoon fresh thyme leaves, carefully stemmed
Fine sea salt and freshly ground black pepper to taste
1 tablespoon dry white wine
1 teaspoon best-quality sherry vinegar
1 tablespoon extra-virgin olive oil
Mixed fresh herbs, for garnish (optional)

1. Place the cottage cheese in the bowl of a food processor and pulse once, just long enough to break up the cheese curds. Add the shallots, garlic, chives, tarragon, parsley, and thyme and process very briefly, pulsing only to blend. Season to taste with salt and pepper. Pulse once again to distribute the seasonings.
2. Transfer the mixture to a 1.5-litre (2½-pint) cheesecloth-lined, perforated mould such as a porcelain *coeur à la crème* mould (or substitute a cheesecloth-lined large sieve) set over a bowl. Cover and refrigerate for at least 24 hours and up to 48 hours.
3. Remove the cheese from the refrigerator. Discard any liquid that has drained from the mould. Transfer the cheese to the bowl of a food processor, add the wine, vinegar, and oil, and pulse to blend. Taste for seasoning. Transfer to a small bowl.
4. Serve either as a dip with raw vegetables, as part of a cheese course, or as a topping for an open-face sandwich, garnished with additional snipped herbs. (The cheese will stay fresh, refrigerated, for up to 2 days. Bring to room temperature to serve.)

MAKES ABOUT 500 ML (16 FL OZ) CHEESE SPREAD

WINE SUGGESTION: An excellent cru Beaujolais – such as a Fleurie or Moulin-à-Vent – would be my choice here.

✧ THE NOBLE SHALLOT ✧   The shallot is the most prestigious member of the onion family. Prized by the French for its delicate nature, both cooked and raw, the flavour that shallot adds to any dish falls somewhere between the aggressive tang of the onion and the subtle power of garlic. It is for this reason that this vegetable flavouring has been nobly selected to play a role in such classic French sauces as Béarnaise. In recipes where the shallot is to be eaten raw, it is essential that the shallot be chopped as finely as possible. The shallot will release a maximum amount of flavour and be more agreeable to eat in small doses. Finely chopped shallots are also excellent in vinaigrettes, or even sprinkled into meat or fish sauces at the last minute to enhance the acidity and flavour of the dish. When buying shallots, avoid any that show signs of sprouting or bruising, they are likely to be tasteless. Be careful to store shallots in a cool place (but not the refrigerator) where they have room to 'breathe', they can spoil easily and a single bad shallot can spoil a whole bunch.

Patricia returns from the market with boxes of colourful primevères, *or primroses.*

*What was paradise but a garden full of vegetables
and herbs and pleasures. Nothing there but delights.*

WILLIAM LAWSON

TOMATO CLAFOUTIS

Why limit clafoutis – that cloud-like creation of fruits baked with a quick and simple batter – to desserts? Colourful with tomatoes, fragrant with fresh thyme, surrounded by a golden egg-and-cheese batter is a favourite summertime dish at our house. I have prepared this with both the traditional round and oval plum tomatoes quite satisfactorily. Serve with a light green salad alongside, and you've got it made. And need I lecture: Only fresh thyme deserves the honour of this dish.

1 kg (2 lb) firm ripe tomatoes
Fine sea salt
2 large eggs plus 2 extra large egg yolks
5 tablespoons crème fraîche or double cream
60 g (2 oz) freshly grated Parmigiano-Reggiano cheese
2 teaspoons fresh thyme leaves, carefully stemmed

1. Preheat the oven to 190°C/375°F/gas mark 5.
2. Core, peel and quarter the tomatoes lengthwise. Place the tomato quarters, side by side, on a double thickness of paper towelling. Sprinkle generously with fine salt. Cover with another double thickness of paper towelling. Set aside for at least 10 minutes, and up to 1 hour, to purge the tomatoes of their liquid.
3. In a small bowl, combine the eggs, extra egg yolks, the crème fraîche, half of the cheese, and half of the thyme leaves. Season lightly with salt and whisk to blend.
4. Layer the tomatoes on the bottom of a 27-cm (10½-in) round baking dish. Pour the batter over the tomatoes. Sprinkle with the remaining cheese and thyme. Place in the centre of the oven and bake until the batter is set and the tart is golden and bubbling, about 30 minutes. Serve warm or at room temperature, cut into wedges.

SERVES 8

WINE SUGGESTION: Any good daily-drinking red is good here. My preference is a young Côtes-du-Rhône.

ROQUEFORT DIP

Half-spread, half-dip, I make this when I'm in the mood for a light cheese that's got a bit of the Roquefort drama on the tongue. It can be served as a dip for raw vegetables (celery is the best), as a spread for crackers or sandwiches, or as part of a cheese course. Prepare it at least one day advance, to allow flavours to mellow.

500 ml (16 fl oz) cottage cheese (full-fat or low-fat)
75 g (2½ oz) Roquefort cheese, at room temperature, broken into pieces
3 tablespoons fresh chives, snipped with scissors
Sea salt and freshly ground black pepper to taste

Place the cottage cheese in the bowl of a food processor and pulse just to break up the curds. Add the Roquefort and chives and process briefly, pulsing once or twice, just to blend. Season to taste. Pulse once again to distribute the seasonings. Transfer to a container, cover securely and refrigerate at least 1 day, to allow flavours to blend and emerge. Bring to room temperature before serving.

MAKES ABOUT 500 ML (16 FL OZ) CHEESE

THE LEGEND OF ROQUEFORT   The legend of Roquefort cheese tells the story of a young shepherd in the rocky Causses region of south-central France. He left an ordinary lunch of bread and sheep's-milk cheese in one of the local limestone caves of the region thinking he would return to it later that day. It was actually several weeks before he retrieved his lunch, discovering an enormous mass of mould. The curious boy tasted the mixture, only to find it was delicious!

Ever since, the maturation period of 3 months to a year takes place in special cool caves in the tiny village of Roquefort-sur-Soulzon. There, limestone cellars 11 stories deep remain an even 8-9°C (45°F), with up to 95 percent humidity, creating a cheese full of character, aroma and flavour. The prized bluish-green-veined Roquefort is actually the third most popular cheese eaten in France, on the heels of Camembert and goats' cheese, or chèvre.

My kitchen is a mystical place, a kind of temple for me.
It is a place where the surfaces seem to have significance, where the sounds
and odors carry the meaning that transfers from the past and bridges to the future.

PEARL BAILEY

MARIE-CLAUDE'S ARMAGNAC CHÈVRE

Marie-Claude Gracia, owner of La Belle Gasconne in the village of Poudenas in south-western France, is one of my favourite French chefs. She likes to serve this regional preparation as an appetizer, with very thin slices of walnut bread and a glass of champagne. The simple combination of fresh, slightly tangy goats' cheese, a touch of sugar, and just a few drops of Armagnac, make for a surprising – almost haunting – palate teaser.

> 1 teaspoon light brown sugar
> Several drops of Armagnac or Cognac
> 125 g (4 oz) very fresh goats' cheese

In a small bowl, combine the sugar and alcohol, stirring to allow the sugar to dissolve. In another small bowl, crush the cheese lightly with a fork. Add the sugar/alcohol mixture and crush again to blend. Taste. Gradually add additional sugar and/or alcohol to taste. Transfer to a ramekin and smooth out with a spatula. (The spread can be prepared up to 1 day in advance, covered and refrigerated. Bring to room temperature before serving.) Serve spread on ultra-thin slices of toasted walnut bread, toasted sourdough bread, or light crackers.

MAKES ABOUT 125 ML (4 FL OZ) CHEESE SPREAD

Poets have been mysteriously silent on the subject of cheese.
G. K. CHESTERTON

CACHAT: PROVENÇAL CHEESE SPREAD

Cachat is an unbelievably tasty cheese spread found at most cheese shops in Provence. The cheesemongers prepare it from leftover bits of cheese, just as the Provençal farmers have for centuries. With the help of such modern gadgetry as the food processor, this is one of the quickest ways I know to give a cheese board a new vibrant flavour. In principle, you can use any bits of just about any variety of leftover cheese. This recipe serves as a simple suggestion of what cheeses to combine. I serve the spread as the cheese course, as part of a cheese course, or as a snack or appetizer, along with Herbed Green Olives (page 49).

About 30 g (I oz) Roquefort cheese, at room temperature
About I25 g (4 oz) goats' cheese, at room temperature
About 2 tablespoons double cream or crème fraîche
I teaspoon eau-de-vie, such as Marc de Provence

If the cheeses are firm, chop them into small pieces. Place all ingredients in the bowl of a food processor and lightly blend, using a quick on-and-off motion. Taste for seasoning and adjust if necessary. The mixture should be slightly chunky and not totally smooth. The flavour should be sharp, almost piquant.

MAKES ABOUT 250 ML (8 FL OZ) CHEESE SPREAD

At the Vaison market: a selection of local olives and tapenades –
various spreads prepared with both black and green olives.

TUNA TAPENADE

Each Tuesday our market in the village of Vaison-la-Romaine is filled with olive and tapenade stands, each merchant trying to outdo the other. This recipe was inspired by a green olive tapenade I sampled one morning in July. Explosively tart with the fresh taste of lemon, this tapenade can be spread on toast as an appetizer, used as a dip for raw vegetables, such as carrots or celery, or at a pinch it can even be tossed with pasta as a quick, last-minute sauce.

1 (190-g/6½-oz) can of tuna packed in olive oil, drained (see Note)
60 g (2 oz) unsalted butter, softened
150 g (5 oz) top-quality green olives (such as French Picholine), drained and stoned
Grated zest of 1 lemon, blanched and refreshed in cold water
2 tablespoons freshly squeezed lemon juice
4 tablespoons fresh basil leaves, finely chopped

With a fork, flake the tuna in the can and transfer to the bowl of a food processor. Add the remaining ingredients and process only until just well blended. The mixture should remain slightly coarse. Taste for seasoning. Transfer to a medium-size bowl and serve at room temperature. (The tapenade can be stored, covered and refrigerated, for up to 3 days.)

MAKES ABOUT 250 ML (8 FL OZ) TAPENADE

NOTE: If the more flavourful tuna packed in olive oil is unavailable, use top-quality white tuna packed in brine. Drain the tuna, discarding the brine.

RUE DE LEVIS 'CAVIAR'

Simplicity never ceases to surprise. How can three pantry ingredients combine to create a taste and texture so appealing? I call this 'spread' of chopped black olives, butter, and coarse sea salt 'Rue de Levis Caviar', since I first sampled it at a restaurant right off Paris's Rue de Levis market and the Parc Monceau in the 17th arrondissement, Le Bouchon de François Clerc. The restaurant makes its own crusty whole wheat bread and serves this spread in little crocks at the table in place of traditional butter.

One would think that with the saltiness of the olives, the coarse sea salt would turn it too aggressively salty. Surprisingly, the salt adds just that right bit of texture, and only serves to open the palate for more to come. Try to use the *sel gris de Guérande*, the famed unrefined sea salt from Brittany. Kosher salt or refined sea salt here would be too dominant. Do not attempt this in the food processor: the resulting spread will be an unappetizing grey, and much too processed. The caviar is most dazzling (no runny streaks of black in the butter) if the olives are fairly dry, so for best results stone and chop the olives and set aside to dry on paper towels for a few hours before making the spread.

60 g (2 oz) best-quality black olives (such as French Nyons), well drained
60 g (2 oz) unsalted butter, softened
½ teaspoon coarse sea salt, preferably *sel gris* from Brittany

1. Stone the olives and finely chop them. Pat dry with paper towels.
2. Place the butter on a plate and mash with a fork. Sprinkle evenly with the salt and the chopped olives. With the fork, carefully mash to incorporate the olives and salt. To keep the colour clear and golden, do not overwork.
3. Transfer to individual crocks or ramekins and smooth out with a spatula. Serve as you would butter. This is particularly good with freshly toasted whole wheat or walnut bread. (The spread can be stored, covered and refrigerated, for up to 1 week. Bring to room temperature before serving.)

MAKES ABOUT 125 ML (4 FL OZ) SPREAD

An assortment of Provençal palate openers, including sausages, homemade bread, and black olives.

ANCHOVY-GARLIC CPISPS

These anchovy-garlic crisps are designed to perk up your appetite, but not assault it. This is a pantry appetizer that can be made in a matter of minutes. Serve as appetizers or chop any leftovers into croutons to toss into salads.

12 anchovy fillets in salt (page 330) or 12 canned anchovy fillets in olive oil, drained
125 ml (4 fl oz) whole milk
3 plump fresh garlic cloves, peeled, degermed and finely chopped
4 tablespoons extra-virgin olive oil
4 slices whole wheat bread, crust removed, cut into strips about 2.5 cm (1 in) wide

1. Preheat the oven to 190°C/375°F/gas mark 5.
2. Rinse the anchovies, discarding any visible bones. Pat them dry and chop finely. Place in a small bowl with the milk and set aside for 15 minutes. Drain, discarding the milk.
3. In a small frying pan, combine the anchovies, garlic and oil. Cook over moderate heat just until the mixture is well-blended and the garlic and anchovies melt into the oil, 2 to 3 minutes.
4. With a pastry brush, brush the strips of bread all over with the anchovy mixture. Place on a non-stick baking sheet and toast in the oven until well browned, turning the bread from time to time, about 5 minutes.
5. Remove the baking sheet from the oven and transfer the strips of bread to a rack to cool. The strips are good warm or at room temperature. They can be stored in an airtight container for up to 1 week.

MAKES ABOUT 20

LEMON-FLECKED OLIVES

The rich meaty tastes of olives and anchovies pair well with the sharp tang of preserved lemons. Here, top-quality anchovy-stuffed olives are tossed with flecks of home-preserved lemons, making for an instant and unusual palate teaser. Guests never fail to ask 'What did you add to these olives?' and then demand the recipe.

> 3 slices of Preserved Lemons (page 319), plus 1 tablespoon liquid from the jar of preserved lemons
> 150 g (5 oz) best-quality anchovy-stuffed green olives, drained (or substitute French Picholine olives, stoned)

Chop the slices of preserved lemon and place them in a small bowl with their liquid. Add the drained olives. Toss to coat the olives with the lemon and liquid. Serve as an appetizer. The olives can be stored (covered securely and refrigerated) up to 1 month.

MAKES ABOUT 150 G (5 OZ) OLIVES

There is no limit to the variety of flavourings added to the green and black olives of Provence: preserved lemon, fresh fronds of fennel, hot pepper, and pickled vegetables.

HARISSA-SEASONED BLACK OLIVES

For those who love the flavour of cumin and cayenne pepper, this olive variation is ideal. I often use these to flavour Anne's Goat Cheese Gratin (page 21) for a pleasant, piquant, change of pace.

> 300 g (10 oz) best-quality black olives (such as French Nyons), unpitted and drained
> 2 tablespoons homemade *Harissa* (page 320), or to taste

In a bowl, combine the olives and *harissa* and toss to blend. Taste for seasoning. Spoon the olives into a jar and shake to blend again. Cover and store, refrigerated, for at least 1 day before sampling and up to 1 month. To serve, bring to room temperature and serve as an appetizer.

MAKES 300 G (10 OZ) OLIVES

ON STORING OLIVES When olives are cured – either with salt, brine, potassium, lye, or ash solution – they are never subjected to high temperatures. Thus, they are a cured, not a cooked product. If you open a jar of olives or have one that has been in the refrigerator for a while, it is possible that a white film has formed on top of the liquid. Not to worry. Simply rinse the olives and store them in water with a dash of salt and vinegar. For even better results, drain the olives, return them to a sterilized jar, and cover them with olive oil. The oil can be recuperated after, used as an olive-infused oil to drizzle over fresh salads and pizzas.

BLACK VERSUS GREEN At the earliest stage of maturity, all olives are green, or unripe. As they age and ripen on the tree, they turn from pale green to reddish brown and then to black. Some varieties are better unripe, and thus are harvested at the green stage, such as the French Picholine or Spanish Manzanilla varieties. For black olives, French olives from Nice or Nyons or Greek Kalamata varieties are a marvel at full maturity. The darker the olive at harvesting, the higher the oil content and the richer the flavour. No matter what the colour when harvested, all olives are bitter and inedible and must be subjected to a curing process – with salt, water, brine, oil, potassium, ash, or lye – to render them delicious.

*I know of nothing more appetizing on a very hot day than to sit
in the cool shade of the dining room with drawn Venetian blinds,
a little table laid with black olives, saucisson d'Arles, some fine tomatoes,
a slice of watermelon, and a pyramid of little green figs baked in the sun.
In this light air, in this fortunate countryside, there is no need
to warm oneself with heavy meats or dishes of lentils. The Midi
is essentially a region of carefully prepared little dishes.*

LEON DAUDET

HERBED GREEN OLIVES

These olives are typical of the appetizers served with drinks before a meal in Provence: A bowl of seasoned olives and a few paper-thin slices of sausage are all you need at cocktail time. The herb mixture only serves as a starting point, for seasoning can be adjusted to personal tastes. I particularly like the interplay of fennel and cumin seed.

300 g (10 oz) best-quality green olives (such as French Picholine), drained
2 fresh bay leaves
½ teaspoon fresh thyme leaves, carefully stemmed
½ teaspoon fennel seeds
½ teaspoon cumin seeds
4 garlic cloves, peeled and crushed
1 tablespoon extra-virgin olive oil
1 teaspoon dried leaf oregano

In a bowl, combine the olives, bay leaves, thyme, fennel, cumin, garlic and oil. Toss to blend. To intensify the flavour of the leaf oregano, rub it between the palms of your hands and let it fall into the olive mixture. Toss once more. Spoon the olive mixture into a jar, and shake to blend again. Cover and store, refrigerated, for at least 1 week and up to 1 month, shaking from time to time for even seasoning. Bring to room temperature before serving.

MAKES ABOUT 300 G (10 OZ) OLIVES

FACING PHOTOGRAPH: *Home-cured and home-seasoned olives and lemon, surrounded by a branch of freshly pickled green olives and fresh thyme, from top: green French Picholine olives seasoned with wild fennel; Chanteduc Black Olives (page 51); green olives seasoned with spicy red peppers; Lemon-Flecked Olives (page 46); Preserved Lemons (page 319); Brine-Cured Black Olives (page 328); and Harissa-Seasoned Black Olives (page 47).*

CHANTEDUC BLACK OLIVES

At Chanteduc we are fortunate enough to have a grove of about 20 olive trees with a pedigree all their own. Our property falls within the geographic limits of the famed olives of Nyons, the only olives honoured with the French AOC, or Appellation d'Origine Contrôlée. The variety of olive is the *tanche*, a plump, purplish-black fruit that is traditionally cured, rather than pressed for its oil.

I always pick the olives around Christmas time, right after the first frost. Once I've cured them – either in brine or in salt – I like to 'doctor' them with varied flavours. This is one of many traditional combinations, with a touch of vinegar to balance the acidity, a good hit of garlic to tempt the appetite, a touch of garden herbs for fragrance and flavour. The flecks of red pepper and oregano make for a simple, appealing appetizer. You can easily adjust it to enliven the cured olives you buy.

300 g (10 oz) best-quality black olives (such as Nyons), unstoned
4 plump fresh garlic cloves, peeled and crushed
2 teaspoons best-quality red wine vinegar
½ teaspoon crushed red peppers (hot red pepper flakes), or to taste
1 tablespoon extra-virgin olive oil
½ teaspoon dried leaf oregano

In a bowl, combine the olives, garlic, vinegar, crushed red peppers and oil. Toss to blend. Rub the oregano between the palms of your hands and let it fall into the olive mixture. Toss once more. Spoon the olive mixture into a jar and shake to blend again. Cover and store, refrigerated, for at least 1 day before sampling, and up to 1 month. To serve, bring to room temperature and serve as an appetizer.

MAKES ABOUT 300 G (10 OZ) OLIVES

✑ **OREGANO, DRIED VERSUS FRESH** ∾ Oregano is the only herb that I prefer dried, rather than fresh. That's because fresh oregano has little flavour and fragrance. Only in drying does the Mediterranean herb truly come to life, imparting a sharp, intense, very mint-like taste and aroma. Be certain to purchase dried leaf oregano (as opposed to the ground version), and rub the broken leaves between the palms of your hands to release its intensity.

FACING PHOTOGRAPH: *Homegrown Salt-Cured Black* Olives de Nyons *(page 326), begin curing with sea salt, fresh bay leaves, thyme, and garlic, which is added later for flavouring.*

We first took possession of Chanteduc on an autumn day such as this, when the leaves were falling
from the vines growing on the stone walls, the grape harvest was over,
and we were looking forward to the opening of the truffle season.

2

SALADS

Fresh greens make me salivate. I can't imagine a truly satisfying, complete meal without salad. In fact, in our home, salad often *is* the meal. Which is why I devote a major portion of my vegetable garden to growing all manner of greens, ranging from Swiss chard (*blette*) to pungent leaves of rocket, to mesclun, that colourful Provençal mix of red and green oak-leaf lettuce, rocket, romaine, chervil, curly endive, and trevise. I've learned to put every herb and bit of green to use somewhere, concocting salads of nothing but herbs (all-tarragon or an All-Star Herb Salad mix of parsley, chives, dill, tarragon, and mint) or a flavourful mix of vegetable tops, including carrot, radish, turnip, fennel, celery, and beetroot tops for The True Salad Fan's Salad. Green beans are a favourite vegetable, and find their way into a variety of salads, as does chicory, a cold-weather standby. Some, like the Cheesemaker's Salad, are there as simple accompaniment, while composed versions such as Saturday Beef Salad honour salad as a meal.

ALL-STAR HERB SALAD

Rather than making herbs part of a green salad, why not make these fresh flavourful greens *the* salad. The idea comes from Paris chef Alain Passard, who years ago served me an all-tarragon salad at his Left Bank restaurant, Arpège. When tarragon is fresh in the market, or your garden overflows with this extraordinarily powerful herb, why not serve it with honour, as a salad all on its own? Years later, chef Passard expanded what I called 'the tarragon tangle' to a full-scale mixed herb salad – just a few well-dressed bites on a small salad plate – as an accompaniment. The idea, really, is to mix and match judiciously. Just don't use so many herbs or they lose their personality. Good combinations include parsley, mint and tarragon. Or, consider an all-mint salad to accompany grilled lamb, the all-tarragon salad to accompany grilled chicken, a sage-heavy salad to accompany roast pork. Other herbs that can be added to the following salad mix include a very judicious addition of hyssop, coriander, sage, chervil and marjoram. Just be sure to include leaves only – no cheating – leaving all stems behind!

1 teaspoon best-quality sherry vinegar

1 teaspoon best-quality red wine vinegar

Fine sea salt to taste

1 tablespoon extra-virgin olive oil

Freshly ground black pepper to taste

60 g (2 oz) fresh flat-leaf parsley leaves, carefully stemmed, rinsed and dried

60 g (2 oz) fresh chives, rinsed, dried and chopped

60 g (2 oz) fresh dill leaves, carefully stemmed, rinsed, dried and chopped

60 g (2 oz) fresh tarragon leaves, carefully stemmed, rinsed, dried and leaves separated

60 g (2 oz) fresh mint, stemmed, rinsed, dried and leaves separated

In a large shallow salad bowl, whisk together the vinegars and salt. Whisk in the oil and pepper. Taste for seasoning. Add all the herb leaves and toss to coat the greens evenly with the dressing. Taste for seasoning. Serve in small portions as an accompaniment to roast chicken, grilled or poached fish.

SERVES 4-6

VARIATION: The dressed salad can also be placed on top of grilled bread that has been brushed with olive oil – in the style of an open-face sandwich.

A varied selection of sage growing outside the pigeonnier, *where the former owner raised pigeons.*

✧ GOING WILD WITH HERBS ∾ Because herbs are very subjective and each person responds differently to any given combination, here are a few basic guidelines for pairing foods with herbs: The idea is to have fun, experiment with different combinations until you find the one that suits a mood or dish. For fish dishes, a light toss of fresh basil, dill or tarragon is excellent. For beef, dill and parsley with a last-minute sprinkling of chives can be a refresher. For lamb, it's amazing what a mixture of dill and mint can do for the flavour of the meat. For vegetables, tarragon and parsley can be a perfect foil for vegetables that have a natural sweetness, such as carrots or tomatoes. For other vegetables that respond more openly to outside flavours, such as the potato, the freedom of choice becomes even broader.

CHANTEDUC WINTER SALAD

In winter months, chicory is a staple in our house. At that time of year, the palate welcomes its clean crispy flavour. This combination of crunchy greens, nutty Parmesan cheese and a tangy lemon always manages to hit the spot!

2 tablespoons freshly squeezed lemon juice
Fine sea salt to taste
2 tablespoons extra-virgin olive oil
Freshly ground black pepper to taste
4 heads of chicory (about 500 g/1 lb)
30 g (1 oz) freshly grated Parmigiano-Reggiano cheese

1. In a large shallow salad bowl, whisk together the lemon juice and salt. Whisk in the olive oil and pepper. Taste for seasoning. Set aside.
2. Rinse the chicory and pat dry. With a small sharp knife, remove and discard the core of each head. Separate each leaf and place in the salad bowl. Toss to coat the leaves evenly. Sprinkle with the cheese and toss again, thoroughly coating the leaves with cheese.
3. Taste for seasoning. Serve immediately, on large dinner plates.

SERVES 4

ɞ BAN THE SALAD PLATE! ɞ I don't know who ever decided that salads should be served on tiny plates or, worse, in tiny bowls. Composed salads need room to breathe, so why not serve them with majesty on a large dinner plate?

THE TRUE SALAD FAN'S SALAD

The title of this salad is a play on words, since in French the word *fane* denotes the tops of root vegetables – such as carrots, radishes, turnips, fennel, celery or beetroot. One evening, chef Joël Robuchon served us a tiny bite-sized salad of mixed root vegetable tops, accompanied by very thin slices of Sheila and Julian's Quick Foie Gras (page 32). The flavours were explosive: The sharp bitterness of the greens helped cut right into the fat of the foie gras, creating an ideal contrast in taste. Since that day my refrigerator has become a repository of ready-to-make salads. And to think as a bona fide salad lover, I wasted years tossing those precious tops!

This recipe is simply a suggestion. Use as many root tops as you can find. Just be certain to snip the tops into very small bite-sized pieces. The salad should be served in very small portions as a counterpoint to rich, fatty foods: Try sautéing rabbit livers or chicken livers quickly in a non-stick pan, then deglaze with a touch of sherry vinegar. Serve the livers alongside the salad. For colour contrast, you can also add very fine juliennes of any of the root vegetables themselves. And remember: Only fresh bright leaves (nothing wilted), and only leaves (no stems allowed!).

> 100 g (3½ oz) tops of very young root vegetables (preferably a mix of carrot, radish, turnip, fennel, celery and beetroot)
> About 2 tablespoons Double Vinegar Vinaigrette (page 318)
> Sea salt and freshly ground black pepper to taste

Wash the root vegetable tops and spin dry. Using scissors, cut the leaves into bite-sized pieces. If necessary, wash and spin dry once again. Place in a large salad bowl, add dressing and toss to coat the greens evenly. Taste for seasoning.

SERVES 4

PROPER TOOLS FOR TOSSING When creating a salad of tiny bite-sized greens such as this, abandon your everyday salad tongs, they're too big and won't properly toss the salad. Instead, use two large serving spoons or soup spoons. They're more compatible with these tiny greens and will do a better job of thoroughly coating the greens with the dressing.

ROCKET & PARMESAN SALAD

Throughout the winter months, rocket – that wild weed which withstands the cold, the wind and even the occasional snow of Provence – is what saves me. On Saturdays, this is our traditional cold-weather lunch – a giant salad of rocket tossed with black olives and cheese, and topped with crispy salty strips of freshly grilled pancetta. In my local market, the salty cured pork is sold as *poitrine-roulé*, a delicious, black-pepper-studded roll of pork breast. If pancetta is not available, substitute a very lean, top-quality bacon. Blanch it for 1 minute in boiling water, then drain thoroughly. Blanching will remove the smoked flavour from the bacon without cooking it.

75 g (2½ oz) thinly sliced pancetta
1 tablespoon freshly squeezed lemon juice
Sea salt to taste
3 tablespoons extra-virgin olive oil
Freshly ground black pepper to taste
A 60-g (2-oz) chunk of Parmigiano-Reggiano cheese
100 g (3½ oz) stemmed rocket leaves (2 bunches), washed and dried
About 24 best-quality black olives (such as French Nyons), stoned

1. Preheat the grill.
2. Cover a grill pan with foil for easier cleaning. Place the pancetta slices side by side on the foil-covered grill pan.
3. Place the grill pan on an oven rack about 7.5 cm (3 in) from the heat. Grill until the pancetta is golden and sizzling, 2 to 3 minutes. Transfer to a double thickness of paper towels to drain. Break into bite-sized pieces. Set aside.
4. In a large shallow salad bowl, whisk together the lemon juice and salt. Whisk in the oil and pepper. Taste for seasoning. Set aside.
5. Using a vegetable peeler, shave the cheese into long thick strips. (If the chunk of cheese become too small to peel, grate the remaining cheese and add to the bowl.) Set aside.
6. Add the rocket to the salad bowl and toss well to coat each leaf thoroughly. Taste for seasoning. Transfer the salad to 4 large dinner plates. Garnish with olives, cheese and pancetta, and serve immediately.

SERVES 4

fines herbes
15Fb kilo
pays: E7

GRATED BEETROOT SALAD

Rich with garlic and a hint of fresh herbs, this is a colourful summertime salad that hits the spot on a hot day. I love to grow beetroots, for they're quite forgiving – even in our harsh Provençal soil – and their vibrant, red-green tops do wonders for brightening up a 'potager'. Use only the freshest baby beetroots – or at least the tiniest you can find in the market – which are sweeter and more flavourful than large ones. Serve this as an accompaniment to cold roast chicken, or as part of a buffet.

VINAIGRETTE

3 plump fresh garlic cloves, peeled and finely chopped

1 tablespoon Dijon mustard

1 tablespoon top-quality red wine vinegar

Fine sea salt to taste

3 tablespoons extra-virgin olive oil

Freshly ground black pepper to taste

500 g (1 lb) fresh raw baby beetroots

1 tablespoon mixed fresh herbs, snipped with scissors (such as a mix of parsley, tarragon, chervil and chives)

1. In a large shallow salad bowl, whisk together the garlic, mustard, vinegar and salt. Whisk in the olive oil and pepper. Taste for seasoning. Set aside.

2. Peel the beetroots. Grate finely in a salad grater, a food mill or a food processor.

3. Transfer to the salad bowl. Toss to coat the beetroots evenly. Add the herbs and toss again. Taste for seasoning. Serve.

SERVES 4

✑ BEETS ARE THE BEST ∾ The beetroot is a vegetable that comes in two parts. Though more commonly used for its violet-red root, the leaves are edible as well (see The True Salad Fan's Salad, page 57). In fact, the contrast in textures and tastes between the leaves and the root can provide an excellent dynamic to any dish.

In the ancient world, the Greeks and Romans ate only the leaves and used the roots for medicinal purposes. Recipes for the root began appearing later on, and in the eighteenth century, the white or 'sugar' beet emerged as a convenient substitute for sugar cane.

When storing fresh beetroots in the refrigerator, separate the tops from the root before wrapping in plastic: Both ends keep longer this way. When buying, look for uniform colour, a lack of blemishes or bruises, and a firm texture.

FACING PHOTOGRAPH: *A local Vaison farmer displays and sells her current harvest of herbs and vegetables.*

*People will do almost anything to be healthy. But what people refuse to do
is eat real food. Why? I don't know. They'll do anything
to avoid cooking broccoli or peeling an orange.*

CAROLYN BERNALARDI, NUTRITIONIST

RED & GREEN SALAD

For pure appetizing colour appeal, give me fresh green food with flecks of red! Green beans prepared in this manner – in boiling water until crisp-tender then plunged into iced water to halt the cooking – are ideal with any vibrant full-flavoured dressing. Add the fresh coriander leaves at the last minute: They will add that hint of orange and sage to the sweet-tender flavour of the beans. Since beans vary in size and tenderness, taste as you cook. Once the beans go from tasting 'raw' to cooked and tender, remove them from the heat.

DRESSING

1 tablespoon best-quality sherry vinegar

Sea salt to taste

3 tablespoons extra-virgin olive oil

2 shallots, finely chopped

1 firm medium tomato

2 tablespoons coarse sea salt

500 g (1 lb) young tender green beans

4 tablespoons fresh coriander leaves, snipped with scissors (or substitute flat-leaf parsley)

1. About 1 hour before serving the salad, prepare the dressing: In a small bowl, whisk together the vinegar and a pinch of salt. Set aside. In another bowl, combine the oil and shallots. Set aside, uncovered, to mellow for about 1 hour.
2. Core, peel, deseed and chop the tomato. Place in a fine-mesh sieve and sprinkle lightly with some of the coarse salt. Set aside to drain.
3. Fill a large pan with 3 litres (5 pints) of water and bring to a boil over high heat.
4. Meanwhile, rinse the beans thoroughly and trim the ends. Cut into 2.5-cm (1-in) lengths. Set aside. Prepare a large bowl of iced water.
5. When the water in the pan has come to a boil, add the 2 tablespoons of sea salt and the beans. Boil, uncovered, until the beans are crisp-tender, about 5 minutes. (Cooking

time will vary, according to the size and tenderness of the beans.) Immediately drain the beans and plunge them into the iced water so they cool down as quickly as possible. (The beans will cool in 1 to 2 minutes. After that, they begin to lose flavour). Transfer the beans to a colander, drain, and wrap in a thick towel to dry. (The beans can be cooked up to 4 hours in advance. Keep them wrapped in the towel and refrigerate, if desired.)

6. To finish: Just before serving, combine the vinegar and oil mixtures, and stir to blend; taste for seasoning. Transfer the beans to a bowl, pour the dressing over the beans, and toss to coat evenly. Add the drained tomatoes and coriander and toss to blend. Taste for seasoning.

7. Serve immediately, as a first course salad or as a vegetable side dish to accompany grilled fish or chicken.

SERVES 4

◡: **CORIANDER CONFUSION** :◡ Coriander provokes a certain amount of confusion, since both the seeds and the leaves are used in cooking, but not to achieve the same purpose. What's more, it goes by so many names: 'cilantro' in Spanish, Mexican and Portuguese cooking, 'Chinese parsley' in Chinese and Japanese cooking, as well as 'Arab parsley', since it is used so freely in Arab cuisine. In South America, one Peruvian tribe is said to so love coriander that their skin gives off its characteristic pungent scent.

The seeds have a milder flavour and are used often in marinades, in pickling, in vinaigrettes, in preparing such French liqueurs as Chartreuse, and in flavouring some cheeses. The seeds also blend well with mushroom dishes, and are a component of such seasoning mixtures as curry and *ras el hanout*, a popular Mediterranean spice blend used to flavour couscous, *tagines* and soups.

As for the leaves, the strong flavour (a combination of orange and sage) suits them for garnishing salads and soups. I prefer to use coriander leaves sparingly, and always on their own. Blend them with other fresh herbs, such as mint, tarragon, sage – and your palate will experience a taste riot! The leaves hold their flavour and colour best when added just before serving. Because of their specific, pungent flavour (detractors say the herb tastes like soap) some cooks prefer to ignore the herb altogether. If that's the case, fresh flat-leaf parsley – its look-alike – is a worthy substitute.

Coriander is a very difficult herb to grow in the garden: It bolts and turns to seed as soon as the weather turns warm. Traditionally, coriander leaves are chewed to neutralize the odour of garlic on the breath. Medicinally, coriander acts as a pleasant stimulant.

TARRAGON GREEN BEAN SALAD

When tiny fresh green beans – *haricots verts* – are in the market I can't get enough of them. Sometimes I'll serve them several nights running, often with a simple grilled salmon or seared swordfish. I prize the combination of freshly picked tarragon, a touch of lemon, a whisper of cream, ingredients that seem delighted to be in the company of crisp, tender green beans.

1 tablespoon freshly squeezed lemon juice
Sea salt to taste
3 shallots, peeled and finely chopped
3 tablespoons crème fraîche or double cream
Freshly ground black pepper to taste
2 tablespoons coarse sea salt
500 g (1 lb) young, tender green beans
4 tablespoons fresh tarragon leaves, snipped with scissors

1. Fill a large pan with 3 litres (5 pints) of water and bring to the boil over high heat.
2. Meanwhile, in a small bowl, whisk together the lemon juice and a pinch of salt. Whisk in the shallots and the crème fraîche or double cream. Taste for seasoning. Set aside.
3. Rinse the beans and trim both the ends. Cut into 2.5-cm (1-in) lengths. Prepare a large bowl of iced water.
4. When the water in the pan has come to the boil, add 2 tablespoons of salt and the beans. Boil, uncovered, until the beans are crisp-tender, about 5 minutes. (Cooking time will vary, according to the size and tenderness of the beans.) Immediately drain the beans and plunge them into the iced water so they cool down as quickly as possible. (The beans will cool in 1 to 2 minutes. After that, they will begin to lose flavour). Transfer the beans to a colander, drain, and wrap in a thick towel to dry. (The beans can be cooked up to 2 hours in advance. Keep them wrapped in the towel and refrigerate, if desired.)
5. If the beans have been refrigerated, bring them to room temperature before serving. To serve, taste the dressing for seasoning. Transfer the beans to a bowl, pour the dressing over the beans and toss to coat evenly. Add the finely chopped tarragon and toss to blend. Taste for seasoning and serve immediately.

SERVES 4-6

YOGURT GREEN BEAN SALAD

This is a favourite 'picnic' recipe, the sort of thing I make when I like to picnic at home. The soothing nature of the yogurt, the gentle sweetness of the beans and the spiciness of the curry create a harmonious trio. Since strengths of curry powder vary dramatically, add the curry powder little by little to the dressing, until the quantity meets your taste. I like to add a touch of tarragon to this at the end, since curry and tarragon is a remarkable pairing.

3 tablespoons full-fat plain yogurt
1 tablespoon freshly squeezed lemon juice
Sea salt to taste
3 tablespoons crème fraîche or double cream
2 teaspoons curry powder (or to taste)
Freshly ground black pepper to taste
500 g (1 lb) young tender green beans
2 tablespoons coarse sea salt
2 tablespoons fresh tarragon leaves, snipped with scissors (optional)

1. In a small bowl, whisk together the yogurt, lemon juice, salt and crème fraîche or double cream. Slowly add the curry powder to taste, stirring well to blend after each addition. Taste for seasoning and set aside.

2. Fill a large pan with 3 litres (5 pints) of water and bring to the boil over high heat.

3. Meanwhile, rinse the beans and trim both the ends. Cut into 2.5-cm (1-in) lengths. Prepare a large bowl of iced water.

4. When the water in the pan has come to the boil, add 2 tablespoons of salt and the beans. Boil, uncovered, until the beans are crisp-tender, about 5 minutes. (Cooking time will vary, according to the size and tenderness of the beans.) Immediately drain the beans and plunge them into the iced water so they cool down as quickly as possible. (The beans will cool in 1 to 2 minutes. After that, they will begin to lose flavour). Transfer the beans to a colander, drain, and wrap in a thick towel to dry. (The beans can be cooked up to 2 hours in advance. Keep them wrapped in the towel and refrigerate, if desired.)

5. If the beans have been refrigerated, bring them to room temperature before serving. To serve, toss the beans and dressing to coat evenly. Taste for seasoning, Add the finely chopped tarragon and toss to blend. Taste for seasoning and serve immediately.

SERVES 4-6

PEAR & WATERCRESS SALAD

Pears and watercress are happy partners: They add a crunchy quality, while the delicate flavour of the pears tone down the pepperiness of the cress. To bring out their maximum flavour, bring the pears to room temperature. Serve this dish as part of a cheese and salad course with an assortment of varied blue cheeses, that might include Roquefort, Fourme d'Ambert and Stilton.

2 firm ripe Comice pears, at room temperature, peeled, cored and cut lengthwise
   into 16 slices
1 tablespoon freshly squeezed lemon juice
Fine sea salt to taste
2½ tablespoons extra-virgin olive oil
Freshly ground black pepper to taste
Large bunch of watercress, cleaned and stemmed

1. About 30 minutes before serving time, prepare the dressing and marinate the pears: In a large shallow salad bowl combine the lemon juice and salt and stir to dissolve the salt. Slowly add the olive oil and stir to blend. Season with pepper. Add the sliced pears and gently toss to coat with the dressing. Set aside to marinate for about 30 minutes.
2. At serving time, add the stemmed watercress and toss to blend thoroughly. Transfer to large serving plates and serve with the cheese assortment (see above).

SERVES 4

WINE SUGGESTION: A fruity fragrant dry white with good acidity, such as an Alsatian Riesling, will play off the contrast between the sweet pears and the salty blue cheeses.

PARMESAN & CELERY SALAD

One rainy October day in Italy's Piedmont region, chef Caesar Giaccone took a friend and me to Belvedere, a small bustling trattoria in the village of Serravalle Laghe. The owner, Laura Brusco, served a version of this salad as a welcoming antipasto: fresh diced celery enhanced with a touch of nutty Italian Parmigiano-Reggiano cheese. I like to prepare this with a slightly lemony sauce, and serve it quite chilled, making for an ultimately refreshing first course. Thin slices of fresh fennel would be a worthy substitute for the celery. Serve with freshly toasted homemade bread, to absorb the flavours.

    2 tablespoons freshly squeezed lemon juice
    Sea salt to taste
    4 tablespoons extra-virgin olive oil
    Freshly ground black pepper to taste
    4 diced celery hearts, with leaves (or substitute thinly sliced fennel, with fronds)
    About 12 shavings of Parmigiano-Reggiano cheese

1. In a small bowl, whisk together the lemon juice and salt. Whisk in the oil and pepper. Taste for seasoning. Add the celery and toss to coat evenly with the dressing. Cover and refrigerate for a minimum of 2 hours, to allow the celery to absorb the flavours of the dressing. Toss occasionally.
2. To serve, place portions of the celery salad in mounds on small salad plates. Sprinkle generously with freshly ground black pepper. Top with shavings of Parmigiano-Reggiano cheese and serve.

SERVES 4

∽ CELERY FOR HANGOVERS ∾ On festive occasions, the Romans would make wreaths of celery leaves and place them on their heads as crowns. The purpose? They believed the head-dresses would negate the effects of the potent wine taken with the meal and, hence, protect them from hangovers.

SALAD OF ROQUEFORT, WALNUTS, CHICORY & LAMB'S LETTUCE

This salad is a hearty and colourful variation on the traditional trio of chicory, Roquefort and walnuts. I sampled it one Sunday at a favoured 'no-name' restaurant, really a funky sort of bistro situated in an antiques barn in the village of Isle-sur-la-Sorgue in Provence. I like the addition of delicate lamb's lettuce, and the creamy dressing in place of a traditional vinaigrette. And if lamb's lettuce is not available, in this instance, fresh watercress leaves would be a worthy substitute.

60 g (2 oz) Roquefort cheese, at room temperature

2 tablespoons crème fraîche or double cream

3 tablespoons freshly squeezed lemon juice

Freshly ground black pepper to taste

2 heads of chicory (about 250 g/8 oz)

150 g (5 oz) lamb's lettuce or watercress

60 g (2 oz) whole walnut pieces

1. In a large shallow salad bowl, make a dressing by whisking together one-quarter of the Roquefort with the cream and lemon juice. Taste for seasoning. Set aside.

2. Rinse the chicory and pat dry. With a small, sharp knife, remove and discard the core of each. Slice each lengthwise into eighths, and place in the bowl.

3. Wash the lamb's lettuce or watercress in several changes of water, being sure to eliminate all sand or dirt. Thoroughly spin dry. Break into individual leaves, discarding the stems. Add to the chicory in the bowl.

4. Add the dressing and toss to coat the leaves thoroughly with dressing. Sprinkle with the walnuts and remaining cheese, crumbled. Toss again.

5. Serve immediately on large dinner plates.

SERVES 4

◡: **THAT LEAF CALLED LAMB'S LETTUCE** :◡ Ever wonder why we call it lamb's lettuce? One day European shepherds observed lambs nibbling greedily at a leaf growing wild in the fields and wondered what all the fuss was about. The shepherds took a taste and the rest is history. Lamb's lettuce – which the French call *mâche* and the Provençal call *doucette* – takes kindly to cold wet weather and is therefore available at the times of year when the selection of other appealing salads may be limited. With its delicate green petals, lamb's lettuce grows in little bunches or 'flowers'. It has a very subtle flavour and the French use it to complement strong flavours in a salad. It has a smooth, agreeable texture and balances out strong cheeses, meats or other more powerful vegetables for any mixed salad. Notably, *mâche* also cuts through the abrasive edge found in chicories, rocket, and endive. To get the best out of lamb's lettuce, trim away any yellow leaves, cut the small stem of dirt off the bottom and wash thoroughly and carefully.

TOUTOUNE'S WINTER SALAD

I think of this salad as a winter vitamin pill – all crunchy, healthy, wholesome. I sampled a version of it one February evening at Chez Toutoune, a long-time favourite Parisian bistro. The white-on-white tone makes one assume there's just a single ingredient, but soon your palate is surprised by the complex mix of flavours, all tangy, perky, and cleansing.

4 heads of chicory, trimmed and cut into matchsticks
2 firm acidic apples, such as Granny Smiths, peeled and cut into matchsticks
4 tablespoons crème fraîche or double cream
2 tablespoons freshly squeezed lemon juice
Sea salt and freshly ground white pepper to taste

1. In a large bowl, combine the chicory and apples.
2. In a small bowl, whisk together the crème fraîche, lemon juice and seasoning. Taste for seasoning.
3. Pour the dressing over the salad and toss to coat the fruit and chicory thoroughly with the dressing.
4. Serve on large dinner plates.

SERVES 4

~ **ON CHICORY** ~ Contrary to what one would think from its bright white and yellow-tinged leaves, chicory grows in the dark in sandy soil. It is a resilient and versatile vegetable. When stored in a plastic bag in the refrigerator, chicory will stay crisp for at least a week. If it has been stored for a few days before actual use, just peel off the first few layers of leaves that may turn green or brown with time. Incidentally, when buying chicory, discolouration of the leaves, especially a green hue, can indicate lack of freshness. In France, chicory is revered as a winter vegetable excellent for garnishing meats and game. Even more common are salads that mingle the delicate bitterness with the sweetness and acidity of apples or oranges.

If a recipe calls for it cooked, heads of chicory are best left whole, otherwise they tend to break up and cook to a purée. For salads and other raw preparations, remove the middle core at the base of the chicory to take out excess bitterness that can be unpleasant and overpowering.

FRENCH CAFÉ SALAD

This is an embellished version of a classic French café salad, often a toss of chicory, Roquefort and walnuts. I've added the pear for a touch of sweetness and smoothness of texture. The fruit also serves as a contrast to the saltiness of the nuts and cheese, the crunch of the chicory. The chives add another dimension, a snappy pungency that wakes up the tastes buds. It's a great luncheon dish, a meal all on its own, quick and easy to prepare and applauded by all salad lovers. If chicory is not readily available, substitute Cos lettuce, sliced on the diagonal.

> 1 tablespoon freshly squeezed lemon juice
> Fine sea salt to taste
> 4 tablespoons walnut oil or extra-virgin olive oil
> Freshly ground black pepper to taste
> 1 firm ripe Comice pear, at room temperature, peeled, cored, and cut into 16
>   lengthwise slices
> 4 heads of chicory, rinsed, trimmed, leaves separated but left whole
> 75 g (2½ oz) Roquefort cheese
> 60 g (2 oz) walnut halves, toasted and cooled
> 3 tablespoons fresh chives, snipped finely with scissors

1. In a large shallow salad bowl, whisk together the lemon juice and salt. Whisk in the oil and pepper. Taste for seasoning.
2. Add the sliced pear and gently toss to coat with the dressing. Add the chicory, Roquefort, walnut halves, and chives, and toss thoroughly, until the ingredients are equally distributed and evenly coated with dressing.
3. Season again with pepper and arrange on individual salad plates.

SERVES 4

⌁ **A NOTE ABOUT GROWING CHIVES** ≻ If you grow chives in your window box or garden, be sure to snip them regularly. They'll grow back more quickly and evenly. When I know I'll be away for a few weeks, I cut them back all the way, and am assured of fresh, green chives on my return.

DANIEL'S CHICKPEA SALAD

Daniel Combe is our winemaker, and he also keeps us supplied with plenty of home-grown chickpeas, which he raises to feed the household pig (with which he makes extraordinary sausages and pâtés.) He knows I am a fan of his earthy, exceptionally tasty beans, and often I'll return home and find a fresh sack of beans at the front gate. This recipe presents a very pure and uncomplicated way of preparing the nutty-flavoured beans, and a variation that is as delicious warm in the winter as it is chilled in the summer.

A few rules: Always buy dried beans from a shop that has good turnover. You're more likely to get beans that are fresher and more flavourful. Be certain to salt the beans only after they have cooked about halfway through. Adding any acid or minerals – including salt – at the beginning will make for tough beans that will never cook all the way through. If you live in an area with very mineral-rich, hard water, you might want to cook beans in filtered or distilled water. Some people add a pinch of bicarbonate of soda to offset the hardness, but use this only for the soaking period. Adding to the cooking period would alter the flavour of the beans. And be sure to chop the garlic as finely as possible, so that as it cooks it all but melts into the sauce of the beans.

Serve this salad as part of a large summer buffet, or as a winter side dish to accompany roast poultry.

> 250 g (8 oz) dried chickpeas
> 2 tablespoons extra-virgin olive oil
> 6 plump fresh garlic cloves, finely chopped
> Bouquet garni: Several sprigs of fresh summer savory, thyme, rosemary and 1 fresh
>   bay leaf, tied in a bundle with cotton twine
> 2 teaspoons fine sea salt, or to taste
>
> VINAIGRETTE
> 1 tablespoon best-quality red wine vinegar
> 1 tablespoon best-quality sherry vinegar
> Sea salt to taste
> 6 tablespoons extra-virgin olive oil
> Freshly ground black pepper to taste
> 1 teaspoon fresh or dried savory leaves

1. Rinse and drain the chickpeas. Place in a large bowl, add boiling water to cover and set aside for 1 hour. Drain and rinse the beans, discarding the water. Set aside.
2. In a large heavy-bottomed pan, combine the olive oil, garlic and the bouquet garni, and stir to coat with the oil. Cook over moderate heat, until the garlic is fragrant and

soft, about 2 minutes. Do not let it brown.

3. Add the chickpeas, stir to coat with oil and cook for 1 minute more. Add 2 litres (3½ pints) of cold water and stir. Cover, bring to a simmer over moderate heat, and simmer for 1 hour. Season with salt. Continue cooking at a gentle simmer until the beans are tender, about 1 hour more. Stir from time to time to make sure they are not sticking to the bottom of the pan. Add additional water if necessary. (Cooking time will vary according to the freshness of the beans.)

4. While the beans cook, prepare the vinaigrette: In a small bowl, combine the vinegars, season with salt and whisk to blend. Add the oil and whisk once more. Season with savory leaves and freshly ground black pepper. Set aside.

5. When the chickpeas are tender, remove them from the heat and drain off any remaining liquid in the pan. Remove and discard the bouquet garni. Transfer the beans to a large bowl and, while they are still warm, add the vinaigrette and toss to blend. Taste for seasoning.

6. Serve either warm or at room temperature. (The salad can be prepared up to 2 days in advance. Bring to room temperature to serve. Toss again and taste for seasoning before serving.)

SERVES 8-10

꙳ A SAVORY TIP ꙳ Savory is often called 'the bean herb' since its sweet flavour interacts naturally with beans – both fresh and dried – and helps brighten their flavour. But it is also reputed to help combat digestive problems associated with a diet rich in beans and cabbage. In herb gardens, summer savory is delicate annual, while winter savory – *sarriette* in French – is an evergreen perennial. Both have quite a spicy, peppery, almost camphor-like taste, like a blend of strong thyme and oregano. Savory should be used sparingly until the palate becomes accustomed to its potency. *Sarriette* grows wild all over Provence, where it is called *poivre d'âne* (donkey's pepper) in French and *pèbre d'aï* in the Provençal language. A fresh or dried sprig of the herb is often used to heighten the flavours of delicate goats'- and sheep's-milk cheeses.

SATURDAY BEEF SALAD

When I make 18-Minute City Steak (page 255) during the week, I always save any leftover meat for this hearty wintertime salad for Saturday lunch. Chunks of rare beef are tossed with a fiery dressing of horseradish, mustard and tiny pickled gherkins (cornichons), along with fresh steamed potatoes.

About 20 small French pickled gherkins, thinly sliced
1 teaspoon Dijon mustard, or to taste
2 teaspoons prepared horseradish
Sea salt and freshly ground black pepper to taste
About 250 g (8 oz) rare cooked beef, cut into bite-sized chunks
1 small red onion, peeled and cut into thin rings
2 tablespoon best-quality red wine vinegar
6 tablespoons extra-virgin olive oil
750 g (1½ lb) firm, waxy, yellow-fleshed potatoes, such as Pink Fir Apple
About 12 leaves of Cos lettuce, washed, rinsed and broken into bite-sized pieces

1. In a large shallow salad bowl, combine the pickles, mustard, horseradish and stir to blend and to coat the pickles evenly. Season with salt and pepper. Add the beef and toss to coat evenly. Set aside.

2. In another large shallow bowl, combine the onion, vinegar and salt and stir to dissolve the salt. Whisk in the oil, season with pepper and taste for seasoning. Set aside about 2 tablespoons of vinaigrette for the lettuce.

3. Scrub the potatoes but do not peel them. Bring 1 litre (1¾ pints) of water to a simmer in the bottom of a steamer. Place the potatoes on the steaming rack. Place the rack over simmering water, cover, and steam until a knife inserted into a potato comes away easily, 20 to 30 minutes.

4. Immediately peel the potatoes. Cut across into thin slices and drop the hot potatoes into the vinaigrette. Toss to blend and coat the potatoes evenly. Taste for seasoning.

5. Combine the potato and the beef mixtures and toss to blend. Set aside at room temperature for at least 1 hour for the flavours to mellow.

6. To serve, taste for seasoning. Toss the 2 tablespoons of vinaigrette with the lettuce. Place a bed of lettuce on 4 large salad plates. Place a mound of salad on the lettuce and serve. (The beef and potato portion of the salad will stay fresh for 2 to 3 days, refrigerated and stored in a sealed container.)

SERVES 4

WINE SUGGESTION: This salad calls out for a fruity young Beaujolais. My favourite is the Beaujolais cru, Saint-Amour.

CHEESEMAKER'S SALAD

Deep in the rugged, misty and mountainous Auvergne region in Central France, one still finds men who live and work in *burons*, tidy two-story grey stone shepherd's huts. Their lives are devoted to the daily ritual of making the rustic, earthy mountain cheese known as Salers. When I visited cheesemaker Raymond Dutrery some years back, we shared slices of his fruity lactic cheese – so intense it tastes of mountain flowers – and talked of what sort of dishes he prepared in his humble dwelling.

When salad time rolled around, Monsieur Dutrery explained that he dressed his lettuce with fresh cream – always on hand – and he loved the way the cream coated the tender lettuce. For the salad, he first softened thin rings of shallots in homemade red wine vinegar, tossed them with tender, delicately flavoured lettuce, then added the cream as a grande finale. The result is a vibrant-flavoured, tangy salad that pairs beautifully with a platter of rich mountain cheeses such as the French Cantal or Salers, or a farmhouse Cheddar.

> 2 shallots, peeled, sliced into thin rings, rings separated
> 1 tablespoon best-quality red wine vinegar
> 1 head of mild, delicately flavoured lettuce, such as butterhead, washed and well-rinsed
> Fine sea salt to taste
> 2 to 3 tablespoons double cream

1. In a large shallow salad bowl, toss the shallots and vinegar to thoroughly coat the shallots. Set aside for at least 15 minutes and up to 4 hours to soften the shallots.
2. At serving time, add the lettuce, toss to coat with vinegar and shallots and season with salt.
3. Add the cream, tablespoon by tablespoon, tossing gently to coat the leaves. Taste for seasoning and serve on large salad plates.

SERVES 4

SLICED ARTICHOKE & PROSCIUTTO SALAD

Four of my favourite ingredients – artichokes, rocket, prosciutto and Parmesan – are linked in this terrific salad. Four intense flavours and textures, a salad that sings of good health. I sampled a more sophisticated, carefully layered version of this salad one evening at an Italian restaurant in Paris – Il Cortilo – but prefer this more casual rendition.

1 tablespoon freshly squeezed lemon juice
Sea salt to taste
3 tablespoons extra-virgin olive oil
Freshly ground black pepper to taste
1 fresh globe artichoke
60-g (2-oz) chunk of Parmigiano-Reggiano cheese
75 g (2½ oz) thinly sliced prosciutto, cut into matchsticks
90 g (3 oz) stemmed rocket leaves (2 bunches), washed and dried

1. In a large shallow salad bowl, whisk together the lemon juice and salt. Whisk in the oil and pepper. Taste for seasoning. Set aside.
2. Prepare the artichoke: As you would break off the tough ends of an asparagus spear, break off the stem of the artichoke to about 2.5 cm (1 in) from the base. Carefully trim and discard the stem's fibrous exterior, leaving the edible and highly prized inner, almost-white stem. Cut off the top quarter of the artichoke. Bend back the tough outer green leaves, one at a time, letting them snap off naturally at the base. Continue snapping off leaves until only the central cone of yellow leaves with pale green tips remains. Lightly trim the top cone of leaves to just below the green tips. Trim any dark green areas from the base. Halve the artichoke lengthwise. With a grapefruit spoon or melon baller, scrape out and discard the hairy choke. Place the artichoke half, cut side down, on a clean work surface. Using a very sharp knife, slice the halved artichoke lengthwise into paper-thin slices. Toss them with the vinaigrette and taste for seasoning.
3. Using a vegetable peeler, shave the Parmesan cheese into long thick strips directly into the bowl. (If the chunk of cheese become too small to peel, grate the remaining cheese and add to the bowl.) Toss to blend. Add the prosciutto and toss to blend. Add the rocket, toss to coat the leaves thoroughly. Add several grindings of fresh pepper and taste for seasoning. Serve immediately on large dinner plates.

SERVES 4

◡ **PROSCIUTTO** ◡ When cutting the prosciutto into matchsticks, do this carefully: You may stack the slices, but do this while the prosciutto is cold, and with a very sharp knife.

Fresh artichokes at the Vaison market.

✌ **ARTICHOKE TIP** ∾ Here's advice I've taken from French chefs: The next time you prepare a fresh artichoke, don't cut the stem, but break it. Place the artichoke on a cutting board, wrap your hand around the stem, and sharply break it off at the edge of the table. Along with the stem, you will remove the tough and fibrous strands that can give an artichoke a chewy and tough texture.

✌ **ON STORING ARTICHOKES** ∾ Not only is an artichoke loaded with vitamins A, B1, B2 and C but it is also equipped with potassium, calcium, phosphorus and iron. Despite its splendid excellent flavour and health virtues, it is a vegetable that does not keep well; hence, prepare them as soon as you can once you bring them home. If you must store before using, keep the artichokes by peeling the outer layer of skin off the stem with a vegetable peeler and placing them in a stout glass or vase of water. The removal of the outer skin will precipitate the absorption of water and prevent the stems from drying out. After all, the artichoke is a member of the thistle family – so why not treat it like the flower it is?

MONKFISH BOUILLABAISSE WITH AÏOLI

I created this vibrant golden soup one summer afternoon after the local fishmonger – Eliane Berenger – presented me with a plump glistening monkfish fresh from the Mediterranean. Here chunks of mild-flavoured, firm-textured monkfish are bathed in a tomato-rich broth punctuated with the sharp, lively flavours of fennel, saffron, garlic and orange zest. A dab of garlic-rich aïoli adds a crowning touch to this modern-day bouillabaisse. Options: grouper, sea bass, cod.

1 kg (2 lb) very fresh monkfish, bone-in
2 tablespoons extra-virgin olive oil
1 head of plump fresh garlic, cloves separated and peeled
1 teaspoon fennel seeds
Bouquet garni: A generous bunch of flat-leaf parsley, celery leaves, fresh bay leaves
  and sprigs of thyme, tied with string
2 teaspoons sea salt, or to taste
2 tablespoons tomato paste
2 tablespoons pastis or anise liqueur
1 can (400 g/14½ oz) whole plum tomatoes in juice
6 plump ripe tomatoes, peeled and quartered
1.5 litres (2½ pints) water
¼ teaspoon cayenne pepper or to taste (optional)
4 small firm fresh fennel bulbs (about 750 g/1½ lb), trimmed, quartered lengthwise
  and cut into bite-sized pieces
A small pinch (about ¼ teaspoon) of saffron threads
Grated zest of 1 orange
3 tablespoons finely chopped fennel fronds or leaves
1 recipe Aïoli (page 82)

1. Fillet the fish: With a fillet knife, cut away the thin membrane covering the outside of the fish. Cut along one side of the central bone to remove the fillet. Repeat with the other side. Cut the monkfish fillet at an angle into 7.5-cm (3-in) escalopes. (Or ask your fishmonger to do this for you.) Place the escalopes on a large platter, cover and refrigerate until serving time. Cut the bone into bite-sized pieces.

2. In a large heavy-bottomed stock pot, heat the oil over moderate heat until hot. Add the garlic, fennel seeds, bouquet garni, salt, and monkfish bones and sweat – cook gently without browning – for 8 to 10 minutes. This will create a condensed, flavourful soup base. Add the tomato paste, anise liqueur, canned tomatoes, fresh tomatoes, water and cayenne pepper, if using. Cover and bring to a boil over high heat. Reduce the heat and simmer for 45 minutes.

3. Remove and discard the bouquet garni and the monkfish bones. Using a hand blender

(continued on next page)

or immersion mixer, roughly purée the liquid in the casserole. (Alternatively, pass the liquid through the coarse blade of a food mill and return it to the casserole.)

4. Add the sliced fennel bulbs, cover, and simmer gently until soft, 15 to 20 minutes more. (The dish can be prepared several hours in advance up to this point, and reheated when adding the monkfish.)

5. At serving time, bring the liquid to a very gentle simmer to ensure that the soup will be thoroughly heated. Add the saffron and the monkfish and reduce the heat, cooking the fish gently until just tender, 3 to 4 minutes more. Taste for seasoning.

6. To serve, transfer portions of the fish and fennel to warmed shallow soup bowls. Spoon the broth over the fish. Sprinkle with orange zest and finely chopped fennel fronds. Pass the aïoli, allowing guests to swirl a teaspoon or two into their soup. Serve with plenty of toasted homemade bread.

SERVES 4-6

WINE SUGGESTION: I enjoy this with an elegant rich white wine, such as a white Châteauneuf-du-Pape from Château Beaucastel.

AÏOLI: GARLIC MAYONNAISE

EQUIPMENT: A mortar and pestle

6 plump fresh garlic cloves
½ teaspoon fine sea salt
2 large egg yolks, at room temperature
250 ml (8 fl oz) extra-virgin olive oil

1. Degerm the garlic: Peel and cut the garlic in half. If there is a green, sprout-like 'germ' running through the centre of the garlic, remove and discard it. Finely chop the garlic.

2. Pour boiling water into a large mortar to warm it; discard the water and dry the mortar. Place the garlic and salt in the mortar and mash together evenly with a pestle to form as smooth a paste as possible. (The fresher the garlic, the easier it will be to crush.)

3. Add the egg yolks. Stir, pressing slowly and evenly with the pestle, always in the same direction, to blend the garlic and yolks thoroughly. Continue stirring, gradually adding just a few drops of the oil, whisking until thoroughly incorporated. Do not add too much oil at the beginning or the mixture will not emulsify. As soon as the mixture begins to thicken, add the remaining oil in a slow and steady stream, whisking constantly. Taste for seasoning. Transfer to a bowl and serve immediately. The sauce can be refrigerated, well sealed, for up to 2 days. To serve, bring to room temperature and stir once again.

MAKES ABOUT 250 ML (8 FL OZ) SAUCE

FACING PHOTOGRAPH: *Golden aïoli.*

Non-cooks think it's silly to invest two hours' work in two minutes' enjoyment;
but if cooking is evanescent, well, so is the ballet.

JULIA CHILD

SUMMER PISTOU

Our wedding anniversary falls at the tail end of summer, the time our good friends Rita and Yale Kramer make their annual visit. Inevitably, they insist upon preparing an anniversary feast, and inevitably, Yale proudly spends the day chopping and peeling, shelling and simmering, making a memorable version of pistou, or summery vegetable soup. Throughout the season, this also happens to be one of my favourite dishes to prepare and to serve: It's an ideal way to get children who won't eat vegetables to devour them, and after many wasp-troubled meals outdoors, I've learned that wasps don't come near the soup! So hurrah again, for pistou.

This is a dish I call my 'telephone recipe', since I usually line up everything I have to do on the table in the courtyard and then dial up for a chat with friends as I prepare the evening feast. There are as many recipes for pistou as there are cooks who prepare it, and I am particular about what should go into mine. I insist upon an abundance of carrots for colour, a mix of fresh white kidney beans as well as borlotti beans, leeks for a touch of elegance, lots of whole garlic, and plenty of green beans. I like the pasta to be as diminutive as possible, so it doesn't overwhelm.

My recipe differs from more traditional versions in that rather than tossing all the vegetables into the mix at one time, I sweat some of the vegetables first in oil, for better colour and depth of flavour. Finally, I love mixing the traditional Gruyère with the untraditional Parmesan, adding yet another layer of flavour to one of summer's greatest dishes. Note that while the soup starts out a brilliant green to begin with, the colour fades as the vegetables cook. This is why a touch of tomato and carrot are nice, and why a verdant hit of pesto not only thickens the soup, but boosts flavour and colour as well.

THE BEANS:
    500 g (1 lb) fresh small white (navy) beans in the pod, shelled, or 250 g (8 oz) dried small white kidney beans (see Note, page 87)
    500 g (1 lb) fresh borlotti beans in the pod, shelled, or 250 g (8 oz) dried borlotti beans (see Note, page 87)
    3 tablespoons extra-virgin olive oil
    3 plump fresh garlic cloves, peeled and finely chopped
    Bouquet garni: Several fresh bay leaves, several sprigs of summer savory and thyme, tied securely with string
    Sea salt to taste

(continued on next page)

Summer Pistou in the making.

THE SOUP

125 ml (4 fl oz) extra-virgin olive oil

2 medium leeks, white and tender green parts only, cut into thin rings

2 medium onions, peeled and coarsely chopped

10 plump fresh garlic cloves, peeled and quartered lengthwise

4 medium carrots, trimmed, peeled, halved lengthwise, and cut into half moons

500 g (1 lb) potatoes, peeled and cubed

Bouquet garni: Several fresh bay leaves, several sprigs of summer savory and thyme, tied securely with string

250 g (8 oz) courgettes, trimmed, halved lengthwise, and cut into half moons

250 g (8 oz) tomatoes, peeled, cored, and chopped

250 g (8 oz) green beans, trimmed and quartered

Sea salt to taste

100 g (3½ oz) very small pasta shapes, such as conchigliette

1 recipe Pistou (page 316)

125 g (4 oz) freshly grated Parmigiano-Reggiano cheese

125 g (4 oz) freshly grated Gruyère cheese

1. Prepare the beans: In a large, heavy-bottomed saucepan, combine the oil, finely chopped garlic and bouquet garni. Stir to coat with oil. Cook over moderate heat until the garlic is fragrant and soft, about 2 minutes. Do not let it brown. Add the fresh or prepared dried beans and stir to coat with oil. Cook for 1 minute more. Add 2 litres (3½ pints) of water and stir. Cover, bring to a simmer over moderate heat and simmer 5 minutes for fresh beans, 30 minutes for dried beans. Season lightly with salt. Simmer 5 minutes more for fresh beans, 30 minutes more for dried beans. Add additional water if necessary.

2. Meanwhile, start the soup: In a 10-litre (17½-pint) stock pot, combine the oil, leeks, onions and garlic over low heat and sweat – cook without colouring – for 2 to 3 minutes, stirring from time to time. Add the carrots, potatoes and bouquet garni, and soften over moderate heat, stirring regularly for about 10 minutes. This will give a lovely colour to the broth and enrich the final flavour of the soup.

3. Remove and discard the bouquet garni from the beans. Add the beans and their cooking liquid to the vegetables in the stock pot. Add the courgettes, tomatoes and green beans, along with 2 litres (3½ pints) cold water. Simmer gently, uncovered, until the beans are tender, about 20 minutes. (Cooking time will vary according to the freshness of the beans. Add additional water if the soup becomes too thick.) Add the pasta and simmer until the pasta is cooked, about 10 minutes more. Taste for seasoning and adjust if necessary.

4. Serve the soup very hot, passing the Pistou as well as the two cheeses to swirl into the soup.

EIGHT TO TEN SERVINGS

WINE SUGGESTION: A Provençal rosé, such as the fine version from Bandol's Domaine Tempier.

NOTE: If using dried beans, rinse them and pick them over to remove any pebbles. Place the beans in a large bowl, add boiling water to cover, and set aside for 1 hour. Drain the beans, discarding the water. Proceed with the recipe from step 1.

ROASTED TOMATO SOUP WITH FRESH HERBS

At the end of summer, when plum tomatoes are still in abundance in our garden as the days grow cooler, this flavourful soup is perfect. The process of roasting the tomatoes is the same one used to prepare homemade sun-dried tomatoes, yet the tomatoes are baked in a slightly hotter oven, and not nearly as long. What you're looking for is similar to what the French call a *confit*, an intensely flavoured reduced essence of tomato. (Yet unlike the true tomato *confit*, these tomatoes are baked with all their pulp and seeds, making for a less dense, more juicy flavour.) This soup is an ideal gift for anyone who gardens and grows tomatoes.

> 1 kg (2 lb) fresh plum tomatoes
> Fine sea salt to taste
> 4 tablespoons finely chopped fresh herb leaves, such as a mix of summer savory, basil, parsley, and thyme
> About 1 litre (1¾ pints) homemade Chicken or Potager Stock (page 321)

1. Preheat the oven to 130°C/275°F/gas mark 1.
2. Trim and discard the stem end of the tomatoes. Halve each tomato, lengthwise. Arrange the tomatoes, cut side up, side by side, on a baking sheet. Sprinkle lightly with salt and the herbs.
3. Place in the oven and bake until the tomatoes are nearly dried and shrivelled, about 2 hours. Check the tomatoes from time to time: They should still be rather flexible, but not at all brittle, and most of their juice should have baked away.
4. Remove the tomatoes from the oven and allow them to cool slightly. Place a food mill (fitted with its coarsest blade) over a large bowl. Transfer the tomatoes to the food mill and purée.
5. Meanwhile, pour the stock into a large stock pot and bring to a boil over high heat. Add the tomatoes, and stir to blend. Reduce the heat and simmer for about 5 minutes to allow the flavours to mingle. Taste for seasoning. Serve in shallow warmed soup bowls, sprinkled with fresh herbs.

SERVES 4

CURRIED CAULIFLOWER SOUP

While working with chef Joël Robuchon on our book, *Simply French*, he presented me with a series of very complex, multi-step soups, dishes that were favourites at his restaurant. Since I was never able satisfactorily to duplicate some of them at home, the soup recipes never made it into the book. *Crème de chou-fleur*, or cauliflower cream soup, served with a jellied caviar base, has long been one of his most popular dishes. Here, I've taken the easiest portion of the recipe – the cauliflower cream – and added an extra dose of curry powder. The result is a haunting, golden-hued soup, one that could serve as an elegant first course for a winter's feast, or as a homey lunchtime main dish.

> 1 kg (2 lb) cauliflower, trimmed and rinsed
> Sea salt to taste
> 1 litre (1¾ pints) chicken stock, preferably homemade (page 321)
> 2 teaspoons curry powder, or to taste
> 1 large egg yolk
> 150 ml (¼ pint) double cream

1. Break the cauliflower into bite-sized florets. Bring a large pot of water to the boil over high heat. Salt, add the cauliflower and blanch for 2 minutes. Drain and refresh under cold running water.

2. In a large saucepan, warm the stock over moderate heat. Taste for seasoning. Add the cauliflower, cover, and simmer until tender, about 20 minutes.

3. Transfer the broth and cauliflower in small batches to the bowl of a food processor. Purée and return to the saucepan. Simmer over moderate heat until reduced to 750 ml (27 fl oz), about 15 minutes. Season to taste with curry powder.

4. In a large bowl, combine the egg yolk and cream. Whisk to blend.

5. Pour a ladleful of the simmering purée into the bowl with the cream mixture. Whisk vigorously. Return the mixture to the saucepan, place over low heat and cook, stirring constantly with a wooden spoon, until the mixture thickens to a creamy consistency, 2 to 3 minutes. The mixture should not boil. Taste for seasoning.

6. Transfer to warmed shallow soup bowls and serve immediately. (The soup can be prepared up to 1 day in advance and reheated. If necessary, thin out with warm water or milk. The curry flavour and colour will intensify with age.)

SERVES 6

AMAZING SORREL SOUP

While travelling around Germany one summer, I sampled many versions of sorrel soup – a flavour I truly adore – but was astonished and puzzled to find the soups were all a brilliant healthy-looking green. One common problem with cooking sorrel is that the herb loses its happy green colour, turning sort of a dull military drab when heated. It was chef Dieter Müller who shared his secret: Blend the sorrel with butter first, adding it only at the end of the cooking time. Even after the soup has sat for a while, it remains green. I love this soup, hot or cold, and have also prepared it with fresh watercress leaves, a worthy substitute.

> 90 g (3 oz) fresh sorrel leaves, stemmed, thoroughly washed and spun dry (or
>   substitute watercress)
> 45 g (1½ oz) unsalted butter, at room temperature
> 2 tablespoons extra-virgin olive oil
> ½ small onion, peeled and sliced into thin rounds
> 180 g (6 oz) starchy potatoes, peeled and diced
> About 1 litre (1¾ pints) chicken or herb stock, preferably homemade
> 250 ml (8 fl oz) double cream
> Sea salt and freshly ground white pepper to taste

1. In a food processor, purée the sorrel, pulsing on and off for 30 to 45 seconds. Add the butter and purée. Transfer to a small bowl, cover, and set aside in a cool area of the kitchen. (Do not refrigerate or the sorrel butter is likely to be too cold to add to the soup at the end.)

2. In a large saucepan, heat the oil until hot but not smoking. Add the onion and sweat over low heat until soft, 3 to 4 minutes. Add the potatoes and cook over low heat until golden, 10 to 15 minutes. Remember not to cook over too high a heat, or they will burn instead of colouring a beautiful golden brown.

3. Add the chicken stock and simmer for about 20 minutes, or until the potatoes are fully cooked. Stir in the double cream. Using a hand blender or immersion mixer, purée the soup directly in the stock pot. (Alternatively, pass the soup through the coarse blade of a food mill or use a blender. Return it to the stock pot.) The potatoes will give thickness and body to your soup without detracting from the sorrel. Taste for seasoning.

4. Just before serving, whisk the sorrel butter into the hot soup, taking care to mix thoroughly and quickly. Serve in heated soup bowls.

SERVES 4-6

COLD TOMATO SOUP WITH BASIL

I could live on tomatoes: I don't think a day goes by that I don't eat them in a salad, on pasta, in a sauce or in soup. When I wander through our vegetable garden in Provence, the very fragrance of a tomato plant makes me salivate, bringing back a lifetime's memories of backyard gardens and sturdy tomato plants, staked teepee-style, laden with an abundance of ripe red fruit. Still, we never seem to have our fill of home-grown tomatoes, so the local farmers always end up filling in the gap. This quick, easy, healthy tomato soup is ideal on those days when the farmer's markets and garden are bursting with tomatoes. Note that, for deeper colour, the onion is not peeled.

EQUIPMENT: A food mill

2 cloves

1 onion, halved

1 kg (2 lb) firm ripe tomatoes, quartered

4 plump fresh garlic cloves, peeled and quartered

1 celery stalk, finely chopped

2 teaspoons sea salt

1 tablespoon extra-virgin olive oil

500 ml (16 fl oz) water or Potager Stock (page 321)

1 bunch of fresh thyme

2 bay leaves, preferably fresh

4 tablespoons basil leaves, rinsed and patted dry, cut into julienne strips

Several tablespoons crème fraîche or double cream or a few drops of extra-virgin olive oil, for garnish (optional)

Stick a clove into each half of the onion and place in a stock pot. Add the tomatoes to the stock pot along with the garlic, celery, salt, oil, water or stock, thyme and bay leaves. Bring to a boil over high heat, reduce the heat and simmer, uncovered, for 20 minutes. Remove and discard the onions, thyme and bay leaves. Pass the soup through the coarse blade of a food mill into a bowl. Taste for seasoning. The soup can be served either hot or cold, sprinkled with fresh basil. For a richer soup, swirl in several tablespoons of crème fraîche or double cream, or a few drops of best-quality olive oil.

VARIATIONS HERE ARE UNLIMITED: Add any of your favourite herbs to the soup as it cooks. At serving time, add any favourite garnish: A *persillade*, or combination of finely chopped garlic and parsley, would heighten the flavour of the soup, hot or cold. Traditional garnishes for a cold gazpacho – cubed cucumbers, croutons, and cubes of fresh red or green pepper – are also a possibility. Finally, for a thicker soup, served warm or cold, reheat the soup and cook a small handful of vermicelli or very fine angel's hair pasta, simmering until the pasta if cooked through.

SERVES 4-6

CHILLED CREAM OF PEA SOUP

A brilliant green soup with a refreshing touch of mint, this chilled, warm-weather soup has the ability to make one feel instantly healthy and revitalized. The secret of maintaining the true green pea colour is to blanch, then refresh the peas in cold water, thus 'setting' the chlorophyll. The refreshing ice bath also helps maintain their crisp crunch. The addition of mint to the blanching water is a small 'tip', but one that – like so many minor cooking *trucs* – makes the difference between food that's flat and one-dimensional and a dish that is layered with nuanced flavours.

Sea salt to taste
Several sprigs of fresh mint
2 kg (4 lb) fresh peas in their pods or about 750 g (1½ lb) fresh shelled peas
1 tablespoon sugar
250 ml (8 fl oz) homemade chicken or vegetable stock, at room temperature
150 ml (¼ pint) double cream
4 tablespoons fresh mint leaves, cut into julienne strips

1. Prepare a large bowl of iced water.
2. In a large pot, bring 3 litres (5 pints) of water to a rolling boil. Add 1½ tablespoons sea salt, the sprigs of fresh mint and the peas, and blanch just until soft, about 10 minutes. (The peas should be cooked longer than you might normally, since you want them to purée easily.)
3. Immediately drain the peas and plunge them into the iced water so they cool down as quickly as possible. Discard the branches of mint. (The peas will cool in 1 to 2 minutes. If you leave them longer, they will begin to lose flavour). Drain the peas thoroughly.
4. In the bowl of a food processor, combine the drained peas, the sugar, and the stock and purée. Add the cream and mix once again. Pass the soup through the coarse blade of a food mill. The soup should be quite thick – the consistency of a split pea soup. Taste for seasoning. Transfer to a bowl and refrigerate for at least 2 hours, to chill.
5. To serve, taste for seasoning, and transfer to chilled shallow soup bowls, garnishing each bowl with slivers of fresh mint.

SERVES 4

ARTICHOKE, PARMESAN & BLACK TRUFFLE SOUP

One blustery February evening several years ago I sampled this sublime sophisticated winter soup at Guy Savoy's restaurant in Paris. It came as part of a multi-course feast that included perfumed oysters bathed in a jellied cream, a perfectly roasted guinea fowl, and this ethereal soup that combined the nutty flavour of artichokes, the richness of Parmesan and the fragrance of fresh black truffles. The soup was truly one of the best dishes I had tasted in months. I would almost like to title the dish 'clandestine,' for its secrets were surreptitiously gathered by my assistant, Alexandra Guarnaschelli, as she worked in Guy Savoy's kitchens as the fish chef.

Since this is a home version, the black truffle is optional. I add fresh black truffle when preparing a festive feast, for artichokes and black truffles enjoy one another's company: Each accentuates the mysterious earthy flavour of the other. Although I prefer to prepare this with fresh artichokes, I'm aware that many cooks may not be adept at turning out perfect artichokes bottoms. I have tried this recipe with bottled artichokes and find the flavour too dull. However, frozen artichokes – usually sold in packets labelled 'artichoke hearts' – are a worthy substitute.

EQUIPMENT: A food mill

4 tablespoons extra-virgin olive oil
Sea salt to taste
2 shallots, finely chopped
4 globe artichokes (See Note) or two 270-g (9-oz) packets of frozen artichoke hearts, defrosted
250 ml (8 fl oz) white wine, preferably a Chardonnay
750 ml (27 fl oz) chicken stock, preferably homemade
One 60-g (2-oz) chunk of Parmigiano-Reggiano cheese
15 g (½ oz) unsalted butter
1 small black truffle, thinly sliced (optional)

1. In a large non-aluminium saucepan, combine 2 tablespoons of oil, a pinch of salt and the shallots and stir to blend. Cook over moderate heat until golden, 2 to 3 minutes. Do not let the shallots brown, or they will turn bitter. Add the artichokes and toss to blend. Add the remaining 2 tablespoons of oil, and cook, uncovered, until the artichokes are soft and impregnated with oil, about 2 minutes more. Add the wine, pouring it all over the surface of the pan, adjust heat to bring the liquid to a gentle simmer and cook, uncovered, until most of the wine – and alcohol – has cooked off, about 7 minutes from the time the liquid comes to a simmer. (The wine not only adds a pleasantly acidic flavour to the soup, but will also prevent the artichokes from turning brown.) Add the chicken stock, adjusting the heat to create a gentle simmer. Cover, and simmer just until the artichokes are soft and

the flavours have had time to mingle, about 20 minutes more. Taste for seasoning.

2. Place a food mill over a large bowl and purée the soup. (Discard any fibrous bits that remain in the mill.) Return the soup to the saucepan. The soup should be a pleasant golden-green and should have the consistency of a slightly runny purée. If the soup appears thin, reduce it slightly over moderate heat. (The soup can be prepared to this point several hours ahead, and reheated at serving time.)

3. Using a vegetable peeler, shave the cheese in long thick strips into a bowl. (If the chunk of cheese becomes too small to shave, grate the remaining cheese and add it to the bowl.) Set aside.

4. To serve, heat the soup and whisk in the butter to add brilliance and to smooth out the texture. Divide the hot soup among four warmed soup bowls. If you are using them, place the truffle slices on top of the soup, followed by the cheese shavings. If done correctly, the shavings should sit delicately on top of the soup, half-melted, but still intact. Serve immediately.

SERVES 4

NOTE: *To trim artichokes for soup* – Prepare a large bowl of cold water. Halve a lemon, squeeze the juice, and add the juice, plus the lemon halves, to the water. With your hands, break off the stem from the base of each artichoke. Bend back the tough outer green leaves, one at a time, and snap them off at the base. Continue snapping off leaves until only the central cone of yellow leaves with pale green tips remain. Lightly trim the top cone of leaves to just below the green tips. Trim any dark green areas from the base. Since you do not need perfect artichoke bottoms for this soup, the vegetable can be sliced lengthwise, making it easier to remove the choke. With a small spoon or a melon baller, scrape out, and discard, the hairy choke from each half. Cut each trimmed artichoke half lengthwise into 8 even slices. Return each slice to the acidulated water. Repeat for the remaining 3 artichokes. Set aside.

Fresh black truffles, ready for slicing.

WINTER PISTOU

Like a symphony of winter flavours, colours and fragrances, this soup plays a warming tune: The squash and carrots add a brilliant tone, the beans an earthy note, while the turnips play percussion, waking the palate like the sound of cymbals. Anointed with a touch of either summer-like pesto or all-season aïoli, it's the soup I make on Saturdays while puttering about the kitchen with a warming fire in the background.

250 g (8 oz) dried small white kidney beans
250 g (8 oz) dried borlotti beans
125 ml (4 fl oz) extra-virgin olive oil
2 medium onions, peeled and cut into thin half-moons
2 medium leeks, white and tender green parts only, cut into thin rings
1 head of plump fresh garlic, peeled and quartered lengthwise
Sea salt to taste
500 g (1 lb) Hubbard or pumpkin squash, seeded, peeled and diced
500 g (1 lb) potatoes, peeled and cubed
250 g (8 oz) turnips or parsnips, peeled and cubed
Bouquet garni: several fresh bay leaves, several sprigs of summer savory and thyme,
    tied securely with string
4 medium carrots, peeled and cut into thick half-moons
1 small can (400 g/14½ oz) whole plum tomatoes in juice
60 g (2 oz) angel's hair pasta, broken into small pieces
1 recipe Aïoli (page 314) or 1 recipe Pistou (page 316)
125 g (4 oz) freshly grated Gruyère cheese

1. Rinse the beans, picking them over to remove any pebbles. Place the beans in a large bowl, add boiling water to cover and set aside for 1 hour. Drain, discarding the water.
2. In a 10-litre (17½-pint) stock pot, combine the oil, onions, leeks, garlic and 1 teaspoon of salt. Soften over medium heat, stirring regularly for about 10 minutes. This will give a lovely green colour to the broth and enrich the final flavour of the soup. Add the drained beans, stir to blend and cook for 2 minutes more. Add the squash, potatoes, turnips, stir to blend and cook 5 minutes more. Add 5 litres (9 pints) of water, the bouquet garni, carrots and tomatoes. Season with salt and simmer gently, uncovered, until the beans are tender, 1½ to 2 hours. (Cooking time will vary according to the freshness of the beans.) Taste for seasoning. Add the pasta and boil until the pasta is cooked, about 10 minutes more. Taste for seasoning
3. Serve the soup very hot, passing the aïoli or pesto and cheese to blend into the soup.

SERVES 6-8

WINE SUGGESTION: A Provençal rosé: My favourite comes from the Domaine Tempier in Bandol.

CARAMELIZED FENNEL SOUP

Cooking is an art that requires patience, timing and exactitude; however, mistakes can also bring about fabulous results. Sometimes I get so absorbed in a new recipe or idea, that I forget about outside distractions. Other times, a quick break from the kitchen can clear my thoughts and help me realize what result I want to produce. I had a straightforward fennel soup in mind, and as my fennel sweated slowly, peacefully, on my stove, I decided to take a trip to the garden for a few herbs. I returned to my stock pot only to discover that the fennel had caramelized in the oil – producing a fragrant, memorable soup, and one that I now make often, 'on purpose'.

> 1 kg (2 lb) fennel bulbs, trimmed and finely chopped
> 6 tablespoons extra-virgin olive oil
> Bouquet garni: A generous bunch of fresh rosemary, parsley, bay leaf, and thyme,
>   tied with string
> 1 litre (1¾ pints) Potager Stock (page 3210) or Chicken Stock (page 322)
> Sea salt to taste

1. In a large heavy-bottomed stock pot, combine the fennel and oil. Cover over low heat and sweat for 10 minutes. Coat the pieces of fennel with the oil, stirring from time to time to make sure they are not sticking to the bottom of the stock pot. Be certain that the fennel does not burn, for it would give your soup a bitter flavour.

2. After about 10 minutes, remove the lid and let the fennel continue to cook over a low heat. Gradually, the pieces should brown and caramelize. Add the bouquet garni and the stock and simmer, covered, for 30 minutes.

3. Remove and discard the herb bundle. Using an immersion mixer, roughly purée the soup directly in the stock pot. (Alternatively, pass the soup through the coarse blade of a food mill or purée coarsely in batches in a food processor, and return it to the stock pot.) The soup should have a creamy consistency, but not totally smooth. Taste for seasoning. Serve piping hot in warm shallow soup bowls.

SERVES 4

QUICK TIP: Cleaning fennel of its outer skin is a tough chore but well worth the result. To avoid excess loss, try using a vegetable peeler instead of a knife. The peeler will remove the skin without taking too much of the fennel along with it.

QUICK CHICKEN-LEMON SOUP

As a young bride in the 1960's my favourite soup was a version of the Greek lemon soup known as *avgolemono*, or chicken stock enriched with rice, thickened with egg yolks and enlivened by a touch of lemon juice. Recently, I revived and revised it, creating a soup that's a relative of Italy's *straciatella* and Greece's *avgolemono*. This soothing warming soup is a favourite mid-week supper dish, one that can be prepared quickly and painlessly. Here the rice and the yolks gently thicken the stock, while the lemon juice brings out the fresh, clean flavours of the poached poultry. Simple as this soup is, it's elegant enough to present to guests when entertaining. Variations are endless: Sometimes I prepare a vegetarian version with Potager Stock (page 321) and substitute fresh mushrooms for chicken. Season at the last minute with your favourite herbs: Tarragon and lemon grass are naturals with both chicken and mushrooms. The soup is also delicious the following day.

1.5 litres (2½ pints) homemade Chicken Stock (page 322) or Potager Stock (page 321)
100 g (3½ oz) short-grain white rice
1 skinless boneless chicken breast, cut into matchsticks
3 tablespoons freshly squeezed lemon juice
3 large egg yolks
60 g (2 oz) freshly grated Parmigiano-Reggiano cheese
Freshly grated nutmeg, to taste
Sea salt to taste
Freshly ground white pepper to taste
Fresh flat-leaf parsley leaves, for garnish

1. In a large stock pot, bring the chicken stock to a boil over high heat. Reduce heat, add the rice and simmer, covered, for 5 minutes. Add the chicken and simmer for 5 minutes more. Taste for seasoning. (The soup can prepared to this point several hours in advance.)
2. Meanwhile in a large bowl, combine the lemon juice and egg yolks and whisk to blend. Add half the cheese and whisk to blend. Set aside.
3. At serving time, add a ladleful of warm (not boiling) soup to the egg mixture and whisk to blend. Pour the mixture back into the stock pot, whisking briskly until well blended. Add a grating of nutmeg and taste for seasoning. Serve in warmed shallow soup bowls, garnished with the remaining cheese and parsley.

SERVES 4

MAGGIE'S VEGETABLE POTAGE

My good friend Maggie Shapiro is a great cook. Every moment I spend in the kitchen with her, I learn some *truc* that she assumes every worldly housewife would know. One rainy September, as our house was bursting at the seams with guests, Maggie took over kitchen duty, with me as her assistant (pen and notebook in hand). Maggie's secret here is to slightly brown all the vegetables first, then add stock, so each element maintains its own character and flavour. The addition of lettuce is a common French custom, and one we should all add to our vegetable soup-making repertoire. This is a simple, non-frivolous, healthy soup, nothing but vegetables, a touch of olive oil, good stock, and a gentle flourish of Parmigiano-Reggiano cheese.

4 tablespoons olive oil

1 leek, white part only, trimmed, scrubbed, and chopped

Sea salt to taste

3 medium carrots, peeled and chopped

2 turnips, peeled and chopped

2 courgettes, peeled and chopped

2 large potatoes, peeled and chopped

½ head of lettuce (such as Cos), washed, dried, and coarsely chopped

A handful of finely chopped cabbage

1 litre (1¾ pints) homemade chicken stock or vegetable stock, (pages 321 and 3220)

One 60-g (2-oz) chunk of Parmigiano-Reggiano cheese

1. In a large heavy-duty stock pot, combine the oil, leek and 1 teaspoon salt and cook until lightly browned, 4 to 5 minutes. Add the carrots, turnips, courgettes and potatoes in small batches, cooking each several minutes before adding the next. Once all the vegetables are lightly browned, add the lettuce and cabbage and stir vigorously until wilted. There should be almost no liquid left at this point. Add hot water just to cover the vegetables and simmer, covered, until the carrots and turnips are soft, about 25 minutes. Taste for seasoning. Add the stock and simmer, covered, gently for 30 minutes more. Taste for seasoning.

2. While the soup simmers, prepare the cheese. Using a vegetable peeler, shave the cheese into long thick strips into a bowl. (If the chunk of cheese becomes too small to shave, grate the remaining cheese and add it to the bowl.) Set aside.

3. Remove the stock pot from the heat. Using a hand blender or immersion mixer, purée the soup directly in the stock pot. (Alternatively, pass the soup through the coarse blade of a food mill or use a blender. Return it to the stock pot.) Taste for seasoning.

4. To serve, ladle the hot soup into warmed soup bowls and place the cheese shavings on top of the soup. Serve immediately.

SERVES 8

A assortment of winter vegetables at the village market.

❧ **WHAT'S IN A SOUP?** ❧ Originally, *soupe* was the word used to describe the slice of bread used to 'sop' up the liquid contents of the cooking pot, or *potage*. In fact, the terms broth and potage were used until the word 'soup' became the fashionable replacement. Soup, as well as potage, is essentially water to which any combination of solid ingredients, meats, vegetables, fish or fruits is added. Thick soups refer to those that are puréed or strained to give a smooth but thick consistency. Otherwise, a soup is clear, and the ingredients are cooked slowly and served in their broth of cooking juices. Originally, soup served the same basic function as an hors d'oeuvre in the meal. It was a liquid-based dish intended to gently awaken the palate and prepare it for the flavours of the meal. In modern cooking, a soup can make a meal of itself and every country has at least one soup associated with its origins. Examples include Russian borscht, French pot-au-feu and bouillabaisse, and Italian minestrone.

GARLIC FAMILY SOUP

With garlic itself in such fine abundance year-round in the markets, the garlic family all but takes over my garden much of the year. In the autumn, I plant shallots and baby onions to enjoy in the spring time. And in summer I plant leeks for autumn . Chives are there for the asking year-round. It's clear that this recipe was born of the need to do something with the vegetable family! Although the final flavour is very creamy, there's not a touch of cream in the dish.

> 6 leeks, white and tender green part, finely chopped
> Sea salt to taste
> 3 litres (5 pints) water
> 2 medium onions (about 300 g/ 10 oz), peeled
> 6 shallots, peeled and halved lengthwise
> Bouquet garni: Several sprigs of fresh parsley and tarragon, several bay leaves and
>   celery leaves, wrapped in the green of a leek and tied with string
> 1 head of garlic, peeled and halved lengthwise
> 4 tablespoons extra-virgin olive oil
> 750 g (1½ lb) starchy potatoes, peeled and diced
> Finely chopped fresh herb leaves for garnish

1. Trim and rinse the leeks, separating the coarse dark-green portion from the white and tender pale-green portion. Chop the white and pale-green portion. Set aside.

2. Prepare the vegetable stock: In a large stock pot combine the green portion of the leeks, a pinch of salt, and the water. Bring to a boil over high heat. Cover, reduce heat to moderate, and simmer for 15 minutes.

3. Meanwhile, slice an onion in half lengthwise. Place each half, cut side down, on a cutting board and cut across into very thin slices. Slice the remaining onion in this manner.

4. In a heavy-bottomed stock pot, combine the reserved portions of the leeks, onions, shallots, bouquet garni, garlic, olive oil and salt. Sweat, uncovered, over moderate heat, until the vegetables are soft and tender, about 10 minutes.

5. Strain the leek broth and pour it over the vegetables. Add the cubed potatoes. Cover and bring to a simmer over moderate heat. Cook for 1 hour. Remove and discard the bouquet garni. Using a hand blender or immersion mixer, purée the soup directly in the stock pot. (Alternatively, pass the soup through the coarse blade of a food mill or use a blender. Return it to the stock pot.) To serve, transfer to warmed shallow soup bowls and garnish with fresh herbs.

SIX TO EIGHT SERVINGS

FACING PHOTOGRAPH: *The essential flavors of Provence: Fresh thyme, basil, rosemary, bay leaves, garlic, onions, and shallots.*

*From my office window at Chanteduc – I can survey our vineyards as well as
Mount Ventoux and the beginning of the Alps to the east.*

4

VEGETABLES

GIVE ME VEGETABLES, VEGETABLES, AND more vegetables. As a side dish, as the main course, as a solo player, as part of a symphony of wholesome gifts from the earth. Serve them hot, serve them cold, bathe them in olive oil and garlic, grill them, roast them, braise or sauté them. From my modest garden and the soil of Provence come tender violet artichokes, juicy sun-ripened tomatoes, shiny oval aubergines, anise-flavoured bulbs of fennel, buttery white beans or *cocos blancs,* fresh spring peas and late spring broad beans. Preparation can be quick and easy – as in Barcelona Grilled Artichokes or Meaty Grilled Mushrooms – long and slow – as in Pure Tomato Confit or Tender Roasted Shallots – or even an elaborate main-dish vegetarian offering – such as Celery Root Lasagne and Monsieur Henny's Aubergine Gratin. Potatoes take their place of honour in gratins, simply roasted with a sprinkling of salt, smashed with oil and herbs, puréed with olive oil and Parmesan, or simply roasted, as in the favoured Fake *Frites.*

BARCELONA GRILLED ARTICHOKES

Artichokes for breakfast? Why not? Especially if you've just finished touring Barcelona's vivid kinetic covered market and stop at the Bar Pinochio for a bracing espresso, a breakfast of thinly sliced pan-grilled artichokes, fresh-from-the-fishmonger langoustines, fried sweets that are sheer decadence. This artichoke dish is quick and versatile, to be served as an appetizer, a quick vegetarian luncheon dish, or as a particularly complementary accompaniment to roasted or grilled fish.

> 1 tablespoon freshly squeezed lemon juice
> Fine sea salt to taste
> 3 tablespoons extra-virgin olive oil
> 2 plump fresh garlic cloves, peeled and finely chopped
> 4 globe artichokes, 8 baby artichokes, or two 270-g (9-oz) packets of frozen artichoke hearts, defrosted

1. In a large shallow salad bowl, whisk together the lemon juice and salt. Whisk in the oil and garlic. Taste for seasoning. Set aside.
2. Prepare the artichokes if using fresh: As you would break off the tough ends of an asparagus spear, break off the stem of the artichoke to about 2.5 cm (1 in) from the base. Carefully trim and discard the stem's fibrous exterior, leaving the edible and highly prized inner, almost-white stem. Cut off the top quarter of the artichoke. Bend back the tough outer green leaves, one at a time, letting them snap off naturally at the base. Continue snapping off leaves until only the central cone of yellow leaves with pale green tips remains. Lightly trim the top cone of leaves to just below the green tips. Trim any dark green areas from the base. Halve the trimmed artichokes or defrosted hearts lengthwise. With a grapefruit spoon or melon baller, scrape out and discard the hairy choke of the fresh ones. Place the prepared artichoke half, cut side down, on a clean work surface.
3. Using a very sharp knife, slice the halved artichokes lengthwise into paper-thin slices. Toss them with the lemon/oil/garlic mixture. (This can be done up to 2 hours in advance. Set aside, uncovered, at room temperature.)
4. To serve, preheat the grill. Transfer the artichokes in a single layer to non-stick baking sheet. Place the baking sheet about 12.5 cm (3 in) from the heat. Grill until the artichokes are golden and sizzling, 2 to 3 minutes. Transfer to a bowl and toss. Taste for seasoning. Serve.

SERVES 4

VARIATION: For a stove-top version, sauté the artichokes in a non-stick pan with the dressing. Once cooked, toss with freshly grated Parmesan cheese and snippets of fresh flat-leaf parsley leaves.

FACING PHOTOGRAPH: *From top to bottom: Braised Whole Garlic (page 130); Barcelona Grilled Artichokes; and Braised Red Onions (page 130).*

MEATY GRILLED MUSHROOMS

Come October, our pine woods are filled with dozens of varieties of wild mushrooms. Everyone in the village seems to know 'the' spot to find the freshest *girolles* (chanterelles) the reddest *lactaire délicieux* (lactarius) the plumpest *boletus* (bolete). Everyone, expect Walter and me. We can go out for hours at a time and spot not a single *champignon*. Finally, we got smart: We tired of everyone telling us how fertile our

A 'back from the market' still life: bright red currants or groseilles, *fresh radishes, and meaty* sanguines *mushrooms (*lactarius deliciousus*), named for the blood-red juice they give off when sliced.*

woods were and began organizing group hunts, with a fine meal to follow. One of our favourite methods for cooking mushrooms is a simple grill, with a difference. The mushrooms are first grilled, then sautéed, making for superbly moist, full flavoured mushrooms without a touch of dryness. I learned the technique from Benoit Guichard, chef Joël Robuchon's right-hand-man in the kitchen. Any good meaty variety of fresh mushroom can be used here, including cultivated white mushrooms, and chestnut mushrooms. These are also good at room temperature, as well as a topping for pizzas or fougasse.

At the Vaison market, a vegetable merchant greets Patricia with a kiss.

> 500 g (1 lb) meaty mushrooms, rinsed and trimmed
> 2 tablespoons extra-virgin olive oil
> Sea salt and freshly ground black pepper to taste
> 1 teaspoon fresh thyme leaves
> 60 g (2 oz) unsalted butter

1. Cut each mushroom lengthwise into 2.5-mm (⅛-in) slices. Brush both sides of each mushroom slice with oil. Season with salt, pepper, and a little of the thyme.

2. Preheat a gas, electric or a ridged cast-iron stove-top grill. Or, prepare a wood or charcoal fire. The fire is ready when the coals glow red and are covered with ash.

3. Place each mushroom on the grill at a 45-degree angle to the ridges of the grill. Grill for 1 minute, pressing firmly down on the mushrooms with a baking sheet, to accentuate the impression of the grill marks. Still grilling the same side of the mushroom, reposition each mushroom at the alternate 45-degree angle. Grill for 1 minute more, pressing firmly down on the mushrooms with a baking sheet. (This will form a very even and attractive grill mark on the mushrooms.) Turn each mushroom over and grill on the other side, positioning the mushrooms again at the two angles, pressing firmly down on the mushrooms with a baking sheet, grilling for a total of 2 minutes more.

4. Meanwhile, in a large frying pan, heat the butter over moderate heat until it sizzles. Add the grilled mushrooms in several carefully arranged layers, sprinkle with the remaining thyme, and finish cooking, covered, until soft and tender, about 5 minutes more. Do not turn the mushrooms, but rather baste regularly with the buttery cooking juices. Serve.

SERVES 4

 WINE SUGGESTION: From the Jura, a light and tasty white Arbois.

ARTICHOKE & BASIL RAGOUT

I make this dish often in early autumn, with end-of-season artichokes and the garden's final burst of basil. I've used wine in place of stock to connect the acidity of the lemon juice and the natural lemony tang of the artichoke, making for a very digestible dish. This is also delicious tossed with fresh pasta: You'll need about 250 g (8 oz).

500 ml (16 fl oz) dry white wine (such as a white Rhône, Riesling, Aligoté, or Chenin Blanc)

250 g (8 oz) fresh flat-leaf parsley leaves, carefully de-stemmed

8 plump fresh garlic cloves, peeled and halved

Sea salt to taste

2 firm ripe tomatoes, cored, skinned and chopped

125 ml (4 fl oz) extra-virgin olive oil

4 globe artichokes plus 1 lemon, prepared, or two 270-g (9-oz) packets of frozen artichoke hearts thawed (see Note, page 95)

4 tablespoons fresh basil leaves, carefully de-stemmed and cut into julienne with scissors or a sharp knife

1. In a 3-litre (5-pint) saucepan, bring the wine to a boil over high heat. Boil vigorously until all the alcohol has cooked off and there is no alcohol aroma wafting from the saucepan, about 8 minutes.

2. With a large chef's knife, finely chop together the parsley, garlic and salt. Transfer to a heavy-duty saucepan. Add the tomatoes, oil and wine. Thoroughly drain the artichoke slices and add to saucepan. Cover, and bring just to a simmer over moderate heat. Reduce the heat to low, cover, and simmer very gently, until the artichokes are soft and offer no resistance when pierced with a knife, 30 to 45 minutes for fresh artichokes, 10 to 15 minutes for thawed. The ragout should not be dry, but should be bathed in a fragrant delicious sauce. Stir in the basil. Taste for seasoning.

3. To serve as a first course or vegetable side dish: transfer to warmed shallow soup bowls, spooning the sauce over the artichokes. Pass plenty of crusty bread for sopping up the sauce. (To serve with pasta: Toss the artichokes with 250 g (8 oz) fresh cooked linguine, using all the liquid as the sauce. The pasta does not require cheese.)

SERVES 4-6

WINE SUGGESTION: Serve the same simple white wine as used in cooking the artichokes.

Zucchini, tomatoes, and peppers – a Provençal trinity.

∽ WHAT'S A RAGOUT? ∿ Sometimes I feel as though the French language was poetically designed around its cuisine. One of my favourite examples is the origins of the word *ragout*. Coming from the French verb *ragouter*, it denotes anything that stimulates or awakens the palate. This idea of reviving a tired palate leads to speculation that stews and ragouts were originally quite spicy, though they have since evolved into elegant dishes. Dating from the sixteenth century, a ragout is classically a stew made from any meat or fish cooked in a thickened sauce with aromatic flavourings. Essentially, there are two types of classical ragouts; first, the 'brown' ragout, the meat or firm fish is seared in oil or butter and then cooked with flour and stock. The other, a 'white' ragout, is cooked without colouration and then treated in the same manner with flour and stock. Naturally, since all ragouts are formed with meats and flour, the final product is always thick and satisfying. The definition of a 'ragout' also extends even further to mean a basic garnish for filling tarts, vol-au-vents and such. For vegetables, the same basic principle applies, a mix of vegetables that are first seared then cooked in their own juices. I like to think of a ragout as an ensemble of tightly bound flavours that emerge tasting greater than the sum of their parts. Here I've gathered my favourite flavours of early autumn to enjoy as a hearty vegetable ragout.

PROVENÇAL ROAST TOMATOES

A variation of roast tomato recipes found in my previous books, I've included the recipe here for it is a classic Chanteduc dish, one that accompanies almost every roast leg of lamb and chicken that I cook in my wood-fired oven. Two common important cooking techniques are used to succeed here: First the tomatoes are seared, meaning browned with intense heat to seal in the juices and impart colour and more flavour. They are then deglazed with homemade vinegar (sometimes a very hot spicy one for extra punch), a process of adding liquid to the pan in which the tomatoes have been seared. This is done to allow the deglazing liquid to absorb the glaze and the browned crusty bits formed on the bottom of the pan. Deglazing should always be done off the heat, to avoid burning those precious juices.

> EQUIPMENT: One oval baking dish large enough to hold all the tomatoes in a single layer (about 25 x 41 cm/10 x 16 in)
>
> 3 tablespoons extra-virgin olive oil
> 12 firm oval tomatoes, cored and halved lengthwise
> Sea salt to taste
> 3 tablespoons best-quality red wine vinegar or *Pili-Pili* Vinegar (see Variation, page 313)
> 3 tablespoons fresh mixed herbs (such as parsley leaves, tarragon, basil and rosemary), snipped with scissors

1. Preheat the oven to 200°C/400°F/gas mark 6.
2. In a very large frying pan, heat the oil over moderately high heat until hot but not smoking. When hot, place as many tomatoes as will easily fit in the pan, cut side down. (If you crowd the pan, the tomatoes will steam, not sear.) Sear, without moving the tomatoes, until they are dark and almost caramelized, 3 to 4 minutes. With a slotted spatula, transfer the tomatoes, cooked-side up, to the baking dish. Overlap them slightly, since they will reduce as they bake. Continue until all the tomatoes are seared. Season the tomatoes lightly with salt. Remove the pan from the heat. Deglaze the remaining fat in the pan with vinegar. Return the pan to moderate heat, scraping the bottom of the pan to loosen drippings into the liquid. Pour over the tomatoes. Sprinkle with fresh herbs.
3. Place the baking dish in the centre of the oven and bake, uncovered, until the tomatoes are soft, shrivelled and even a bit dark around the edges, about 30 minutes.
4. Serve hot, warm, or at room temperature.

SERVES 8

VARIATION: This recipe lends itself to endless variation. As a change of pace and an even more substantial dish, top the tomatoes with a dollop of Pistou (page 316) and a grating of Parmesan cheese before placing them in the oven.

JUNE VEGETABLE RAGOUT WITH HERB GARDEN PISTOU

One June morning the extraordinarily fresh array of vegetables on display at my vegetable merchant in Vaison-la-Romaine nearly knocked me out with their sheer beauty. I wanted to bring them all home, and so I did, combining the purple-tipped artichokes (known as *poivrades*), plump broad beans, last-of-season peas and asparagus. I had made some basil-garlic sauce the day before, and still had some in the refrigerator, so added the lively sauce to this sunny ragout. The wine – both its fruit and its acid – links the varied flavours of the vegetables.

> 2 medium onions (about 300 g/10 oz), peeled
> 6 tablespoons extra-virgin olive oil
> 1 head of plump fresh garlic, cloves peeled but left whole
> Sea salt to taste
> Bouquet garni: Small bunch of summer savory (or substitute thyme) and parsley, tied
>   in a bundle with string
> 8 fresh artichoke hearts, quartered
> 1 kg (2 lb) fresh broad beans in their pods (500 g/1 lb shelled beans, first skin removed)
> 3 tomatoes, skinned, cored, deseeded and coarsely chopped
> 375 ml (13 fl oz) white wine, such as Sauvignon Blanc
> 1 kg (2 lb) fresh peas in their pods, shelled (500 g/1 lb), blanched and refreshed
> 20 fresh asparagus tips, blanched and refreshed
> 1 recipe Pistou (page 316), to serve

1. Slice each onion in half lengthwise. Place each half, cut side down, on a cutting board and cut across into very thin slices.

2. In a large unheated frying pan combine the onions, oil, garlic, salt and bouquet garni and toss to coat the ingredients with the oil. Cover and, over a low heat, sweat until the onions are soft, about 10 minutes. Add the artichokes, broad beans, tomatoes and wine and simmer, uncovered, for 10 minutes to cook off the alcohol. Add the blanched peas and asparagus and cook for 1 minute more.

3. Serve immediately, passing a bowl of Pistou and plenty of crusty homemade bread.

SERVES 4

WINE SUGGESTION: Since this dish could be served as a main course, it deserves its own wine. Use the same wine as for cooking, such as a Sauvignon Blanc.

BLANCH AND REFRESH: Blanch vegetables for 1 to 2 minutes in boiling salted water, then refresh them for 1 minute in iced water, so they will retain their lovely green colour, even if they are to be recooked and served warm.

PATRICIA'S SPEEDY RATATOUILLE

I think of this dish as my speedy ratatouille, since it's made in a flash and still possesses many of the great qualities of a painstakingly prepared ratatouille. No matter how big a batch I make, it disappears with great haste. It's equally good warm or cold, served as a vegetable dish or tossed with pasta. Just be certain that you use firm young courgettes fresh from the garden. Old, worn and wrinkled courgettes have no place here. Adding a drop of vinegar at the end lends a sharp touch, particularly refreshing when served slightly chilled on a very hot day.

> 3½ tablespoons extra-virgin olive oil
> 10 small very fresh courgettes (about 1 kg/2 lb), cut into thin rounds
> 2 teaspoons fresh thyme leaves, carefully stemmed
> Sea salt to taste
> 3 plump fresh garlic cloves, finely chopped
> 5 medium tomatoes or 12 small oval plum tomatoes (about 1 kg/2 lb) skinned, cored, deseeded and chopped
> 2 tablespoons tomato paste
> 2 teaspoons best-quality red wine vinegar

1. In a very large frying pan over moderately high heat, heat the oil until hot but not smoking. Add the courgettes and 1 teaspoon of thyme leaves and sauté, shaking the pan from time to time, until the courgettes are cooked through but still firm and just beginning to brown slightly, about 5 minutes. (The courgettes need not be in a single layer, but the rounds should not be piled high in the pan.) The courgettes are done at the point they really begin to taste like cooked courgette and before they lose their brilliant green colour.

2. Add the salt and the garlic and cook for 1 or 2 minutes more, just until the garlic begins to brown. (The salt will force the courgettes to give off liquid, which will prevent the garlic from burning.) Add the tomatoes and tomato paste, and, still over moderately high heat, continue cooking, uncovered, until ingredients are well-blended and very little liquid remains in the pan, about 10 more minutes.

3. Add the remaining teaspoon of thyme and the vinegar. Taste for seasoning. Serve warm or at room temperature.

SERVES 6-8

Cooking should be a carefully balanced reflection of all the good things of the earth.

JEAN AND PIERRE TROISGROS

TURNIP & CUMIN PURÉE

It's time for turnips – with their subtle, ginger-like flavour – to stand on their own. All too often, this firm dense root vegetable is relegated to the stock pot or acts as a minor character in boiled beef and vegetables, or pot-au-feu. Here – all on their own – turnips are paired with a gentle dose of cumin. Serve this with roast pork or with a simple roast duck.

> 2 tablespoons butter
> 750 g (1½ lb) turnips, peeled and cubed
> Sea salt to taste
> A pinch of sugar
> About 250 ml (8 fl oz) homemade Chicken Stock (page 322)
> ½ teaspoon cumin seeds

1. In a large frying pan, heat the butter over moderate heat until it sizzles. Add the cubed turnips, salt lightly, add a pinch of sugar, and sauté, tossing until the turnips are lightly browned all over, about 7 minutes.
2. Cover with chicken stock and cook over low heat until almost all of the liquid is evaporated, about 30 minutes.
3. Transfer to a food mill or the bowl of a food processor and purée. Season to taste with cumin. Taste for seasoning.
4. Serve warm, as a side vegetable dish. (The purée can be prepared several hours in advance. Keep warm in the top of a double boiler set over simmering water.)

SERVES 4

PURE TOMATO CONFIT: OVEN-ROASTED TOMATOES

Nothing can match the pure wholesome flavour of tomatoes, and no method amplifies tomato essence like a reduction. These are the sun-dried tomatoes of the 1990s, fresh tomatoes that are baked for hours in a very slow oven until much of their moisture evaporates, creating tomatoes with a dense haunting rich, and pleasantly tangy, flavour. Be sure to adjust the oven to the lowest possible heat, so that the tomatoes actually melt more than bake. I use the tomatoes in soups, salads, on sandwiches, for pasta, or anywhere I want a rich pure tomato flavour. Although fresh herbs have a tendency to burn when baked, both the liquid provided by the oil and the low oven temperature prevent this from happening.

> 1 kg (2 lb) fresh plum tomatoes, skinned, cored, deseeded and quartered lengthwise
> Fine sea salt and freshly ground black pepper to taste
> A pinch of icing sugar
> 2 sprigs of fresh thyme, stemmed
> 4 plump fresh garlic cloves, slivered
> 2 tablespoons extra-virgin olive oil

1. Preheat the oven to the lowest possible setting, about 110°C/230°F/gas mark ¼.
2. Arrange the tomato quarters side-by-side on a baking sheet. Sprinkle each side lightly with salt, pepper and icing sugar. Scatter the thyme leaves over the tomatoes and place a garlic sliver on top of each quarter. Drizzle with olive oil. Place in the oven and cook until the tomatoes are very soft, about 1 hour. Turn the tomatoes, baste with the juices, and cook until meltingly tender, and reduced to about half their size, about 2 hours in total. Check the tomatoes from time to time: They should remain moist and soft. Remove from the oven and allow to cool thoroughly.
3. Transfer the tomatoes to a jar, cover with the cooking juices and oil, cover securely, and refrigerate, up to 1 week.
4. Use in salads, on sandwiches, for pasta, or anywhere you want a rich pure tomato flavour.

MAKES ABOUT 500 G (1 LB) TOMATOES

↙ **TWO WAYS TO PEEL A TOMATO** ∾ I follow two schools of thought on peeling tomatoes: When serving tomatoes raw – as in a salad – I peel them with a vegetable peeler, using a back-and-forth sawing motion to remove the peel. This way, the tomatoes are not subjected to heat and retain their delicious raw flavour. When tomatoes will eventually be cooked – as in this preparation – blanch them in boiling water for 1 minute, refresh them in cold water, and the peel will slip off with ease.

It was in France that I first learned about food.
And that even the selection of a perfect pear, a ripe piece of Brie, the freshest butter,
the highest quality cream were as important as how the dish
you were going to be served was actually cooked.

ROBERT CARRIER

MONSIEUR HENNY'S AUBERGINE GRATIN

One spring weekday just before Easter I was chatting with my butcher, Monsieur Henny. Along with my leg of lamb, he wrapped up a container of aubergine-and-tomato gratin from his *traiteur* or delicatessen counter. The simple gratin was a revelation: He had taken baby aubergines, sliced them in half and placed them cut side up in a gratin dish. A brush of olive oil, a sprinkling of fresh herbs, and fresh halved tomatoes, cut side down, nested on top of the aubergine. A long roasting in a hot oven and voilà! a marvellously dark, caramelized vegetable gratin, full of the rich flavour of a fine ratatouille. When the dish comes bubbling and fragrant from the oven, even you are convinced the dish was laborious and even complicated. I think of it as my 'slice and for-get it' gratin, for it takes no more than three or four minutes of preparation time. The possibilities with the dish are endless: I've added my own touch, a dusting of freshly grated Parmesan, to provide a bit of body and to bind the flavourful juices that flow from the tomatoes and the aubergine. If there is any leftover, recycle by topping it with tomato sauce, fresh herbs and another sprinkling of cheese. The dish is best made with tiny aubergines, weighing no more than 150 g (5 oz): They generally have more flavour and are less likely to be bitter.

2 tablespoons extra-virgin olive oil

3 small aubergines, each weighing about 150 g (5 oz) or the equivalent weight in larger aubergines, trimmed at stem end

Fine sea salt to taste

3 tablespoons mixed fresh herbs, finely chopped, such as leaves of rosemary, sage, thyme and basil

Pinch of dried oregano

60 g (2 oz) freshly grated Parmigiano-Reggiano cheese

1 kg (2 lb) fresh tomatoes, cored and halved across

1. Preheat the oven to 230°C/450°F/gas mark 8.

2. Drizzle 1 tablespoon of oil over the bottom of a shallow 2-litre (3½-pint) gratin dish. If

the aubergines are small, slice them in half lengthwise. (If they are large, cut them into four lengthwise slices.) Place the aubergines, skin side down, in a single layer in the gratin dish. Lightly score the aubergines with a sharp knife. Sprinkle with salt, the finely chopped fresh herbs and the oregano. Sprinkle with about half the cheese. Place the tomato halves, cut side down, on top of the aubergine in a single layer. Brush the tomato skins with the rest of the oil, and sprinkle with the remaining cheese.

3. Place the gratin dish in the centre of the oven and bake until the vegetables are soft and almost falling apart, about 1 hour. The tops of the tomatoes should be almost black and the juices from the aubergine and tomato should turn thick and almost caramelized.

4. Serve warm or at room temperature, as a side dish or main vegetable dish. Use a spatula to cut and serve measured portions.

SERVES 4-6

WINE SUGGESTION: A bright young red is ideal here, Chianti, Côtes-du-Rhône, a Californian Zinfandel.

꙳ ON AUBERGINES ꙳ Aubergines are tricky, because everything is hiding beneath the protective outer skin. In selecting the best aubergines, pick them up and test the weight: The best are firm, and heavy for their size. Select the smallest available, since large aubergines are, for the most part, overgrown. Oversized aubergines not only lose their tenderness, but also contain larger seeds that contribute to a bitter aftertaste. (This is why I am opposed to salting aubergines to 'rid them of bitterness'. If the aubergine is fresh in the first place, it will never be bitter.) I am also of the 'never peel an aubergine' school: Why discard something that's so beautiful and tastes so delicious? Note that the aubergine's porous, fat-free flesh is also capable of absorbing impressive quantities of oil, water or any liquid substance. This is why I find cooking them in the oven the best way to enjoy aubergines without drenching them in olive oil. It also helps them to release their natural juices without drying them out. Baste the aubergines as they cook for added moisture and flavour.

Watch a French housewife as she makes her way slowly along the loaded stalls …
searching for the peak of ripeness and flavor.… What you are seeing is a true artist at work,
patiently assembling all the materials of her craft, just as the painter squeezes
oil colours onto his palette ready to create a masterpiece.

KEITH FLOYD

BRAISED & GRATINÉED FENNEL

In Provence, fennel grows wild along the roadsides and is an easy garden vegetable. I often raid the garden of the delicate fronds for salad, being careful not to overdo it. For the fronds help provide the light and energy that keep this bulb vegetable growing. Since fennel is one of my favourite vegetables, no one need coax me to prepare this dish. Anything that comes bubbling from the oven with a nice coating of cheese wins my appetite! Much of the work can be done in advance: The fennel is lightly browned, then braised in a touch of broth. The drained fennel is then gratinéed at the last minute under the grill. The same dish could be prepared with many other vegetables, including celery, carrots, cauliflower and cabbage, with approximately the same cooking times.

6 tablespoons extra-virgin olive oil
1 kg (2 lb) fennel bulbs, trimmed and quartered lengthwise
Sea salt to taste
750 ml (27 fl oz) Potager Stock (page 321) or Chicken Stock (page 322)
60 g (2 oz) freshly grated Parmigiano-Reggiano cheese

1. In large pan, heat the oil over moderately high heat until hot but not smoking. Add the fennel and a touch of salt. Sweat, uncovered, over moderate heat until the fennel begins to brown lightly and becomes impregnated with the oil, about 5 minutes.
2. Add the stock, cover and simmer gently until the fennel is meltingly tender throughout, about 30 minutes. If any broth remains in the pan, remove the fennel and reduce the liquid over high heat until just a few tablespoons of thick sauce remain. Taste for seasoning. (The fennel can be prepared up to 2 hours in advance up to this point. Return the fennel to the pan. Cover and set aside).
3. To finish, preheat the grill. Transfer the fennel slices in a single layer to a large gratin dish and sprinkle with cheese. Place the baking dish under the grill, about 8 cm (3 in) from the heat. Grill until the cheese is melted and fragrant, the fennel sizzling, 1 to 2 minutes.
4. Serve immediately as a vegetable side dish. This is particularly delicious with a roast

turkey or chicken, pork or grilled fish, or all by itself as a vegetable main dish.

SERVES 4-6

TIP: Never discard the delicate feathery fronds that sprout from the top of a bulb of fennel. They can be finely chopped and tossed into salads or scattered over this gratin as the fennel comes from oven.

ᔚ A WORD ON FENNEL ᔚ 'Florence' fennel is the term used to describe bulb fennel – *fenouil* in French and *finnochio* in Italian. It's a vegetable that responds brilliantly to braising, stewing, and even grilling. The compelling anise taste is tempered by the sweetness of the juices and the mellow translucent texture. Etymologically, fennel comes from *feniculum* or *fenum* meaning 'little hay.' This is perhaps an allusion to the wispy fronds at the top of the bulb. When storing fresh fennel, it is best to trim the larger stems, leaving only a few small fronds intact. Otherwise, the stems continue to extract moisture from the bulbs, leaving the interiors spongy and stringy.

The secret of good cooking is, first, having a love of it. . . . If you're convinced
that cooking is drudgery, you're never going to be good at it,
and you might as well warm up something frozen.

JAMES BEARD

CELERIAC LASAGNE

Life works in strange ways. One day I was in New York cooking several recipes from my book *Bistro Cooking* for television. The show was on potato gratins, so I selected a potato and celeriac gratin. I hadn't make the dish for years, and had forgotten how much I loved the combination of the tangy gratin with a touch of tomato, cream and cheese. I couldn't wait to return home to Paris to recreate a new gratin using celeriac. The very day of my return I dined at the wonderful Parisian restaurant, L'Ambroisie, where chef Bernard Pacaud prepared a 'lasagne' of very thinly sliced celeriac, layered with white truffles, foie gras and wild mushrooms. I went back to the tomato-cream mixture of my first gratin, but inspired to take the Italian accent of the dish even further, replaced the traditional Gruyère cheese with freshly grated Parmesan. I always keep several batches of tomato sauce in my freezer, so dishes such as this are less of an ordeal. This lasagne can make a one-dish meal all on its own. Or, serve it as I have, with Bonito in Parchment with Warm Pistou (page 203).

About 1.5 kg (3 lb) celeriac
2 tablespoons freshly squeezed lemon juice
3 tablespoons sea salt
500 ml (16 fl oz) Tomato Sauce (page 000)
175 ml (6 fl oz) crème fraîche or double cream
Butter for preparing the gratin dish
125 g (4 oz) freshly grated Parmigiano-Reggiano cheese

1. Preheat the oven to 200°C/400°F/gas mark 6.
2. Peel the celeriac and cut it in half to make it more manageable. Using a mandoline, electric mandoline or vegetable slicer, cut it into paper-thin slices.
3. In a large pan, bring 6 litres (10 pints) of water to a rolling boil. Add the lemon juice, salt and the celeriac, stirring to prevent it from sticking. Cook until tender but still firm, about 7 minutes. Drain thoroughly, carefully pressing out any excess water.
4. Meanwhile, in a medium-size saucepan combine the tomato sauce and cream. Warm over low heat and taste for seasoning.

5. Butter a 2-litre (3½-pint) gratin dish. Layer one-third of the drained celeriac on the bottom of the gratin dish. Top with one-third of the tomato sauce, and one-third of the cheese. Repeat two more times, until all the celeriac, tomato-cream sauce and cheese have been used. (The dish can be prepared to this point several hours in advance. Bring to room temperature before baking.)

6. Place in the centre of the oven and bake until golden brown, about 40 minutes. Serve immediately, cut into thick wedges.

SERVES 6-8

❧ ON CELERIAC ❧ Celeriac is actually a vegetable of extremes: It is often served raw (as in a classic French *céleri rémoulade*, a julienne of celeriac tossed in a tangy mayonnaise) or in the form of a creamy purée or soup. There are other ways to enjoy this root vegetable, and this lasagne is one my favourites. Attacking the vegetable can be intimidating because it's round and covered with a thick skin. Like turnips, celeriac actually has several layers of skin that need to be thoroughly peeled before being used. The best way to begin is to cut off the top and bottom so it rests steadily on the cutting board. Then, with a sharp knife or vegetable peeler, cut around the edges from top to bottom, turning the celery as needed. Make sure to cut through and to discard all the brown and light brown skin. Remove any large brown spots as well. The interior should be an off-white colour. If peeled ahead of time, the celery will discolour and dry out. Store in water with a bit of lemon juice or vinegar until ready to use.

FRESH WHITE BEANS WITH GARLIC & HERBS

Fresh white *cocos blancs,* encased in pale celadon-green pods and the mottled red *cocos rouges* encased in brilliant red pods, grow all over Provence in the summer. I love to serve the white beans as a simple salad, at room temperature, or as a warm dish to accompany roast lamb. I always mix both red and white beans for fresh summer pistou, for more complex flavours and varied colours. Haunt your local farmers' market for fresh beans – they'll reward you with their creamy nutty flavours and you'll love the aromas that waft from the kitchen as fresh beans, garlic and herbs fill the room with their mingled fragrances.

500 g (1 lb) fresh small white (navy) beans in the pod, shelled, or 250 g (8 oz) dried
  small white beans, cooked

500 g (1 lb) fresh borlotti beans in the pod, shelled, or 250 g (8 oz) dried borlotti
  beans, cooked

3 tablespoons extra-virgin olive oil

3 plump fresh garlic cloves, finely chopped

About 2 litres (3½ pints) cold water

2 fresh bay leaves

Large bunch of fresh thyme

1 teaspoon fine sea salt, or to taste

extra-virgin olive oil to drizzle

1. For dried beans: Rinse the beans, picking them over to remove any pebbles. Place the beans in a large bowl, add boiling water to cover and set aside for 1 hour. Drain, discarding the water.

2. For both fresh and dried beans: In a large heavy-bottomed pan, combine the olive oil and garlic and stir to coat the garlic with the oil. Cook over moderate heat, until the garlic is fragrant and soft, about 2 minutes. Do not let it brown. Add the beans, stir to coat with oil, and cook for 1 minute more. Add 2 litres (3½ pints) of cold water, and stir in the bay and thyme. Cover, bring to a simmer over moderate heat, and simmer for 15 minutes for fresh beans for 30 minutes for dried beans. Season with salt. Continue cooking at a gentle simmer until the beans are tender, about 15 minutes more for fresh beans or 30 minutes more for dried beans. Stir from time to time to make sure they are not sticking to the bottom of the pan. Add water if necessary. (Cooking time will vary according to the freshness of the beans.) Taste for seasoning. Remove and discard the bay leaves and thyme.

3. At serving time, pass a cruet of extra-virgin olive oil to drizzle over the beans.

SERVES 4-6

FACING PHOTOGRAPH: *A farmer with his homegrown produce.*

The onion is the truffle of the poor.
ROBERT J. COURTINE

ONION⁊PARMESAN GRATIN

I call this a dream recipe: One that's low on labour, big on flavour. And it can be prepared quickly, with items a cook generally has to hand. This versatile vegetable dish – which tastes both light and rich at the same time – was inspired by chef Alain Passard, who serves it often in his elegant Parisian Left Bank restaurant, Arpège.

I find this onion gratin works miracles as a slightly sweet and mild accompaniment to strong-flavoured dishes such as Beef Daube with Mustard, Herbs and White Wine (page 258). The gratin is a good companion for both white and red wines, and can easily be prepared several hours in advance, then gratinéed just seconds before serving.

The cloves, by the way, are a surprise ingredient and add a pleasantly unexpected flavour. For best results, grind the cloves in a food mill or coffee grinder just before use.

1 kg (2 lb) onions, peeled
60 g (2 oz) unsalted butter
½ teaspoon fresh thyme leaves
¾ teaspoon whole cloves, freshly ground
Fine sea salt to taste
2 large egg yolks
3 tablespoons double cream
60 g (2 oz) freshly grated Parmigiano-Reggiano cheese

1. Slice an onion in half lengthwise. Place cut side down on a cutting board and slice crosswise into very thin slices. Slice the remaining onions in this manner. Set aside.
2. In a large non-stick frying pan, combine the butter, onions, thyme, ground cloves and salt. Cover and sweat over very low heat until the onions are very soft, about 10 minutes. Taste for seasoning.
3. Transfer the onion mixture to a medium-size porcelain baking dish (such as a 27-cm/10½-in dish) and even it out with the back of a spoon. (The gratin can be prepared several hours in advance up to this point. Store, covered, at room temperature.)
4. Just before serving, preheat the grill.
5. In a small bowl, combine the egg yolks and cream and whisk with a fork to blend. Stir in the cheese. Pour the mixture over the onion mixture in the baking dish. Place the baking dish under the grill, about 5 cm (2 in) from the heat. Grill until the top is sizzling, fragrant and golden, about 1 minute.

6. Serve immediately, as a vegetable course or as an accompaniment to such dishes as Beef Daube with Mustard, Herbs and White Wine (page 258).

SERVES 4

🌳 WINE SUGGESTIONS: This gentle harmonious dish reminds me of France's Loire Valley. The region's Savennières comes to mind, with its fruity, pleasantly acidic flavour. But, indeed, any good red wine with a fine acid balance – a Beaujolais or Côtes-du-Rhône – would be fine.

: THE MAGIC OF CLOVES :   Cloves are actually the sun-dried unopened nail-like pink flower-buds of an evergreen tropical tree native to Southeast Asia. The word 'clove' comes from the Latin *clavus*, which literally means 'nail'. In French, a clove is *un clou de girofle*, a nail of the clove tree. (In fact when someone is tiny and thin, they compare them to a *clou de girofle*.)

Originally found in the Spice Islands, cloves were already in use in Asia long before they were discovered by the Dutch in the seventeenth century. Long known for medicinal value, cloves are still used to prevent nausea, and to soothe aching eyes. Clove oil – distilled from the leaves and the flower-buds – is used as a flavouring, an insecticide, and to numb toothaches.

Though some compare the taste of clove to cinnamon or mace, its flavour is quite unique. The heat of cooking or a long marination helps to temper its intense spiciness. While in cooking the clove is primarily used for baking and for sweet wines, cloves are equally delicious when added to slow-cooked beef stews (where they bring out the flavour of beef nicely), meat sauces, even pickling vegetables. Traditionally, onions are studded with cloves when preparing soups or stocks. You will find cloves added to cold meats, such as sausages and hams, where they help aid digestion.

Here I've experimented with mixing the clove's tangy bite with the warm comfort of milk. The pairing is dynamic. Always purchase cloves whole and grind them yourself in a spice or coffee grinder. Never keep whole cloves for more than a year, for even the whole spice will lose its power and zest.

In cooking, as in the arts, simplicity is a sign of perfection.
CURNONSKY

BRAISED RED ONIONS

Vermilion red onions, roasted slowly in a warm oven are a fine accompaniment to a simple roast pork, grilled sausages or roast chicken. I like to make a large batch and then use them on sandwiches and pizzas.

6 large red onions, in their skins
1 tablespoon extra-virgin olive oil
4 tablespoons water
Sea salt and freshly ground black pepper to taste

1. Preheat the oven to 130°C/275°F/gas mark 1.
2. Place the onions in a shallow baking pan, drizzle with oil and water. Place in the centre of the oven and bake, basting every 15 minutes, until soft, about 2 hours.
3. To serve, remove the onion skins and either slice or leave whole. Season with salt and pepper.

SERVES 6

VARIATION: For delicious braised garlic, cut off and discard the top third from whole heads of garlic in their skins. Substitute for red onions.

CELERY⸱PARMESAN GRATIN

Often I feel like a one-woman band, singing the praises of the world's most abused vegetable: celery. My garden in Provence harbours a special plot for growing the proud stalks, ready for transforming gratins, soups and salads. Try letting celery star all on its own, as in this simple refreshing gratin: You're not likely to regret it.

EQUIPMENT: One oval gratin dish, about 35.5 x 23 x 5 cm (14 x 9 x 2 in)

> Unsalted butter for buttering the gratin dish
> Sea salt
> 1.25 kg (2½ lb) diced celery hearts, with leaves
> 125 ml (4 fl oz) crème fraîche or double cream
> Freshly ground black pepper to taste
> 90 g (3 oz) freshly grated Parmigiano-Reggiano cheese

1. Preheat the grill and generously butter the gratin dish.
2. In a large pan, bring 6 litres (10 pints) of water to a rolling boil. Add 3 tablespoons of salt and the celery. Cook until it is tender but still firm, about 7 minutes. Drain thoroughly.
3. Toss the celery and cream in the gratin dish, and even out with the back of a spoon. Season generously with pepper and sprinkle with the cheese.
4. Place the gratin dish about 12.5 cm (5 in) from the heat. Cook until the cheese is melted and golden brown, 2 to 3 minutes.
5. Serve immediately.

SERVES 6-8

Our favourite street musician, Philippe, at the local market.
In honour of guest Julia Child's eightieth birthday,
he came up the hill with his barbary organ
for a special performance at Chanteduc.

*Large, naked raw carrots are acceptable as food only to those
who lie in hutches eagerly awaiting Easter.*
FRAN LEIBOWITZ

CARROTS PROVENÇAL

Our friend Maggie Shapiro has been a frequent house guest over the years, and with each visit she seems to leave behind a recipe that becomes part of our repertoire. When she gave me this one, which she first ate years ago when her housekeeper Irma prepared it, she said 'Once you've tasted these, you'll never prepare carrots any other way.' She's right. This beautiful dish – with a colourful contrast of black and orange – has become our traditional Thanksgiving vegetable. It's one with a personal Provençal touch, prepared with olives picked from our own trees. The carrots can be served warm or at room temperature, which means that of course you can make them in advance. If baby carrots are available, use them cut in half lengthwise.

2 tablespoons extra-virgin olive oil
1 kg (2 lb) carrots, peeled and sliced diagonally
1 head of plump fresh garlic, peeled and halved
Sea salt to taste
About 30 best-quality black olives (such as French Nyons), drained, stoned and
    halved

1. In a large frying pan, heat the oil over moderately high heat until hot but not smoking. Add the carrots, stir to coat with oil, and reduce heat to moderate. Cover and braise for 20 minutes, stirring regularly.
2. Add the garlic, season with salt and stir. Continue cooking over low heat until the carrots are almost caramelized and the garlic is soft and tender, about 15 minutes more.
3. Sprinkle with the olives, stir, and taste for seasoning. Serve hot or at room temperature.

SERVES 8-10

VARIATION: Carrots and tarragon are natural partners: Try substituting about 4 tablespoons chopped fresh tarragon leaves for the black olives.

TENDER ROASTED SHALLOTS

Shallots grace the table with elegance and distinction. In this roasted version, the shallots are first simmered in milk, a procedure that serves to both soften and sweeten the root vegetable. This is a very tender vegetable accompaniment, one that is particularly delicious with Spit-Roasted Brine-Cured Pork (page 269).

> 18 shallots, in their skins
> 500 ml (16 fl oz) whole milk
> 1 tablespoon extra-virgin olive oil
> ½ teaspoon best-quality red wine vinegar
> Sea salt to taste

1. Preheat the oven to 200°C/400°F/gas mark 6.
2. In a shallow heatproof and ovenproof casserole, combine the shallots and milk. Bring to a simmer over moderate heat. Cover and simmer gently for 10 minutes.
3. Drain the shallots, discarding the milk. Return them to the casserole and cover with foil. Place in the centre of the oven and roast until tender, about 35 minutes.
4. Remove from the oven, and add the oil and vinegar with salt to taste. Toss to blend.
5. Serve whole, in their skins, as a vegetable accompaniment.

SERVES 4-6

*Corine and Josiane Meliani of Les Gourmandines,
Vaison-la-Romaine's quality produce shop.*

POTATOES ROASTED IN SEA SALT

In French, this potato preparation is known as *pommes de terre en diable* or *pommes de terre au sel* after the method of roasting tiny whole potatoes in their skins with just a sprinkling of sea salt in an unglazed clay pot known as *la diable* or 'the devil'. The results of this ultra-simple preparation are astonishing: The potatoes emerge fragrant, with the skins just a bit crackly. The flesh of the potato soft, yet not mushy, and filled with the perfume of sea salt. As the potatoes cook, the clay absorbs some of their moisture, leaving behind a rich, almost primordial, earthy flavour.

The dried clay pots generally come in several shapes. Sometimes they are twin round flat-bottomed vessels, with a pair of elongated clay handles. Other times they resemble a bean pot, with a flat bottom, a bulbous shape and very tiny opening and a very tiny lid. I have an entire collection of these pots, some old, some new, since whenever I prepare this recipe, I never seem to manage to make enough potatoes for the crowd. I generally roast the potatoes in a clay pot in the oven, but traditionally, the potatoes were cooked in the *diable* set in cinders in the fire. They can also be cooked on top of the stove, over a very low flame using a heat diffuser.

This recipe allows for endless variations: I keep it very simple, with just a sprinkling of salt, tucking a few fresh bay leaves in for good measure. One might add whole garlic cloves in their skins, whole shallots in their skins or a bunch of fresh thyme.

Once the potatoes emerge from the clay cooker, they can be sampled with the sauce of whatever they are cooked with, a touch of olive oil, fresh butter, homemade mayonnaise, aïoli, the sky's the limit. The other beauty of this recipe is that the potatoes somehow know, instinctively, that they are not going to go into the oven alone. They sense that they will have to share the oven's heat so they retain a very flexible attitude towards cooking time and temperature.

> About 4 teaspoons sea salt
> 1 kg (2 lb) small, yellow-fleshed potatoes (such as Pink Fir Apple), scrubbed

1. Preheat the oven to 190°C/375°F/gas mark 5.
2. Sprinkle about 2 teaspoons of salt on the bottom of a dry clay cooker. Place the potatoes in the pot. Sprinkle with the remaining 2 teaspoons of salt. Cover. Place the clay cooker in the oven and roast. Once the potatoes present no resistance when pierced with a two-pronged fork, they are done, about 45 minutes. If the oven is reduced, they will happily stay there until you are ready for them.
3. To serve, bring the clay pot to the table and uncover, so guests can take in the pleasing, earthy aroma emerging from the pot.

SERVES 6-8

SMASHED POTATOES

After the fad of creamy mashed potatoes began to fade, Parisian palates moved on to what I call 'smashed' potatoes and the French call *pommes écrasées*. Rather than reducing the potatoes to a purée, they are simply crushed with a fork and enriched with butter and oil. The dish shows up everywhere, from bistro tables to grand palaces, and plays a versatile role as a warming accompaniment to roast pork, chicken, lamb or fish. It's a method that flatters the fragrance and flavour of very nutty, fruity, earthy yellow-fleshed potatoes. In France we use the fingerling *la ratte* or yellow-fleshed Charlotte.

Be sure to have a large well-heated bowl on hand in which to crush the potatoes. The glory of this dish is the fragrance that wafts from the rising steam, so prepare and serve at the very last moment.

> 1 kg (2 lb) firm, yellow-fleshed potatoes, scrubbed and peeled
> Coarse sea salt to taste
> 125 g (4 oz) unsalted butter
> 2 tablespoons extra-virgin olive oil
> 2 tablespoons fresh flat-leaf parsley, leaves only, snipped with scissors
> Fine sea salt to taste

1. Place the potatoes in a large pot and fill with cold water to cover by at least 3 cm (1 in). For each litre (1¾ pints) of water, add 1 tablespoon (10 g) of coarse sea salt. Simmer, uncovered, over moderate heat until a knife inserted into a potato comes away easily, 20 to 30 minutes. Make sure the potatoes are fully cooked, or they will not mash properly. Drain the potatoes as soon as they are cooked. (If allowed to cool in the water, the potatoes will taste re-heated.)

2. Transfer the potatoes to a large warm serving bowl and dot with the butter and oil. With a large fork or a potato masher, coarsely crush the mixture to blend. Do not let it form a purée. Season with fine sea salt and parsley and serve immediately.

SERVES 4-6

GARLIC LOVER'S VARIATION: Simmer a head of garlic in cream until soft, then purée in blender. When mashing the potatoes, add the garlic cream along with the butter and oil.

⌁ NEXT DAY TIP ⌁ Should you have any leftover potatoes, they are delicious cut into chunks and tossed in dressing – either fresh mayonnaise seasoned with herbs or a herb-flecked vinaigrette.

FAKE *FRITES*

Steamed and then roasted, these potatoes have the look and flavour of freshly cooked chips, minus the excess fat. The potatoes can be steamed several hours in advance and roasted at the last minute. The steaming allows a fine moist coating of starch to form on the surface of the potato, providing a very crisp texture when baked. Baking time will of course vary according to the variety of potato used, as well as the cut. I like to cut my potatoes into fat, hefty chips. Serve with a simple roast, such as 18-Minute City Steak (page 255) or Spit-Roasted Brine-Cured Pork (page 269).

> 1 kg (2 lb) baking potatoes, such as Maris Piper or Bintje, peeled and cut into thick chips 1.75 cm (¾ in) by 7.5 cm (3 in) long
> 2 to 3 tablespoons extra-virgin olive oil
> Fine sea salt to taste

1. Preheat the oven to 250°C/475°F/gas mark 9.
2. Bring 1 litre (1¾ pints) of water to a simmer in the bottom of a steamer. Place the potatoes on the steamer over simmering water, cover, and steam just until a knife inserted into a potato comes away easily, 10 to 12 minutes. (The potatoes should not be cooked through, or they will tend to fall apart.)
3. Transfer the steamed potatoes to a bowl and drizzle with oil. Carefully toss to coat evenly with oil. (The potatoes can be prepared up to this point several hours in advance. Set aside at room temperature.)
4. With a large slotted spoon, transfer the potatoes in a single layer to a non-stick baking sheet. Discard any excess oil or liquid. Place the baking sheet in the oven and bake – turning so they brown evenly – until the potatoes are crisp and a deep golden brown, 15 to 20 minutes.
5. Remove from the oven, season generously with salt, and serve immediately.

SERVES 4-6

⌁ THE POTATO OF CHOICE ⌁ Almost any potato can be roasted in this manner, but my potato of choice is the firm, yellow-fleshed Charlotte, the size of an egg. The variety has existed only since the early 1980s, when farmers from Brittany made an immediate hit with this very tender, creamy, fine-fleshed potato. The most famous ones now come from the island of Noirmoutier, where their earthy flavour marries so well with the rare sea salt that is the gift of the island's shores. My second choice here is the tiny *ratte* variety, known in France since the ninth century but newly made famous in France in the 1980s. The *ratte* is a very tiny potato (some are not much bigger than an almond) of uneven shape, with very fine golden skin and a very waxy, smooth flesh with a mild, buttery, earthy flavour.

GRATIN DAUPHINOIS

To wash or not to wash the potatoes, that is the question. There are two schools of thought on rules for a perfect gratin. Some cooks never wash the potatoes, preferring a starchier dish that creates a more unctuous liaison of starch, cream, and cheese to coat the potatoes. Others feel the clean potato flavour is enhanced by a careful rinse. I prefer the starchy version, but try it both ways, and decide for yourself. This is a variation on my favourite and simplest of gratins, first published in the first edition of my *Food Lover's Guide to Paris*. In France, I like to use the Charlotte potato. Just be sure they are nice and firm-fleshed potatoes. And make sure the cheese is a good Gruyère.

EQUIPMENT: One 2-litre (3½-pint) ovenproof dish

1 plump fresh garlic clove, peeled and halved
1 kg (2 lb) firm-fleshed potatoes, peeled and sliced very thinly
125 g (4 oz) freshly grated Gruyère cheese
500 ml (16 fl oz) whole milk
125 ml (4 fl oz) crème fraîche or double cream
Sea salt and freshly ground black pepper to taste

1. Preheat the oven to 190°C/375°F/gas mark 5.
2. Rub the inside of the baking dish with garlic.
3. In a large bowl, combine the potatoes, three-quarters of the cheese, the milk, crème fraîche, salt and pepper. Mix well. Spoon the mixture into the baking dish, pouring the liquid over the potatoes. Sprinkle with the remaining cheese.
4. Place in the centre of the oven and bake until the potatoes are cooked through and the top is crisp and golden, about 1¼ hours.

SERVES 4-6

What I say is that, if a man really likes potatoes,
he must be a pretty decent sort of fellow.

A. A. MILNE

JR'S GRATIN DAUPHINOIS

Chef Joël Robuchon is one of the greatest cooks I know, and his version of any dish is sure to bring diners to their knees. Not one ever to stint on butter or cream, he embellishes his potato gratin with plenty of both. Robuchon also cooks his potatoes in the creamy mixture first, making for a gratin that is ultimately rich and unctuous.

EQUIPMENT: One 2-litre (3½-pint) ovenproof dish

500 ml (16 fl oz) whole milk
250 ml (8 fl oz) crème fraîche or double cream
125 g (4 oz) freshly grated Gruyère cheese
Sea salt and freshly ground black pepper to taste
Freshly grated nutmeg to taste
1 kg (2 lb) firm-fleshed potatoes, peeled and sliced very thinly
1 plump fresh garlic clove, peeled and halved
45 g (1½ oz) unsalted butter

1. Preheat the oven to 190°C/375°F/gas mark 5.
2. In a large saucepan, bring the milk to the boil over moderate heat. Add the crème fraîche, and three-quarters of the cheese. Stir to blend. Season with salt, pepper and a grating of nutmeg. Add the potatoes and mix well with a wooden spoon. Cook over low heat, stirring from time to time, until the potatoes are soft, about 20 minutes. Taste for seasoning.
3. Rub the inside of the baking dish with garlic. Transfer the potatoes and their liquid to the baking dish. Sprinkle with the remaining cheese and the butter.
4. Place in the centre of the oven and bake until the potatoes are cooked through and the top is crisp and golden, about 1¼ hours. Serve immediately.

SERVES 4-6

POTATO, OLIVE OIL & PARMESAN PURÉE

Homey and elegant in the same breath, a perfect potato purée is pure, smooth, creamy gastronomic pleasure. This version is embellished with a touch of olive oil and enriched with flavourful Parmesan cheese. Here I steam rather than boil the potatoes, for a richer potato flavour. Serve this with a simple roast chicken and a nice bottle of red wine.

EQUIPMENT: Food mill

1 kg (2 lb) baking potatoes
375-500 ml (12-16 fl oz) whole milk
Fine sea salt to taste
About 4 tablespoons extra-virgin olive oil
30 g (1 oz) freshly grated Parmigiano-Reggiano cheese

1. Scrub and peel the potatoes. Bring 1 litre (1¾ pints) of water to a simmer in the bottom of a steamer. Place the potatoes on the steamer over simmering water, cover, and steam until a knife inserted into a potato comes away easily, 20 to 30 minutes. (Make certain the potatoes are cooked through, or they will be very difficult to put through the food mill.)

2. Meanwhile, in a large saucepan, bring the milk just to the boil over high heat. Set aside.

3. Pass the potatoes through the medium grid of a food mill into a large, heavy-bottomed saucepan. Add a pinch of salt and the olive oil – little by little – stirring vigorously with a wooden spoon until the oil is thoroughly incorporated and the mixture becomes fluffy and light. Slowly add about three-quarters of the hot milk in a thin stream, stirring vigorously, until the milk is thoroughly incorporated.

4. Place the pan over low heat, and continue to stir vigorously. If the purée seems a bit heavy or stiff, add additional oil and milk, stirring all the while. Stir in the cheese. Taste for seasoning. (The purée may be made up to 1 hour in advance. Place in the top of a double boiler over simmering water. Stir occasionally to keep smooth.)

SERVES 6-8

⌁ HEALTH NOTE ⌁ Boiling potatoes robs them of over half of their potassium content. To obtain maximum health benefits, steam them.

BRAISED ASPARAGUS

In the early spring, all of France waits for the first asparagus to appear from Provence. While the soil in Provence tends to be chalky and rocky, there are also vast patches of rich, sandy soil ideal for cultivating long, elegant rows of asparagus. Add to the equation the wealth of warm spring sun and you have an enviable asparagus culture. While fat, ivory-white asparagus are traditional, today many different varieties are found, including classic green asparagus and the delicate violet-tipped variety with white stems shading to a delicate spring green.

The inspiration for this recipe comes from Paris chef Alain Passard: I spent a day in his kitchen early one spring, and noticed that rather than blanching asparagus, as is the French tradition, he braised them slowly in golden butter from Brittany, making for a vegetable that is particularly moist and rich with that grassy, pure asparagus flavour. During the slow braise the asparagus give up their mineral-like juices which concentrate and mingle with the butter, bathing the asparagus in a truly intense sauce. This method can be used with any variety of asparagus, just be certain they are all the same size, so they cook evenly.

> 45 g (1½ oz) unsalted butter
> 1 kg (2 lb) medium-size green asparagus, tough ends trimmed
> Fine sea salt and freshly ground black pepper to taste
> Coarse sea salt to taste

1. In a large frying pan, melt the butter over medium heat. Add the asparagus and shake the pan until they fall into a single layer in the bottom of the pan. Raise the heat slightly and cook until the butter starts to sizzle, 1 to 2 minutes. Season with fine sea salt and pepper.
2. Reduce the heat to low. With a spatula, rotate the asparagus as they cook, turning them so they brown slightly on all sides. Cook for an additional 10 to 12 minutes, or until tender. Taste for seasoning. With a slotted spoon, gently transfer the asparagus to a serving plate. Sprinkle with a small amount of coarse sea salt. Serve immediately.

SERVES 4-6

5

PASTA

WHERE WOULD THE MEDITERRANEAN PALATE be without pasta? The line-up of Provençal ingredients – ripe black olives, fresh Mediterranean clams, plump red tomatoes, rosemary, and thyme – all seem destined to share top billing with wheaty strands of pasta. During the winter months, I'll cook up a sauce of sausage, fennel, and red wine to toss with spirals of fusilli, turn up the heat with a batch of Spicy Red Pepper Spaghetti, or warm our souls with rich helpings of Spaghetti alla Carbonara, inspired by a favorite trattoria in Rome. Should we unearth a fragrant black truffle in the vineyard, it will surely find its way into Hervé's Truffle Butter Pasta, a dish inspired by our local truffle expert, Hervé Poron. I rarely make fresh pasta at home anymore, since Giuseppina Giacomo, the village shopkeeper we've dubbed 'Madame Pâtes Fraîches' provides us with golden sheets of fresh egg pasta for forming into rectangles of lasagne, or cutting into strands of fettucine for tossing with creamy Roquefort cheese, lemon zest, and a touch of fresh rosemary. Our local green olives go into a variation on the popular Puttanesca, while Monday evenings we'll be found near the fire, downing helpings of Monday Night Spaghetti, laced with an avalanche of fresh herbs – parsley, sage, rosemary, basil, and thyme.

FACING PHOTOGRAPH: *Old stone steps lead to the master bedroom, where a louvered shutter allows for a cool evening breeze. When the rosemary is freshly trimmed, the adjacent rooms are perfumed with the herb's heady, oil-rich scent.*

FETTUCINE WITH ROQUEFORT, LEMON ZEST & ROSEMARY

It's really a shame that so much goes down the drain – pasta cooking water, that is. The starch and delicate flavour of the liquid, when used judiciously, can enhance the texture and flavour of many pasta dishes. I sampled a version of this dish one evening in Germany, at the Michelin three-star restaurant of Heinz Winkler. The next day, chef Winkler kindly demonstrated his version, one that's surprisingly light despite the addition of rich Roquefort cheese. In fact, this is one of the lighter pastas I know, with just a gentle hint of Roquefort, amplified by a generous dose of nutmeg, a ration of butter, a soupçon of lemon zest. It's a 'midnight' pasta if ever there was one, for making when you're starved and in a hurry! Even those who are not Roquefort fans will want 'seconds'.

45 g (1½ oz) unsalted butter, at room temperature

45 g (1½ oz) Roquefort cheese, at room temperature

500 g (1 lb) fresh or dried fettuccine or tagliatelle

3 tablespoons sea salt

About 250 ml (8 fl oz) pasta cooking water

Freshly grated nutmeg to taste

Zest of 1 lemon

1 tablespoon fresh rosemary leaves, finely chopped (8 fl oz) pasta cooking water

Freshly ground black pepper to taste

1. Preheat the oven to the lowest possible setting, about 110°C/230°F/gas mark ¼. Place a large heatproof bowl in the oven to warm.

2. In a small bowl, mash the butter and Roquefort with a fork until soft and well-blended. Set aside.

3. In a large pan, bring 6 litres (10 pints) of water to a rolling boil. Add the salt and the pasta, stirring to prevent the pasta from sticking. Cook until tender, 1 to 2 minutes. Carefully drain the pasta, leaving a few drops of water clinging to the pasta so that the sauce will adhere. Reserve 250 ml (8 fl oz) of cooking water.

4. Add the pasta to the warmed bowl, and add the butter-Roquefort mixture, tossing the pasta slowly and gently until the pasta absorbs all of the mixture. Slowly add the cooking water, tablespoon by tablespoon, until the pasta is evenly coated with sauce. (Rather than thinning out the sauce, the starchy water will actually work to thicken it.) Season generously with nutmeg and toss with the lemon zest and rosemary. Taste, then season with pepper. Toss once more. Transfer to warmed shallow soup bowls and serve.

SERVES 4-6

WINE SUGGESTIONS: This is lovely with an Italian white wine: a golden-smooth Umbrian Orvieto, a Frascati from the Roman hills or a nicely chilled Vernaccia di San Gimignano.

FUSILLI WITH SAUSAGE, FENNEL & RED WINE

This hearty cold-weather pasta is a full-flavoured blend of well-seasoned pork sausage and a hint of fennel, all held together with a silky red wine sauce. Just before serving a few eggs are tossed with the pasta – carbonara-style – as a gentle binder, producing a dense clinging sauce. Search out the best sausage meat you can find, preferably a well-seasoned pork sausage sold either in bulk or in links (in which case you'll need to remove the meat from the casings). I make this dish both with fusilli – the little corkscrew pasta – or with the quill-like penne. They're both an ideal shape for trapping pieces of sausage, giving you equal amounts of sauce and pasta with each bite. In this recipe it is a good idea to reserve a bit of pasta cooking water to even out the sauce at the very end. Note that red wine replaces traditional water or stock in the sauce, adding additional balance, character and flavour to the dish.

500 g (1 lb) sausage meat, broken into small pieces
1 teaspoon fennel seeds
3 tablespoons tomato paste
500 ml (16 fl oz) dry red wine, such as Chianti
2 eggs, at room temperature
500 g (1 lb) dried pasta, such as fusilli or penne
Sea salt and freshly ground black pepper to taste
30 g (1 oz) freshly grated Parmigiano-Reggiano cheese
About 250 ml (8 fl oz) pasta cooking water

1. In a frying pan large enough to hold the pasta later on, brown the sausage with no additional fat over low heat for 3 to 4 minutes. With the end of a spatula, continue to break up the sausage pieces into fine bits of meat. Add the fennel seeds and tomato paste, toss to blend, and cook for 3 to 4 minutes to allow the flavours to blend.
2. Slowly add the wine, pouring it all over the surface of the pan. Adjust the heat to bring the liquid to a gentle simmer and cook, uncovered, until most of the wine – and alcohol – have cooked off, about 15 minutes from the time the liquid comes to a simmer.
3. Meanwhile, place the eggs in a small bowl and whisk to blend. Whisk in the cheese and a generous grinding of pepper. Set aside.
4. In a large pan, bring 6 litres (10 pints) of water to a rolling boil. When the water boils, add 3 tablespoons salt and the pasta, stirring to prevent the pasta from sticking. Cook until tender but firm to the bite, 9 to 11 minutes. Carefully drain the pasta, leaving a few drops of water clinging to the pasta so that the sauce will adhere. Reserve 250 ml (8 fl oz) of cooking water.
5. Add the pasta to the frying pan with the sausage meat and use two forks to toss thoroughly, evenly coating the pasta with the sauce. Remove the pan from the heat and, working quickly with two forks, stir in the egg mixture and continue to toss until each piece of pasta is evenly coated with sauce. (The pasta should not be dry: If it is, add the pasta water, tablespoon by tablespoon, tossing after each addition, to create a smooth clinging sauce.)
6. Serve immediately in warmed shallow soup bowls. Pass the pepper mills.

SERVES 4-6

WINE SUGGESTION: This pasta can take a big wine: I love it with a fine Piedmont red, such as a Dolcetto d'Alba.

PENNE 'RISOTTO'

This recipe was inspired by a visit to French chef Alain Ducasse's country hotel-restaurant, La Bastide de Moustiers, a lovely three-hour drive – across Provence's most stunning lavender fields – from our home. Before dinner, I chatted with the resident chef, Sonja Lee, about the evening's menu. She began talking about penne cooked like risotto and I conjured up an instant image of a bowl of dense, perfectly cooked pasta, penetrated with the rich flavours of a tomato sauce. Rather than boiling the pasta in water, the penne is actually cooked like risotto: It is browned lightly in oil, tossed with a thick coating of tomato paste, then cooked slowly, by adding spoonfuls of broth, stirring and tossing until it is cooked through and only a veil of sauce remains. The end result is a pasta that is deeply flavoured and so unusual. Ask your guests to guess how it was cooked: I'll bet few will get the right answer. The recipe is said to originate with the workers in the olive oil mills along the Mediterranean coast. Each time I prepare the dish, I vary it. For a vegetarian pasta, I substitute a rich herb broth for chicken stock. I once prepared this with a rich duck stock, and everyone kept looking for the bits of meat they were sure had been added to the sauce.

> 500 g (1 lb) dried tubular pasta, such as penne
> About 2.5 litres (4 pints) homemade Potager Stock (page 321) or Chicken Stock (page 322)
> 125 ml (4 fl oz) extra-virgin olive oil
> 2 tablespoons fresh rosemary leaves, finely chopped
> ¼ teaspoon crushed red peppers (hot red pepper flakes), or to taste
> ½ teaspoon fine sea salt
> 4 tablespoons tomato paste
> 2 teaspoons homemade red wine vinegar
> 60 g (2 oz) freshly grated Parmigiano-Reggiano cheese

1. In a large saucepan, heat the stock and keep it simmering, with barely an occasional bubble, while preparing the pasta.
2. In a heavy-duty frying pan large enough to hold all the pasta (it need not be in a single layer), heat the oil over moderately high heat. When hot but not smoking, add all the pasta with the rosemary and peppers, stirring continuously until the pasta begins to brown lightly around the edges, 3 to 4 minutes. Season with salt, and add all the tomato paste, stirring constantly until the pasta is uniformly coated with the sauce.
3. Slowly add a ladleful of stock, stirring until most of the liquid is absorbed. Adjust heat as necessary to maintain a gentle simmer. The pasta should cook slowly, and should always be covered in at least a light film of stock. Continue adding ladlefuls of stock, stirring frequently and tasting regularly, until the pasta is tender and firm to the bite, about

17 minutes total. Add the vinegar and toss. Taste for seasoning. Add about half the cheese and toss to blend. Serve immediately, in warmed shallow soup bowls. Pass a bowl with the remaining cheese to sprinkle over the pasta.

SERVES 4-6

WINE SUGGESTIONS: I like a dense meaty wine with this dish. Try a Gigondas from Provence, an Australian Shiraz, a spicy Rhône-style red from California, or a Montepulciano d'Abruzzo from Italy.

⌁ **HOT WATER OR COLD?** ⌁ Following rules I somehow learned as a child, I always began with cold tap water – rather than hot – when filling a pan with water to bring to a boil. One day I decided to research the reason for this time-wasting habit: As it turns out, the concern stems for the lead in pipes, which would leach out more readily in hot water than cold. Today, most lead pipes have been replaced by other harmless materials. So today, it's okay to fill your stock pots with steaming tap water. See how quickly even a 'watched' pot will boil!

MONDAY NIGHT SPAGHETTI

Most stores are closed in Vaison-la-Romaine on Monday, and this is when I turn to the garden and pantry for sustenance. The bold fresh flavours of just-picked herbs, a touch of spicy red pepper and the soothing flavour of tomato sauce make this a favourite. Make sure the herbs are fresh, and use a good variety in the sauce, and lots of rosemary, basil, and thyme as garnish.

500 g (1 lb) spaghetti

3 tablespoons extra-virgin olive oil

6 plump fresh garlic cloves, finely chopped

½ teaspoon crushed red peppers (hot red pepper flakes), or to taste

Sea salt to taste

One 765-g (28-oz) can of peeled plum tomatoes in juice, or one 765-g (28-oz) can of crushed tomatoes in purée

Bouquet garni: Generous bunch of fresh rosemary, parsley, bay leaf, thyme and sage, tied with string

1 teaspoon best-quality red wine vinegar

A handful of finely chopped fresh rosemary, parsley, thyme, sage, and basil, for garnish

Freshly grated Parmigiano-Reggiano cheese, for the table

1. In an unheated frying pan large enough to hold the pasta later on, combine the oil, garlic and crushed red peppers and salt, stirring to coat with the oil. Cook over moderate heat just until the garlic turns golden, but does not brown, 2 to 3 minutes.

2. If using whole canned tomatoes, purée in a blender or food processor, or place a food mill over the frying pan and purée the tomatoes directly into it. Crushed tomatoes can be added directly from the can. Add the bouquet garni. Season with additional salt, stir to blend and simmer, partially covered (to capture the herbed infusion), until the sauce begins to thicken, about 15 minutes. Remove and discard the herb bundle. Taste for seasoning.

3. Meanwhile, in a large pan, bring 6 litres (10 pints) of water to a rolling boil. Add 3 tablespoons sea salt and the spaghetti, stirring to prevent the pasta from sticking. Cook until tender but firm to the bite, 11 to 14 minutes. Drain thoroughly.

4. Add the drained pasta to the sauce. Toss, add the vinegar, cover, and let rest off the heat for 1 to 2 minutes to allow the pasta to absorb the sauce. Add about half the finely chopped fresh herbs and toss again. Transfer to warmed shallow soup bowls, and sprinkle with the remaining herbs. Serve immediately, passing a bowl of cheese.

SERVES 4-6

WINE SUGGESTION: Serve a sturdy red wine that will stand up to the spice of the sauce, such as a Dolcetto d'Alba or a spicy Côtes du Rhône.

SPAGHETTI WITH GREEN OLIVE PUTTANESCA

On one visit to our market in Vaison-la-Romaine, I counted no less than 20 different varieties of green olives, seasoned with herbs, spices and vegetables, cured in many different ways. The fresh pungency of green olives is often ignored in cooking, where black olives often take a front seat. Here is a Provence-inspired variation on the classic spaghetti alla puttanesca, substituting green olives for black, and fresh thyme for parsley, offering a new dimension to an old favourite.

3 tablespoons capers
3 tablespoons extra-virgin olive oil
3 plump fresh garlic cloves, finely chopped
½ teaspoon crushed red peppers (hot red pepper flakes), or to taste
One 765-g (28-oz) can of peeled plum tomatoes in juice, or one 765-g (28-oz) can of
    crushed tomatoes in purée
20 top-quality green olives (such as French Picholine), drained, stoned, and chopped
Sea salt to taste
500 g (1 lb) spaghetti
1 tablespoon fresh thyme leaves

1. Drain the capers, rinse well and soak in cold water for 10 minutes to remove excess salt.
2. In an unheated frying pan large enough to hold the pasta later on, combine the oil, garlic and crushed red peppers. Cook over moderate heat just until the garlic turns golden but does not brown, 2 to 3 minutes.
3. If using whole canned tomatoes, place a food mill over the frying pan and purée the tomatoes directly into it. Crushed tomatoes can be added directly from the can. Add the olives and the drained capers. Season with salt, stir to blend, cover, and simmer until the sauce begins to thicken, about 15 minutes. Taste for seasoning.
4. Meanwhile, in a large pot, bring 6 litres (10 pints) of water to a rolling boil. Add 3 tablespoons sea salt and the spaghetti, stirring to prevent the pasta from sticking. Cook until tender but firm to the bite, 11 to 14 minutes. Drain thoroughly.
5. Add the drained pasta to the pan with the sauce. Toss, cover and let rest off the heat for 1 to 2 minutes to allow the pasta to absorb the sauce. Add the thyme and toss again. Serve immediately in warmed shallow soup bowls. Traditionally, cheese is not served.

SERVES 4-6

WINE SUGGESTION: A dependable Chianti, such as those from the Antinori or Ricasoli estates.

INDIVIDUAL COURGETTE LASAGNE WITH SPICY PIZZA SAUCE

The inspiration for this dish comes from colleagues Johanne Killeen and George Germon of Al Forno restaurant in Providence, Rhode Island. This version is actually 'constructed' in individual portions at serving time. Simply count on two strips of lasagne per serving.

4 tablespoons extra-virgin olive oil

3 tablespoons fresh rosemary leaves, finely chopped

½ teaspoon crushed red peppers (hot red pepper flakes), or to taste

10 plump fresh garlic cloves, slivered

Sea salt to taste

One 765-g (28-oz) can of peeled plum tomatoes in juice, or one 765-g (28-oz) can of crushed tomatoes in purée

200 g (7 oz) firm fresh courgettes, scrubbed, trimmed, and thinly sliced (do not peel)

½ teaspoon dried leaf oregano

2 tablespoons balsamic vinegar

8 sheets of dried lasagne (do not use the precooked variety)

1. In an unheated frying pan combine the 3 tablespoons of oil, the rosemary, crushed red peppers, garlic and salt. Cook over moderate heat just until the garlic turns golden, but does not brown, 2 to 3 minutes. If using whole canned tomatoes, place a food mill over the pan and purée the tomatoes directly into it. Crushed tomatoes can be added from the can. Stir to blend, and simmer, uncovered, until the sauce begins to thicken, about 15 minutes.

2. While the sauce is simmering, prepare the courgettes: In a large, non-stick frying pan, heat the remaining 1 tablespoon of oil over moderately high heat. When the oil is hot but not smoking, add the courgettes and sauté just until golden, about 5 minutes. Transfer to a colander to drain any excess oil, season with salt and toss with oregano. Add the courgettes to the sauce in the frying pan and toss. Add the balsamic vinegar and toss. Cover, and let rest over low heat 1 to 2 minutes to allow the courgettes to absorb the sauce.

3. Meanwhile, in a large pan bring 6 litres (10 pints) of water to a rolling boil. Add 3 tablespoons of salt and the lasagne, stirring to prevent the pasta from sticking. Cook until tender but firm to the bite, about 4 minutes. Drain thoroughly.

4. Place a spoonful of the sauced courgettes on a warmed dinner plate. Top with a layer of lasagne. Add a second layer of sauce, a second layer of lasagne, and a third layer of sauce. Repeat with additional servings, until all the pasta and sauce have been used. Serve.

SERVES 4

WINE SUGGESTION: Either a young Italian red, such as a Barbera d'Alba, or a white, such as Pinot Grigio.

CATALAN FRIED NOODLES

Nearly each day in Provence I am reminded of the unity of Mediterranean cuisine and the realization that the related cuisines have virtually no borders. While garlic mayonnaise, or aïoli, is generally tied to Provence, I've had endlessly delicious versions in Spain, particularly in Barcelona, where it shows up as a tapas topping for potatoes and always with the ever-popular *fideos*, a pasta side-dish that's prepared much like the Italian risotto. I serve it on days I'm looking for a quick and filling dish with a great hit of garlic. I first sampled this dish at Barcelona's El Dorado Petit, where they tossed the pasta with cubes of monkfish and serve it with a garlic-rich sauce.

250 g (8 oz) *fideos* noodles (or dried angel-hair pasta, capelli d'angelo, or vermicelli), broken into 5-cm (2-in) lengths

2 tablespoons extra-virgin olive oil

250 ml (8 fl oz) Chicken Stock (page 322)

1 recipe Aïoli (page 314)

1. Preheat the oven to 180°C/350°F/gas mark 4.

2. In a large bowl, toss the pasta with the oil. Spread evenly on a rimmed non-stick baking sheet. Place in the centre of the oven and bake, shaking from time to time, until golden brown, 5 to 7 minutes. Do not allow the pasta to burn. Remove from the oven and set aside.

3. In a large saucepan, bring the stock to a boil over high heat. Add the browned noodles, stir to blend and cook, covered, until most of the liquid is absorbed, about 5 minutes.

4. Stir in several tablespoons of garlic mayonnaise. Serve immediately, transferring to warmed shallow soup bowls. Pass a bowl with additional garlic mayonnaise to add to the noodles.

SERVES 4

WINE SUGGESTIONS: To counter the intensity of the aïoli, you'll want a thirst-quenching wine: A young red from the Rhône, a rosé from Provence, or a pale white Italian Verdicchio.

No man is lonely while eating spaghetti: it requires so much attention.
CHRISTOPHER MORLEY

SPICY RED PEPPER SPAGHETTI

Brilliant red sweet peppers from the potager or the market remain gems of Provence's summer bounty. Here, red peppers are seared with onions, garlic and a touch of pepper, enriched with chicken stock, then turned into a slightly coarse purée. The method of tossing the pasta – first with the cheese, then with the sauce – results in a pasta with greater depth of flavour, since the pasta first absorbs the cheese, then the rosy sauce. I often make a double batch for the freezer, for those days when I'm pressed for time in the kitchen.

4 red sweet peppers
500 g (1 lb) onions
4 tablespoons extra-virgin olive oil
Sea salt to taste
2 plump fresh garlic cloves, finely chopped
½ teaspoon crushed red peppers (hot red pepper flakes), or to taste
500 ml (16 fl oz) chicken or vegetable stock, preferably homemade (page 322)
500 g (1 lb) spaghetti
90 g (3 oz) freshly grated Parmigiano-Reggiano cheese

1. Halve the peppers, trim and discard the core, veins and seeds. Chop the flesh coarsely and set aside.
2. Slice an onion in half lengthwise. Place cut side down on a cutting board and cut across into very thin slices. Slice the remaining onions in this manner. Set aside.
3. In a large frying pan, heat the oil over moderate heat until hot but not smoking. Add the peppers and a pinch of salt and cook, stirring regularly until softened, about 5 minutes. Add the onions, garlic, red pepper flakes and another pinch of salt and cook over moderate heat until the onions begin to soften, about 5 minutes more. (Do not let the onions brown.) Add the stock and simmer, uncovered, over moderate heat until thickened, about 30 minutes.
4. Transfer the mixture in small batches to a food processor or blender, being careful to remove the plunger or lid, so the liquid does not splatter. Process to a coarse purée. Return to the saucepan in batches and reheat gently over low heat.
5. Meanwhile, in a large pan, bring 6 litres (10 pints) of water to a rolling boil over high heat. Add 3 tablespoons of sea salt and the spaghetti, stirring to prevent the pasta from

sticking. Cook until tender but firm to the bite, 11 to 14 minutes. Drain thoroughly.
6. Add the drained pasta to a large bowl and add about half the cheese. Toss gently and thoroughly, until all the cheese has been absorbed. Add the pepper sauce and toss again, until all of the sauce has been absorbed. Taste for seasoning. Serve immediately, in warmed shallow bowls. Pass a bowl with the remaining cheese to sprinkle over the pasta.

SERVES 4-6

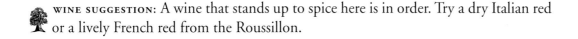 WINE SUGGESTION: A wine that stands up to spice here is in order. Try a dry Italian red or a lively French red from the Roussillon.

∽ SOME LIKE IT HOT! ∽ Be careful when adding hot ingredients to the container of a food processor or blender: Always add in small batches, and remove the lid or plunger so that the hot air and steam can escape. This way, less splattering, easier clean ups!

∽ DON'T THROW AWAY THAT STARCH! ∽ Traditionally, the promise of a classical French sauce is to deliver strong flavour and smooth texture. Most sauces are thickened with a starch – in most cases flour – and finished with additional reducing for a more concentrated flavour or with butter to give a glossy effect. Water drained from pasta provides a natural source of starch that acts as a thickening agent: So let the starch that is normally thrown away add body and life to the pasta sauce (see the recipes on pages 147 and 149).

HERVÉ'S TRUFFLE BUTTER PASTA

ervé Poron is our local truffle expert: He runs one of the world's largest truffle preserving operations. From November to March, his little factory in Puymeras is in full operation, as he and his staff weigh, clean, trim and measure the bountiful local truffle crop. On one visit, he gave me a sample of the truffle butter he had

created. I tossed it on fresh pasta made by Giuseppina Giacomo, owner of the village pasta shop, and was instantly convinced that this is one of the finest ways to consume black truffles. Their fragrance and rich flavour are accentuated by the butter and fully absorbed into the pasta.

I think of this as the classic black cocktail dress of food: Simplicity as well as perfection. If you are truly smitten with the essence of truffles, prepare your own pasta, but first store the eggs enclosed in a jar with the truffles for a day or two. Pasta prepared with the eggs will take on a rich truffle flavour of its own. Since the dish is very rich, serve in small portions.

Fresh truffles infuse fresh eggs with their mysterious flavor and fragrance.

> Sea salt to taste
> 500 g (1 lb) fresh fettuccine or tagliatelle
> 125 g (4 oz) unsalted butter
> 30 g (1 oz) fresh black truffles, finely chopped

1. In a large pan, bring 6 litres (10 pints) of water to a rolling boil. Add 3 tablespoons sea salt and the pasta, stirring to prevent the pasta from sticking. Cook until tender, about 1 minute. Drain thoroughly.
2. Meanwhile, in a frying pan large enough to hold the pasta later on, melt the butter over lowest possible heat. Add the truffles and toss to blend.
3. Add the drained pasta to the frying pan with the sauce. Toss, cover and let rest off the heat for 1 to 2 minutes to allow the pasta to absorb the sauce.
4. Transfer to warmed shallow soup bowls and serve immediately.

SERVES 6

WINE SUGGESTION: A rich white is ideal here: Try one prepared with the viognier grape, such as one from California or the Rhône valley.

FACING PHOTOGRAPH: *Fresh truffle 'sandwich': St. Marcellin cow's milk cheese is sliced in half, fresh sliced black truffles are slipped between the halves, then all is grilled just until the cheese melts. Delicious!*

CHECCHINO DAL 1887'S SPAGHETTI ALLA CARBONARA

Spaghetti carbonara seems to have as many versions as there are cooks who prepare it. The best one I ever tasted was at Trattoria Checchino dal 1887 in Rome. They present it sauced with a blend of eggs, a good hit of freshly ground black pepper, matchsticks of crisp pancetta, and a mixture of Pecorino and Parmigiano-Reggiano cheeses. Despite its popularity, spaghetti alla carbonara, is often disappointing. Deceptively simply, it is an easily put together dish that demands great attention to detail. Think of it as a two-step process, where you have to work quickly. First, thoroughly coat the pasta with the pancetta and oil, then – off the heat – toss with the seasoned eggs. When I do it, I send everyone out of the kitchen, so I can concentrate 100 percent.

> 4 large eggs, at room temperature
> Sea salt and freshly ground black pepper to taste
> 5 tablespoons extra-virgin olive oil
> 100 g (3½ oz) pancetta, very thinly sliced and cut into matchsticks
> 500 g (1 lb) spaghetti
> 30 g (1 oz) freshly grated Pecorino cheese
> 30 g (1 oz) freshly grated Parmigiano-Reggiano cheese

1. Place the eggs in a small bowl and whisk until smooth. Whisk in a pinch of salt and a generous grinding of pepper. Set aside.

2. In a frying pan large enough to hold the pasta later on, combine the oil and pancetta and sauté gently over moderate heat, just until the pancetta begins to crisp and turn a very light brown, 4 to 5 minutes. Set aside.

3. In a large pot, bring 6 litres (10 pints) of water to a rolling boil over high heat. Add 3 tablespoons of sea salt and the pasta, stirring to prevent the pasta from sticking. Cook until tender but firm, or al dente, 11 to 14 minutes. With tongs or a slotted spoon, transfer the pasta to a colander to drain. Toss well to eliminate as much water as possible.

4. Add the spaghetti to the pancetta in the frying pan, and over low heat thoroughly toss to coat the pasta with the oil. Remove the pan from the heat and, working quickly, stir in the egg mixture and continue to toss until the mixture is thoroughly blended and each strand of pasta is coated with the thick satiny golden sauce. (If the pan is too hot, you will have scrambled eggs: To avoid this be certain to add the eggs off the heat.) Serve immediately, in warmed shallow soup bowls. Pass the cheeses and the pepper mill.

SERVES 4-6

WINE SUGGESTION: A dry white, from the Castelli Roman vineyards near Rome or a zesty white Pinot Grigio.

PROVENÇAL PENNE

In Provence, cooks often enliven their tomato sauce with a bit of orange zest, a practice I've followed for years. Going one step further, I enjoy bathing bulb fennel in a tomato-and-orange sauce, making for a dish that pleases the eye as well as the palate.

4 tablespoons extra virgin olive oil
1 medium onion, finely chopped
2 garlic cloves, finely chopped
½ teaspoon crushed red peppers (hot red pepper flakes), or to taste
1 fresh bay leaf
Sea salt to taste
1 fennel bulb (about 250 g/8 oz), trimmed and cut into matchsticks
One 765-g (28-oz) can of peeled plum tomatoes in juice, or one 765-g (28-oz) can of
    crushed tomatoes in purée
Zest of 1 orange (preferably organic), cut into matchsticks
500 g (1 lb) dried tubular pasta, such as penne
3 tablespoons fresh flat-leaf parsley leaves, snipped with scissors

1. In an unheated frying pan large enough to hold the pasta later on, combine the oil, onion, garlic, crushed red pepper, bay leaf and a pinch of salt, and toss to coat with the oil. Place over moderate heat, cooking just until the garlic turns golden but does not brown, 2 to 3 minutes. Add the fennel, stirring so the ingredients blend together and are evenly coated in the oil. Cover and sweat for 10 minutes over a moderate heat. Toss the fennel with a wooden spoon from time to time to ensure that none sticks or burns.
2. If using whole canned tomatoes, place a food mill over the frying pan and purée the tomatoes directly into it. Crushed tomatoes can be added directly from the can. Add the orange zest. Stir to blend and simmer, uncovered, until the sauce begins to thicken, about 15 minutes. Taste for seasoning. Remove and discard the bay leaf.
3. Meanwhile in a large pan, bring 6 litres (10 pints) of water to a rolling boil. Add 3 tablespoons of salt and the pasta, stirring to prevent it from sticking to the bottom. Cook until tender but still firm to the bite. Drain thoroughly.
4. Add the drained pasta to the frying pan with the fennel sauce. Toss. Cover and reduce the heat to low, and let rest for 1 to 2 minutes, stirring to coat the pasta with the sauce. Taste for seasoning. Add the parsley and toss again. Transfer to warmed shallow soup bowls and serve immediately.

SERVES 4-6

 WINE SUGGESTION: A good-quality red that can stand up to the spice and the orange is ideal, such as a Chianti Classico from Tuscany or a California Zinfandel.

What you eat and drink is 50 percent of life.
GÉRARD DEPARDIEU

PATRICIA'S SPAGHETTI WITH CLAMS

Nearly two decades of living in France has helped give me a sense of building flavours in the kitchen. Often, a simple step – such as straining or reducing a liquid – can transform a dish from one that's ordinary to one that delivers big substantial flavours. Here, the extra step of steaming the clams, then reducing the clam liquor for a refined sauce results in a subtle, elegant fusion of flavours. The sweetness of the clam liquor balances nicely with the tomato's acidity, resulting in a wonderfully refined clam flavour.

> 1 kg (2 lb) small fresh little neck or carpet-shell clams (about 40 clams)
> Sea salt and freshly ground black pepper to taste
> 500 ml (16 fl oz) homemade Tomato Sauce (page 325)
> 500 g (1 lb) spaghetti
> 2 tablespoons fresh thyme leaves

1. If necessary, purge the clams. Since most clams come from sandy areas, they tend to be sandy themselves. To test for grittiness, steam open a few open and taste them. If they are gritty, purge them in salt water, thoroughly dissolving 1 tablespoon salt per litre (1¾ pints) of cold water. Scrub the shells under cold running water, then purge in the water for 3 hours at room temperature. Pick up the clams with your fingers, leaving behind the grit and sand. (You will be amazed at the amount of sand they give up.) Scrub the clams thoroughly under cold running water with a stiff brush. Discard any with broken shells or shells that do not close when tapped. Transfer them to a shallow dish and season generously with freshly ground pepper.

2. Prepare a large steamer: Fill the bottom portion with 250 ml (8 fl oz) water and bring to a boil. Transfer the clams to the steamer basket and steam, removing the clams one by one as they open. The entire process should take less than 10 minutes. Discard any shells that do not open. Reserve the liquid in the bottom of the steamer: This is your clam liquor. Remove the clams from their shells. Discard the shells and place the clam meat in a small bowl. Place a double thickness of moistened cheesecloth over a strainer, and pour the clam liquor through the cheesecloth directly over the clams. Rinse the clams in the clam liquor, to help remove any recalcitrant sand, and, at the same time, to plump the clams in their own juices. With a slotted spoon, transfer the clams to another small bowl and cover so they do not dry out. Pour the clam liquor once more through the cheese-

cloth-lined strainer into a covered frying pan large enough to hold the pasta later on.

3. Place the frying pan over high heat and reduce the clam liquor to about 4 tablespoons, 6 to 7 minutes. Whisk in the tomato sauce and simmer for 2 to 3 minutes to fuse the flavours. (The recipe can prepared up to this point several hours in advance. Reheat gently at serving time, tasting for seasoning.)

4. Cook the pasta: In a large pan, bring 6 litres (10 pints) of water to a boil. Add 3 tablespoons of salt and the pasta, and cook just until tender but still firm to the bite, 11 to 14 minutes. With a slotted spoon, transfer the pasta to a colander to drain. Toss well to eliminate as much water as possible.

5. Add the drained pasta to the frying pan with the clam-flavoured tomato sauce and toss thoroughly. Add the reserved clams. Cover and warm gently over very low heat, allowing the pasta to absorb the sauce, 1 to 2 minutes. Taste for seasoning. Transfer to warmed individual shallow bowls, sprinkle with thyme and serve immediately.

SERVES 4-6

WINE SUGGESTIONS: The tomato sauce all but dictates a red wine here: Try an Italian Barbera, a Californian Zinfandel, or a light red Côtes-du-Rhône.

✑ HAPPY AS A CLAM! ↝ Actually the expression is 'Happy as a clam at high tide'. Since clams live in sand, they can't be gathered while the sand is under water.

6

BREAD

ON ANY GIVEN DAY IN PROVENCE I CAN BE found in the kitchen first thing each morning, mixing, kneading, concocting a bread, a biscuit, the makings of a bread tart or a pizzalike fougasse. I know of few acts that give a cook as much spiritual nourishment as making bread. With a batch of dough assembled in just minutes, I am rewarded with a feeling of true accomplishment before the sun is fully risen, before I've set down the road for a run or a trip to the market. Bread is patient, bread is flexible, bread is responsive. There's bread for breakfast (such as Baby Chocolate Brioche), bread for sandwiches we'll take on the train back to Paris (Golden Parmesan-Pepper Loaf) and those ideal for the cheese tray that accompanies each dinner (Fig, Apricot, Walnut, & Raisin Rye). In the winter months I crave the rich, warming density of a slice of Rita's Rye, while at Christmas time Provençal Olive Oil Brioche feeds the need for tradition. Pine Nut Rolls remind me of summer and the sun, while Oatmeal Biscuits appear on the menu when we're in the mood for a blue cheese feast, accompanied by a sip of sweet *vin doux naturel* from the nearby Domaine La Soumade.

FACING PHOTOGRAPH: *Walter unloads* ceps de vigne, *spent trunks of vines used as fuel for the outdoor bread oven that Patricia tends in the courtyard of their farmhouse.*

POMPE À L'HUILE: PROVENÇAL OLIVE OIL BRIOCHE

Years ago I made an olive oil brioche – known as *pompe à l'huile* – to celebrate our first Christmas in Provence. For some unknown reason, I put the recipe on the back burner, so to speak, and forgot about it. I resurrected it recently, and in the period of a single week, made more than half a dozen versions.

I paired the golden dough with quickly seared foie gras in a syrupy sherry as I had savoured in Spain; I wrapped it around a truffled pork sausage and baked it, serving a traditional mustard sauce alongside; served it with cheese and sweet-and-sour Mostarda (page 331) in place of dessert. Each morning, guests came down to breakfast and headed for the bread drawer, cutting off thick slices of brioche, to toast and sample with homemade apricot jam. Few recipes are as versatile as this one.

I'm a brioche lover, but pretty much stopped making it because of the high butter content. This recipe – using only extra-virgin olive oil as the fat – is ideal for today's world. It's light, only mildly sweet, is right at home on the breakfast, lunch and dinner table. In short, a hit!

1 teaspoon active dry yeast
1 teaspoon sugar
250 ml (8 fl oz) lukewarm water (about 40°C/105°F)
4 tablespoons extra-virgin olive oil
2 large eggs, at room temperature
2 teaspoons fine sea salt
Grated zest of 1 orange, preferably organic
Grated zest of 1 lemon, preferably organic
1 tablespoon orange flower water (optional)
About 675 g (1¼ lb) plain flour
1 beaten egg yolk, for glazing

1. In the bowl of a heavy-duty electric mixer fitted with a dough hook, combine the yeast, sugar and water, and stir to blend. Let stand until foamy, about 5 minutes. Stir in the olive oil, eggs, salt, orange and lemon zests and orange flower water (or substitute 1 tablespoon water), and stir to blend.

2. Add the flour, a little at a time, mixing at the lowest speed until most of the flour has been absorbed and the dough forms a ball. Continue to knead until soft and satiny but still firm, 4 to 5 minutes, adding additional flour as necessary to keep the dough from sticking.

3. Transfer the dough to a bowl, cover tightly with plastic wrap and place in the refrigerator. Let the dough rise in the refrigerator until doubled or tripled in bulk, 8 to 12 hours.

(continued on next page)

(The dough can be kept for 2 to 3 days in the refrigerator. Simply punch down the dough as it doubles or triples.)

4. About an hour before you plan to bake the brioche, remove the dough from the refrigerator. Punch down the dough, roll it into a circle and shape in the form of a crown, forming a small hole in the centre of the crown. Place on a non-stick baking sheet and place a small tea cup in the hole to keep it from closing up as the dough rises. Cover with a clean towel and let rise until about double in bulk, about 1 hour.

5. Preheat the oven to 200°C/400°F/gas mark 6.

6. Remove the towel and the tea cup and brush the dough with the egg yolk glaze. Place the baking sheet in the centre of the oven. Bake until the brioche is a deep golden brown, about 30 minutes, turning the baking sheet from time to time if the oven is heating unevenly.

7. Remove the brioche from the oven and transfer to a rack to cool. If stored in a sealed plastic bag, the brioche will stay fresh for 2 to 3 days.

MAKES 1 LARGE BRIOCHE

VARIATIONS: In Provence, the olive oil brioche may be seasoned with about 1 teaspoon of fennel grains, or even rolled into two layers, flavoured with several tablespoons of quince jam – *confiture de coings* – in between the layers.

❧ **A CHRISTMAS TRADITION** ❧   In the region of Aix-en-Provence it's known as the *gibassié*, in Manosque they call it *fougasse*, in the northern part of the Vaucluse, it may be called *pogne*, but by any name the *pompe à l'huile* is sacred in Provence, an essential element of Christmas-eve dinner. Prepared with the first-pressed olive oil of the season, the brioche was traditionally arranged in the bakery on straw baskets in threes, as a symbol of the Trinity.

❧ **THE HONOUR OF BREAD** ❧   For the French, bread is a staple of any good meal. Different types of bread are baked fresh daily all over France, and because of its common appeal there are many expressions surrounding bread. My favourites include: *Long comme un jour sans pain* (As long as a day without bread) or *Il a mangé son pain blanc le premier* (literally, he ate the white bread first – an expression that refers to someone who takes the best first and leaves the rest for last). More simply, *gagner son pain* (win his bread) is how someone makes a living, or wins his daily bread.

*Bread is the warmest, kindest of words. Write it always
with a capital letter, like your own name.*

RUSSIAN CAFÉ SIGN

PINE NUT ROLLS

Early one July, friends invited us to dine at the Château Eza in Eza, an enchanting hill town near Monte Carlo. The evening had a special allure: We were beginning a two-week vacation, we were with friends we had not seen in a long time and the meal offered many pleasant surprises. The best of which was the assortment of breads, including these tiny pine nut rolls. Pine nuts, of course, come from the parasol pines one sees looming all over the Mediterranean, so it seemed like a perfectly natural flavouring there. I love the creamy, almost haunting flavour of pine nuts. But beware: They become rancid if not properly stored. Be sure to buy from a reputable merchant, and store them in the freezer until they will be used. For best results, toast them for 2 to 3 minutes in a warm oven to bring out their mystical flavour.

> 1 recipe basic bread dough, prepared through step 3 (page 185)
> 125 g (4 oz) pine nuts, toasted and cooled

1. About 1½ hours before you plan to bake the rolls, remove the dough from the refrigerator. Punch down the dough, place it in a bowl, cover with a clean towel and let rise at room temperature for about 1 hour.

2. Preheat the oven to 230°C/450°F/gas mark 8.

3. Separate the dough into 15 even portions, each weighing about 60 g (2 oz). Press several teaspoons of pine nuts into each portion of dough and shape each into a neat round, pulling the dough around itself to form a tight ball. Place each portion of dough on a baking sheet. Cover with a clean towel and let rise for 30 minutes.

4. Remove the towel and place the baking sheet in the centre of the oven. Using a large plant sprayer filled with water, spray the bottom and sides of the oven with water. Spray 3 more times for the next 6 minutes. (The spray will help give the rolls a good crust.) Bake until the dough turns a deep golden brown, 20 to 25 minutes, turning the baking sheet from time to time if the oven is heating unevenly.

5. Remove the baking sheet from the oven and transfer the rolls to a rack to cool. The rolls should be consumed the day they are prepared.

MAKES ABOUT 15 ROLLS

He lay back for a little in his bed thinking about the smells of food …
of the intoxicating breath of bakeries and dullness of buns. … He planned dinners,
of enchanting aromatic foods … endless dinners, in which one could alternate flavour
with flavour from sunset to dawn without satiety, while one breathed
great draughts of the bouquet of brandy.

EVELYN WAUGH

BABY CHOCOLATE BRIOCHE

I can't think of a better way to begin a Sunday morning than with a few cups of thick espresso coffee and one of these delicate fragrant individual chocolate-filled brioches. This simple brioche recipe (a milk-based variation of Provençal Olive Oil Brioche page 167) is best prepared a day in advance, allowing the dough to rise slowly in the refrigerator overnight. The long, leisurely rise makes for a more tender and flavourful brioche. Inevitably, some chocolate will seep out as the rolls bake, but don't worry, it builds character! I prefer to sweeten these with local lavender honey from my market in Vaison: The marriage of honey and chocolate was definitely made in heaven!

 1 teaspoon active dry yeast
 2 tablespoons lavender honey (or other fragrant honey)
 250 ml (8 fl oz) lukewarm whole milk (about 40°C/105°F)
 4 tablespoons extra-virgin olive oil
 2 large eggs, at room temperature
 2 teaspoons fine sea salt
 About 675 g (1¼ lb) plain
 90 g (3 oz) bittersweet chocolate, preferably Lindt Excellence, divided into 12
  portions

FOR THE GLAZE:
 1 egg yolk
 1 tablespoon whole milk
 1 tablespoon sugar

1. In the bowl of a heavy-duty electric mixer fitted with a dough hook, combine the yeast, honey and milk, and stir to blend. Let stand until foamy, about 5 minutes. Stir in the olive oil, eggs and salt, and stir to blend.
2. Add the flour, a little at a time, mixing at the lowest speed until most of the flour has been absorbed and the dough forms a ball. Continue to knead until soft and satiny but

still firm, 4 to 5 minutes, adding additional flour to keep the dough from sticking.

3. Cover the bowl tightly with film and refrigerate. Let the dough rise until doubled or tripled in bulk, 8 to 12 hours. (The dough can be kept for 2 to 3 days in the refrigerator. Simply punch down the dough as it doubles or triples.)

4. About an hour before you plan to bake the rolls, remove the dough from the refrigerator. Punch down the dough and divide into 12 even portions, each weighing about 90 g (3 oz). With the palm of your hand, flatten each portion into a disc. Press a piece of chocolate into each portion of dough and shape into a neat round, pulling the dough around itself to form a tight ball so that the chocolate is completely covered with the dough. Place the portions of dough on a baking sheet, cover with a clean towel and let rise for 30 to 45 minutes.

5. Preheat the oven to 200°C/400°F/gas mark 6.

6. Prepare the glaze: Place the egg yolk in a small bowl and beat lightly with a fork. Add the milk and sugar and blend. Remove the towel and brush each piece of dough with the glaze. Place the baking sheet in the centre of the oven. Bake until the rolls are a deep golden brown, 15 to 20 minutes, turning the baking sheet from time to time if the oven is heating unevenly. Some chocolate may seep from the rolls, which is normal.

7. Remove the rolls from the oven and transfer to a rack to cool. Let rest for 10 to 15 minutes before serving. If stored in a sealed plastic bag, the brioche will stay fresh for 2 to 3 days.

MAKES ABOUT 12 INDIVIDUAL ROLLS

VARIATIONS: These little brioches can be made with a variety of flavourings. Additional sweet fillings might include almonds or hazelnuts rolled in honey or a combination of candied orange or lemon zest, or chopped prunes or dates. For a savoury brioche, try filling them with olives, tapenade, or a mixture of fresh herbs, such as thyme, summer savory and rosemary.

Bleu d'Auvergne (vache)

Roquefort (brebis)

Fourme d'Ambert (vache)

Bleu des Causses (vache)

OATMEAL BISCUITS

Whenever I travel to Britain, I forgo dessert in favour of biscuits, cheese and a little glass of port. When the biscuits are crumbly and delicate, the cheese pungent and ripe, the port aged just right, the combination is ultimately memorable. These same biscuits – what Americans call crackers – are lovely with a sharp farmhouse Cheddar, an aged French Cantal, or any of the range of blue cheeses. To make the combination thoroughly European, serve a spoonful of Mostarda (page 331) alongside. The dough in this recipe is particularly easy and forgiving.

100 g (3½ oz) plain flour
100 g (3½ oz) fine oatmeal
½ teaspoon fine sea salt
2 teaspoons brown sugar, firmly packed
½ teaspoon baking soda
75 g (2½ oz) unsalted butter, chilled and cubed
1 teaspoon freshly squeezed lemon juice
3 to 4 tablespoons whole milk

1. Preheat the oven to 200°C/400°F/gas mark 6.
2. In a food processor, combine the flour, oatmeal, salt, brown sugar, and baking soda and process just until blended. Add the butter and pulse just until the mixture resembles coarse crumbs, about 10 pulses. Through the feed tube, add the lemon juice and 3 tablespoons of milk and pulse just until the dough begins to hold together, about 10 times. Add additional milk if the mixture is too dry. Do not over-process. The dough should not form a ball.
3. With a pastry scraper, transfer the dough to a floured work surface. Roll about 3 mm (⅛ in) thick. Using a 5 cm (2 in) scalloped pastry cutter, cut out the dough. Transfer the rounds to non-stick baking sheets. Pierce each round four or five time with the tines of a fork to create an attractive design.
4. Place in the oven and bake until firm in texture, slightly puffed up, and lightly browned around the edges, 12 to 15 minutes. If your oven has a tendency to bake unevenly, rotate the baking sheets from top to bottom and front to back halfway through the baking period. The biscuits should rise slightly.

Josiane Deal, owner of Lou Canestéou, our local cheese shop.

(continued on next page)

FACING PHOTOGRAPH: *An assortment of blue cheeses and a carafe of the local sweet fortified* vin doux naturel *to accompany Oatmeal Biscuits.*

5. Remove from the oven and let cool on the baking sheets for 1 minute, to firm up. Using a metal spatula, transfer the biscuits to wire racks to cool completely. The biscuits can be stored in an airtight container at room temperature for 1 week.

MAKES ABOUT 24 BISCUITS

WINE SUGGESTIONS: Although port is a natural here (I like Churchill's Tawny Port, aged 10 years or, of course, any good vintage port) I also enjoy a rich Spanish sherry, such as Gonzalez Byass' Oloroso Dulce; a chilled, sweet fortified French wine, such as a *vin doux naturel* from Domaine La Soumade in Provence; or a sweet, sherry-like Marsala, such as a barrel-aged Soleras or Riserva from De Bartoli.

ON OATMEAL Oatmeal is a grain that instantly calls an image to mind: sitting at the breakfast table on a cold winter's day, with bowl of steaming hot porridge, topped with cinnamon and bits of brown sugar. One of the best comfort foods in existence. In fact, beyond that, oatmeal is more complex than it first appears. 'Rolled oats' are, as the term implies, oats that have been flattened with a roller so they are easier to eat. An oat kernel, or oat 'groat', a term used to describe an oat kernel with only the hull removed, was originally rolled and blended as part of one big flake. The oats consumed at breakfast, most commonly 'quick oats', are rolled and steel-cut to an even thinner consistency so that they can be cooked quickly and eaten immediately. Quick oats are not recommended for bread recipes, they are too thin and delicate to hold their own. Not only is oatmeal delicious, but it is an excellent source of soluble fibre, iron and minerals.

ON BAKING SODA Baking soda, or sodium bicarbonate, has an almost indefinite shelf-life as long as it is not exposed to humidity. It is used as a leavener in baking when joined with an acidic ingredient, such as buttermilk, lemon juice or vinegar, sour cream or molasses. The baking soda neutralizes some of the acidity and, by that process, causes the baked ingredient to rise.

GOLDEN PARMESAN-PEPPER LOAF

I first sampled a version of this zesty aromatic bread in England at The Seafood Restaurant, Rick Stein's magnificent waterside fish restaurant in the Cornish village of Padstow that looks out into the Atlantic Ocean. My variation is made along the lines of *pain de mie*, a fine-crumbed, refined bread with almost no crust, a rather grown-up version of what we consider 'white bread'. The addition of butter and milk makes for a softer, more delicate bread, a golden brown loaf that slices and toasts beautifully. I love to serve this bread toasted, with blue cheese and a glass of port.

EQUIPMENT: One 22.5 x 12.5 cm (9 x 5 in) loaf tin or covered *pain-de-mie* mould

Butter for buttering the tin
1 teaspoon active dry yeast
1 teaspoon sugar
375 ml (13 fl oz) lukewarm whole milk
1½ teaspoons salt
60 g (2 oz) unsalted butter, melted
550-750 g (1¼-1½ lb) strong flour
60 g (2 oz) freshly grated Parmigiano-Reggiano cheese
1 teaspoon freshly ground black pepper

1 Butter the loaf tin or the mould and cover of a *pain-de-mie* pan. If using a loaf tin, butter a piece of foil to use as a cover. Set aside.

2. In the bowl of a heavy-duty electric mixer fitted with a dough hook, combine the yeast, sugar and milk, and stir to blend. Let stand until foamy, about 5 minutes. Add the salt and butter and stir to blend.

3. Add the flour, a little at a time, mixing at the lowest speed until most of the flour has been absorbed and the dough forms a ball. Add the cheese and pepper. Continue to knead at the lowest speed until soft and satiny but still firm, 4 to 5 minutes, adding additional flour to keep the dough from sticking. Scrape the dough hook. Form the dough into a ball and return to the bowl. Cover and let rise until double in bulk, about 2 hours.

4. Punch down the dough and transfer to the baking tin. With your fingertips, press the dough down smoothly, being sure it fills the corners. Cover tightly. Let rise at room temperature until about double in bulk, about 2 hours. About 30 minutes before the dough is ready to be baked, preheat the oven to 190°C/375°F/gas mark 5.

5. Cover the bread tin with buttered foil or the pain-de-mie mould with its buttered cover. Place in the centre of the oven and bake until the bread is golden brown, about 45 to 55 minutes. Remove from the oven, unmould and place on a rack to cool.

MAKES 1 LOAF

There is a communion of more than our bodies when bread is broken
and wine is drunk. And that is my answer when people ask me:
Why do you write about hunger, and not wars or love?

M. F. K. FISHER

SESAME, FLAX & SUNFLOWER SEED BREAD

I bake bread every few days, usually a sourdough loaf filled with various seeds or grains, which provide an extra bit of wholesomeness, flavour and crunch. Since I know that not everyone has the time or desire to keep a sourdough starter active, I have developed a yeast version of my daily loaf. It uses only a small amount of leavening (so there's more wheat, less yeast flavour) and takes on its substantial character from long rising in the refrigerator. This loaf is kneaded by mixer – rather than by hand – creating a glutinous, high-rising, more polished loaf with even air holes.

1 teaspoon active dry yeast

1 teaspoon sugar

1 litre (1¾ pints) lukewarm water

1 tablespoon fine sea salt

About 1.25 kg (2½ lb) strong flour

90 g (3 oz) hulled sesame seeds

90 g (3 oz) flax seeds

90 g (3 oz) sunflower seeds

1. In the bowl of a heavy-duty electric mixer fitted with a flat dough hook, combine the yeast, sugar and 125 ml (4 fl oz) of water and stir to blend. Let stand until foamy, about 5 minutes.

2. Stir in the salt and another 125 ml (4 fl oz) of the water, and mix at low speed for 1 minute. Mix in the remaining water. Slowly add 550 g (1¼ lb) of the flour and mix until incorporated, about 3 minutes. Slowly add the remaining flour, and mix for about 3 minutes. A slow, steady addition of flour will make for a dense, well-constructed loaf. Add the sesame seeds, flax seeds and sunflower seeds. Mix for 1 minute more, until the dough pulls away from the sides of the bowl and begins to form a loose but cohesive ball. Scrape the dough hook.

3. Cover the bowl with plastic film and refrigerate until doubled in bulk, about 8 hours.

4. Transfer the dough to lightly floured work surface and knead by hand for 2 minutes. Return the dough to the bowl, cover and refrigerate until doubled again, about 8 hours or overnight.

5. Punch the dough down. Place in a clean bowl, cover and set aside at room temperature in a draught-free spot until doubled, 3 to 4 hours.

6. Shape the dough into a large round loaf. Place a large floured cloth in a large loaf tin or rectangular basket and place the dough, smooth side down, in the tin or basket. Loosely fold the cloth over the dough. Let rise at room temperature until doubled, about 1¼ hours.

7. At least 40 minutes before placing the dough in the oven, preheat the oven to 250°C/475°F/gas mark 9. If using a baking stone, place it in the oven to preheat.

8. Lightly flour a rimless baking sheet, turn the dough over on to the sheet. Slash the top of the dough several times with a razor blade, so it can expand regularly during baking. With a quick jerk of the wrists, slide the bread on to the baking stone, or place the baking sheet in the oven. Using a garden mister, generously spray the bottom and sides of the oven with water. Then spray 3 more times during the next 6 minutes. (The steam created will help give the loaf a good crust, and will give the dough a boost during rising). Once the bread is lightly browned – after about 10 minutes – reduce the heat to 220°C/425°F/gas mark 7 and rotate the loaf so that it browns evenly. Bake until the crust is a dark golden brown and the loaf sounds hollow when tapped on the bottom, about 45 minutes more, for a total baking of about 55 minutes. Transfer to a rack to cool. Do not slice the bread for at least 1 hour, for it will continue to bake as it cools.

MAKES I LOAF

꒰ **A WORD ON FLAX** ꒱ Flax seed has taken on new importance in recent years as it has been found to be excellent in combating high cholesterol levels. Obviously, it is also quite rich in fibre. The stalk of the flax plant is still used in the fabrication of cloth, and when treated and prepared for weaving, it is a rich golden yellow. Thus, the term 'flaxen-haired maiden' from fairy tales. Flax seed is commonly found at health-food stores.

Talk of joy: There may be things better than beef stew and
baked potatoes and homemade bread – there may be.
DAVID GRAYSON

CRUSTY WHEAT & POLENTA BREAD

I am always searching for new natural flavours for my repertoire of breads. One day I had polenta on my mind and created this version, which is rich in corn flavour but not heavy, as many corn breads can be. Serve this golden crusty bread with Sheila and Julian's Foie Gras (page 32); or use in toasted cheese sandwiches or as a special bread for the cheese course.

> 1 teaspoon active dry yeast
> 1 teaspoon sugar
> 175 ml (6 fl oz) lukewarm milk
> 1 tablespoon fine sea salt
> 1 tablespoon extra-virgin olive oil
> 300 ml (½ pint) lukewarm water
> About 800 g (1¾ lb) strong flour
> 300 g (10 oz) polenta

1. In the bowl of a heavy-duty electric mixer fitted with a dough hook, combine the yeast, sugar and milk and stir to blend. Let stand until foamy, about 5 minutes. Add the salt, oil and water, and stir to blend.

2. Very slowly add about two-thirds of the flour to the mixing bowl – a bit at a time – working at the lowest possible speed, mixing well after each addition. Add the polenta – a bit at a time – still at lowest speed, mixing well after each addition. Add as much of the remaining bread flour as necessary, mixing at the lowest speed, until most of the flour has been absorbed and the dough begins to form a ball. Continue to knead for a full 5 minutes at the lowest speed.

3. Cover the bowl with plastic film and refrigerate. Let the bread rise in the refrigerator until doubled in size, about 8 hours.

4. The next day, remove the dough from the refrigerator, punch it down, and cover again with plastic film. Let rise at room temperature until about doubled in size, 2 to 3 hours.

5. Punch down the dough and knead it for about 30 seconds. Shape the dough into a tight rectangle by rolling the ball of dough and folding it over itself. Place a large floured cloth in a large loaf tin or rectangular basket, sprinkle generously with cornmeal and

place the dough, smooth side down, in the tin or basket. Loosely fold the cloth over the dough. Let rise at room temperature until doubled in size, about 1¼ hours. (Alternatively, form into two round loaves and let rise on a baking sheet, covered with a clean towel.)

6. At least 40 minutes before placing the dough in the oven, preheat the oven to 250°C/475°F/gas mark 9. If using a baking stone, place it in the oven to preheat.

7. Lightly flour a rimless baking sheet, and turn the dough over on to the sheet. Slash the top of the dough several times with a razor blade, so it can expand evenly during baking. With a quick jerk of the wrists, slide the dough on the baking stone or place the sheet in the oven. Using a garden mister, generously spray the centre of the oven with water (don't worry about the bread turning soggy). Then spray 3 more times during the first 6 minutes of baking. (The steam created will help give the loaf a good crust and will give the dough a boost during rising.) Once the bread is lightly browned – about 10 minutes – reduce the heat to 200°C/400°F/gas mark 6 and rotate the loaf so it browns evenly. Bake until the crust is a dark golden brown and the loaf sounds hollow when tapped on the bottom, about 20 to 25 minutes more, for a total baking time of about 30 to 35 minutes.

8. Remove the bread from the oven and transfer to a cooling rack. Do not slice the bread for at least 1 hour, for it will continue to bake as it rests. The bread can be stored in a sealed plastic bag for 3 to 4 days.

MAKES 1 LARGE LOAF OR 2 MEDIUM LOAVES

⌇ **WHAT'S IN A WORD?** ⌇ A lot of words are thrown around loosely without any investigation of their real meaning. Semolina? Polenta? Cornmeal? Semolina is the general term used to describe any cereal that is coarsely ground into granules. Though most semolina is made from a durum wheat base, others, such as white semolina, are ground from rice. In this case, yellow semolina is ground from maize to make both polenta and cornmeal. Polenta is coarsely ground maize and yields a grainy texture when cooked. Cornmeal is almost powdery in comparison and is consequently used for different methods of cooking breads and cakes.

WALNUT, RYE & CURRANT LOAF

Bread, cheese and wine. I could live on it! And nothing brings out the flavour of a rich golden cheese like a perfectly dense, firm and crusty toasted slice of bread studded with walnuts and currants. Here's my favourite version. (If dried currants cannot be found, substitute raisins.) Note that, as in all my bread recipes, a minimum of yeast is used here, so the bread tastes of wheat and rye, walnuts and currants, not yeast. One teaspoon equals about half a packet of yeast.

> 1 teaspoon active dry yeast
> 1 teaspoon sugar
> 625 ml (22 fl oz) lukewarm water
> 2 teaspoons fine sea salt
> 150 g (5 oz) rye flour
> About 750 g (1½ lb) srong flour
> 1 tablespoon honey
> 125 g (4 oz) walnut pieces
> 125 g (4 oz) dried currants (or substitute raisins)

1. In the bowl of a heavy-duty electric mixer fitted with a flat dough hook, combine the yeast, sugar and water and stir to blend. Let stand until foamy, about 5 minutes.

2. Add the salt, the rye flour and then the wheat flour, a little at a time, mixing at the lowest speed until most of the flour has been absorbed and the dough forms a ball. Add the honey and continue to knead until soft and satiny but still firm, 4 to 5 minutes, adding additional flour to keep the dough from sticking. Add the walnuts and the currants and mix until evenly blended. Scrape the dough hook. (If the walnuts and currants are not evenly mixed into the dough by machine, knead them in by hand.)

3. Cover the bowl with film and refrigerate until double in bulk, about 8 hours, or overnight.

4. Transfer the dough to a lightly floured work surface and knead by hand for 2 minutes. Return the dough to the bowl, cover and let rise at room temperature until double in bulk, 2 to 3 hours.

5. Shape the dough into a large round loaf. Place a large floured cloth in a large loaf tin or rectangular basket and place the dough, smooth side down, in the pan or basket. Loosely fold the cloth over the dough. Let rise at room temperature until doubled in bulk, 2 to 3 hours.

6. At least 40 minutes before placing the dough in the oven, preheat the oven to 250°C/475°F/gas mark 9. If using a baking stone, place it in the oven to preheat.

7. Lightly flour a rimless baking sheet, turn the dough over on to the sheet. Slash the top of the dough several times with a razor blade, so it can expand evenly during baking.

With a quick jerk of the wrists, slide the bread onto the baking stone, or place the sheet in the oven. Using a garden mister, generously spray the bottom and sides of the oven with water. Then spray 3 more times during the next 6 minutes. (The steam created will help give the loaf a good crust, and will give the dough a boost during rising.) Once the bread is lightly browned – after about 10 minutes – reduce the heat to 200°C/400°F/gas mark 6 and rotate the loaf so that it browns evenly. Bake until the crust is a dark golden brown and the loaf sounds hollow when tapped on the bottom, about 30 minutes more, for a total baking of about 40 minutes. Transfer to a rack to cool. Do not slice the bread for at least 1 hour, as it will continue to bake as it cools.

MAKES 1 LOAF

A loaf of Sesame, Flax & Sunflower Bread (page 176), with three local cheeses.
Left to right: Cow, sheep and goat.

If God had not made brown honey,
men would think figs much sweeter than they do.
XENOPHANES

FIG, APRICOT, WALNUT & RAISIN RYE

I love the way recipes develop. One afternoon in April I was reorganizing my pantry and came across several small bags of dried fruit. There wasn't enough in any of the bags to amount to much, so I gathered them all up to create a dense loaf that goes well with fresh cheese, especially our fresh local goats' cheese. But the guests who were at our house that weekend wouldn't wait for the cheese course: They wanted this bread for breakfast, lunch and dinner. What better compliment can you pay a cook? Of course I complied! You don't need to follow the amounts and varieties of dried fruits and nuts to the letter. Use what you have on hand, mixing and matching dried fruits and nuts to your taste. Just be sure they are of top quality.

> 1 teaspoon active dry yeast
> 1 teaspoon sugar
> 625 ml (22 fl oz) lukewarm water
> 10 dried apricots (about 60 g/2 oz), quartered
> 75 g (2½ oz) sultanas
> 4 dried figs (75 g/2½ oz), quartered
> 30 g (1 oz) walnuts, quartered
> About 750 g (1½ lb) strong flour
> 150 g (5 oz) rye flour
> 2 teaspoons fine sea salt
> 1 tablespoon raw honey

1. In the bowl of a heavy-duty electric mixer fitted with a flat dough hook, combine the yeast, sugar and water and stir to blend. Let stand until foamy, about 5 minutes.
2. Meanwhile, in a small bowl, combine the dried fruits and nuts and toss with 1 tablespoon flour. This will prevent them from sticking together and allow them to be more evenly distributed through the dough. Set aside.
3. Add the flours and the salt to the yeast mixture, a little at a time, mixing at the lowest speed until most of the flour has been absorbed and the dough forms a ball. Add the honey and continue to knead until soft and satiny but still firm, 4 to 5 minutes, adding additional flour to keep the dough from sticking. Add the dried fruit and nuts and mix

(continued on next page)

just until incorporated into the dough. Scrape the dough hook. (If the fruits and nuts are not evenly mixed into the dough by machine, knead them in by hand.)

4. Cover the bowl with plastic wrap and refrigerate until doubled in bulk, about 8 hours.

5. Transfer the dough to a lightly floured work surface and knead by hand for 2 minutes. Return the dough to the bowl, cover and let rise at room temperature until doubled in bulk, 2 to 3 hours.

6. Shape the dough into a large round loaf. Place a large floured cloth in a large loaf tin or rectangular basket and place the dough, smooth side down, in the pan or basket. Loosely fold the cloth over the dough. Let rise at room temperature until doubled in bulk, 2 to 3 hours.

7. At least 40 minutes before placing the dough in the oven, preheat the oven to 250°C/475°F/gas mark 9. If using a baking stone, place it in the oven to preheat.

8. Lightly flour a rimless baking sheet, turn the dough over on to the sheet. Slash the top of the dough several times with a razor blade, so it can expand regularly during baking. With a quick jerk of the wrists, slide the bread on to the baking stone, or place the sheet in the oven. Using a garden mister, generously spray the bottom and sides of the oven with water. Then spray 3 more times during the next 6 minutes. (The steam created will help give the loaf a good crust, and will give the dough a boost during rising.) Once the bread is lightly browned – after about 10 minutes – reduce the heat to 200°C/400°F/gas mark 6 and rotate the loaf so that it browns evenly. Bake until the crust is a dark golden brown and the loaf sounds hollow when tapped on the bottom, about 30 minutes more, for a total baking of about 40 minutes.

9. Transfer to a rack to cool. Do not slice the bread for at least 1 hour, for it will continue to bake as it cools.

MAKES I LOAF

BREAD DOUGH

This my simple basic dough that I use in preparing pizzas, the base of rolls (Pine Nut Rolls, page 169) and bread tarts, such as Onion-Caraway Bread Tart (page 191).

1 teaspoon active dry yeast
1 teaspoon sugar
325 ml (11 fl oz) lukewarm water
2 tablespoons extra-virgin olive oil
1 teaspoon fine sea salt
About 500 g (1 lb) strong flour

1. In the bowl of a heavy-duty electric mixer fitted with a dough hook, combine the yeast, sugar and lukewarm water, and stir to blend. Let stand until foamy, about 5 minutes. Stir in the oil and salt.

2. Add the flour, a little at a time, mixing at the lowest speed until most of the flour has been absorbed and the dough forms a ball. Continue to knead at the lowest speed until soft and satiny but still firm, 4 to 5 minutes, adding additional flour to keep the dough from sticking.

3. Transfer the dough to a bowl, cover tightly with plastic wrap and place in the refrigerator. Let the dough rise in the refrigerator until doubled or tripled in bulk, 8 to 12 hours. (The dough can be kept for 2 to 3 days in the refrigerator. Simply punch down the dough as it doubles or triples in bulk.)

4. Proceed with the individual recipes for rolls, bread tarts, and pizzas.

MAKES ENOUGH DOUGH FOR 15 ROLLS, 1 BREAD TART, OR 4 SMALL PIZZAS

I was taught from childhood the sanctity of food.
Not a piece of bread could be thrown away without kissing it
and raising it to one's eyes as with all things holy.

ATTIA HOSAIN

RITA'S RYE

Year's ago, my friend Yale Kramer sent me this recipe, one he dedicated to his wife, Rita. He baked it late one night, then presented it to her as a gift in the morning. 'I think it is delicious as a breakfast bread to go with Gruyère or Gouda and it is, in my opinion, the perfect bread for *croque monsieur*,' he wrote. Later, when I prepared it for all of us at Chanteduc, he added to his commentary: 'This is definitely a speciality bread, not a dinner bread, but one for toasting with butter, or as part of a cheese course.' Yes!

> 1 teaspoon active dry yeast
> 1 teaspoon sugar
> 750 ml (27 fl oz) lukewarm water
> 1 tablespoon fine sea salt
> About 550 g (1¼ lb) rye flour
> 550-750 g (1¼ to 1½ lb) strong flour
> 4 tablespoons caraway seeds
> 1 tablespoon fennel seeds
> 2 tablespoons lavender honey

1. In the bowl of a heavy-duty electric mixer fitted with a flat dough hook, combine the yeast, sugar and 250 ml (8 fl oz) water, and stir to blend. Let stand until foamy, about 5 minutes.

2. Add the salt and remaining 500 ml (16 fl oz) water and mix to blend. Slowly add the rye flour and mix at the lowest possible speed until the flour is thoroughly incorporated. Slowly begin adding the wheat flour, caraway, fennel seeds and honey, continuing to mix at the lowest speed until the dough begins to form a ball. Continue to knead until soft and satiny but still firm, 4 to 5 minutes, adding additional flour to keep the dough from sticking. The dough should barely clean the sides of the bowl. Scrape the dough hook.

3. Cover and set aside at room temperature to rise until about double in bulk, 2 to 3 hours. Punch down and let rise more time, until doubled in bulk, 2 to 3 hours.

4. Shape the dough into a large round loaf. The dough will be quite sticky. To make it easier to handle the dough, dust your hands with flour before working with it. Place a large floured cloth in a large loaf tin or rectangular basket and place the dough, smooth

Assorted breads for sale at the Vaison market.

side down, in the tin or basket. Loosely fold the cloth over the dough. Let rise at room temperature until doubled in bulk, 2 to 3 hours.

5. At least 40 minutes before placing the dough in the oven, preheat the oven to 250°C/475°F/gas mark 9. If using a baking stone, place it in the oven to preheat.

6. Lightly flour a rimless baking sheet, turn the dough over on to the sheet. Slash the top of the dough several times with a razor blade, so it can expand regularly during baking. With a quick jerk of the wrists, slide the bread on the baking stone or place the sheet in the oven. Using a garden mister, generously spray the bottom and sides of the oven with water. Then spray 3 more times during the next 6 minutes. (The steam created will help give the loaf a good crust and will give the dough a boost during rising.) Once the bread is lightly browned – after about 10 minutes – reduce the heat to 200°C/400°F/gas mark 6 and rotate the loaf so that it browns evenly. Bake until the crust is a dark, golden brown and the loaf sounds hollow when tapped on the bottom, about 30 minutes more, for a total baking of about 40 minutes. Transfer to a rack to cool. Do not slice the bread for at least 1 hour, for it will continue to bake as it cools.

ONE LOAF

CARAWAY CORN‑RYE BREAD

This is a 'memory lane' recipe. One of my favourite tastes from childhood is caraway and rye, often in the form of firm round rolls topped with coarse salt. Here is my grown-up interpretation. Rye flour has very little gluten and is often difficult to work with, for it tends to become quite sticky. By beginning with a rye 'sponge' the bread is easier to work.

SPONGE

1 teaspoon active dry yeast

1 teaspoon sugar

1 cup of lukewarm water

about 200 g (7 oz) rye flour

THE BREAD

500 ml (16 fl oz) water

1 tablespoon fine sea salt

90 g (3 oz) polenta or cornmeal

125 g (4 oz) rye flour

About 550 g (1¼ lb) strong flour

6 tablespoons caraway seeds

1 egg plus 1 tablespoon water

1 teaspoon coarse sea salt

1. Prepare the sponge. In the bowl of a heavy-duty electric mixer fitted with a flat dough hook, combine the yeast, sugar and water, and stir to blend. Let stand until foamy, about 5 minutes. Add the rye flour and mix at the lowest possible speed until the flour is thoroughly incorporated. Scrape the hook. Leave the sponge in the bowl. Cover securely and refrigerate 8 hours or overnight.

2. Remove the sponge from the refrigerator. Return the bowl to the mixer and add to the sponge the 500 ml (16 fl oz) water, the salt, the polenta or cornmeal, and the final 125 g (4 oz) of rye flour, a little at a time, mixing at the lowest speed until all of the flour has been absorbed. Slowly begin adding the wheat flour and 5 tablespoons of the caraway seed, continuing to mix at the lowest speed until the dough begins to form a ball. Continue to knead until soft and satiny but still firm, 4 to 5 minutes, adding additional flour to keep the dough from sticking. Scrape the dough hook.

3. Shape the dough into a large round loaf. Place a large floured cloth in a large loaf tin or rectangular basket and place the dough, smooth side down, in the tin or basket. Loosely fold the cloth over the dough. Let rise at room temperature until doubled in bulk, 3 to 4 hours.

4. At least 40 minutes before placing the dough in the oven, preheat the oven to 250°C/475°F/gas mark 9. If using a baking stone, place it in the oven to preheat.

5. Bake the loaf: Lightly flour a rimless baking sheet, turn the dough over on to the sheet. Slash the top of the dough several times with a razor blade, so it can expand evenly during baking. Glaze with the egg and water mixture. Sprinkle with the remaining 1 tablespoon of caraway seeds and 1 teaspoon coarse sea salt. With a quick jerk of the wrists, slide the bread on to the baking stone, or place the sheet in the oven. Using a garden mister, generously spray the bottom and sides of the oven with water. Then spray 3 more times during the next 6 minutes. (The steam created will help give the loaf a good crust, and will give the dough a boost during rising.) Once the bread is lightly browned – after about 10 minutes – reduce the heat to 200°C/400°F/gas mark 6 and rotate the loaf so that it browns evenly. Bake until the crust is a dark, golden brown and the loaf sounds hollow when tapped on the bottom, about 30 minutes more, for a total baking of about 40 minutes. Transfer to a rack to cool. Do not slice the bread for at least 1 hour, for it will continue to bake as it cools.

MAKES 1 LOAF

‿ **AN ANISE-RICH SPICE** ∾ Caraway seeds are a spice most notably appreciated by the Germans. They use them to perfume breads, sauerkraut and their famous liqueur *kümmel*, in which caraway plays the lead role. However, this liking for the rich anise-flavoured spice makes its way into a wide span of world cuisines, including that of the Dutch, who add the fragrant seeds to certain cheeses such as Gouda, and to the Alsatians, who add it to Münster.

Although caraway responds well to cooking and baking, it should not heated for an extended period of time: The seed can turn bitter and upset the balance of a dish. In fact, in slow-cooking recipes – borscht, for example – it is to be added only during the last few minutes of cooking.

In Hungary and England, caraway is added to such menu staples as cooked potatoes and 'seed cakes', small sugar-coated pound cakes, that attained the height of popularity in Victorian times. These cakes are even referred to in great literary works of the time – examples include Dickens's David Copperfield: 'I cut and handed the seed-cake.'

Caraway, or 'carvey' in Scotland from the French *carvi*, was also eaten by itself as both a digestive aid and an after-meal breath sweetener. The French have numerous nicknames for the spice, including 'mountain cumin', 'fool's aniseed' and 'meadow cumin'.

ONION CARAWAY BREAD TART

I've always had a love affair with homemade bread, but ever since I moved to France that romance has been fed to an even greater extent – almost like yeast – by the bread-loving world that surrounds me. At Chanteduc, we fire up the wood-burning bread oven as often as time permits, and that's when I go to town! Bread tarts are such a simple solution to both appetizers and desserts, that I make them frequently.

This onion and caraway variation – a bit reminiscent of my German upbringing in Milwaukee, Wisconsin – makes for a lovely first course or even a main luncheon dish, accompanied by a tossed green salad. The tart is enhanced with a generous hit of freshly ground black pepper, preferably the top-grade Tellicherry pepper, with its complex balanced elegant flavours. The peppercorn has hints of ginger and pine, and although it's a rich and bold seasoning, it is far from aggressive.

> 4 medium onions (about 750 g/1½ lb), peeled
> 6 tablespoons extra-virgin olive oil
> 1 teaspoon sea salt
> 2 teaspoons sugar
> Bouquet garni: Several sprigs of fresh rosemary and 1 fresh bay leaf, tied in a bundle with string
> Freshly ground black pepper to taste, preferably Tellicherry
> 1 large egg
> 1 teaspoon caraway seeds
> 1 recipe Basic Bread Dough (page 185), prepared with 1 teaspoon caraway seeds

1. Slice an onion in half lengthwise. Place each half, cut side down, on a cutting board and cut across into very thin slices. Slice the remaining onion in this manner.

2. At least 40 minutes before baking the tart, preheat the oven to 230°C/450°F/gas mark 8.

3. In a large shallow frying pan, combine the onions, oil, salt, sugar and bouquet garni and toss to coat the onions with oil. Cover and sweat over the lowest possible heat until the onions are very soft and slightly golden, about 30 minutes. Taste for seasoning.

4. Crack the egg into a small bowl, whisk to blend, then stir the egg into the onion mixture. Add the caraway seeds and toss to blend.

5. Punch down the prepared dough and shape into a rectangle. On a lightly floured surface, roll the dough into a 30 x 40-cm (11½ x 15½-in) rectangle, or one large enough to fit a standard non-stick baking sheet. Place the dough on the baking sheet and press it flat to evenly fit the pan.

6. Spread the onion mixture evenly on the bread dough, going right to the edge. Place in the centre of the oven and bake until the bread is firm and the onion mixture golden, about 25 minutes. Remove from the oven, transfer to a cutting board and cut into squares or rectangles. Serve immediately.

SERVES 10-12

FOUGASSE

The lyrical, ladderlike bread known as fougasse is my Provençal pizza. I take my favorite bread dough, shape it into individual breads, then flavour them with whatever delicious toppings I might have on hand – black or green olives, home-cured anchovies, marinated baby artichokes, capers, bits of fresh goat cheese, a touch of hot *pili pili* oil, or simply a brush of honey or olive oil and a scattering of fresh thyme and coarse sea salt. The most traditional fougasse is flavoured with bits of browned pork fat (what we call cracklings), but one also finds sweet versions prepared with a butter-rich dough or brioche-like butter and egg dough flavoured with orange flower water. The origin of the word is a mystery, though in the rest of France a *fouace* can refer to any sort of flat, baked galette, either sweet or savory.

1 recipe Bread Dough (page 185)

Fougasse from the Vaison market.

1. At least 40 minutes before placing the assembled fougasse in the oven, preheat the oven to 250°C/475°F/gas mark 9).

2. Punch down the prepared dough and divide it evenly into 5 pieces. Shape each piece into a ball. On a lightly floured surface, roll each ball of dough into a 20 x 12.5 cm (8 x 5 inch rectangle. Using a pastry scraper, cut lengthwise slashes into the bread, with 3 slashes at the bottom half of the dough and a single slash at the top, so that the slashes resemble the veins of a leaf.

3. Sprinkle a baking sheet with flour and carefully transfer the rectangles of dough to the baking sheet. Gently pull apart at the slashes. Cover with a clean towel and let rest for 10 minutes.

4. Assemble the fougasse: Brush lightly with olive oil or honey, then sprinkle with preferred toppings.

VARIOUS SAVOURY TOPPING SUGGESTIONS: Brush the dough with olive oil, then – either alone or in combination – sprinkle dough with the following: pitted and halved black or green olives; drained capers; drained anchovy fillets; soft goat's cheese, crumbled; a thin layer of tomato sauce; drained marinated artichokes.

VARIOUS SWEET TOPPING SUGGESTIONS: Brush the bread with melted honey, then add – either alone or in combination – hopped walnuts; whole almonds; strips of chopped dried figs, apricots, kumquats, candied orange or lemon peel; sprinkle with whole fennel seeds, if desired.

Patricia prepares fougasse in her farm kitchen.

Patricia purchases fish at the Vaison market.

7

FISH & SHELLFISH

OUR LANDLOCKED VILLAGE MAY BE HOURS from the Mediterranean, yet the profusion of miniature whitebait, anchovies, sea bass, monkfish, dorade, and tuna in the Vaison market attests to the Provençal appetite for the fruits of the sea. And thanks to the wonders of modern transportation, lobster, crab, scallops, and oysters from Brittany waters are mine for the asking. Local fishmonger Eliane Berenger is a constant wealth of recipes and tips, while the glistening array of ultra-fresh fish at the stalls at the Tuesday market entice one to feast on Monkfish 'Carpaccio', to take roast fish whole (such as silvery Bonito in Parchment with Warm Pistou), to bake it buried in salt (as in Whole Fish Roasted in a Crust of Sea Salt), or to sear Pancetta-Wrapped Cod. Mint from the garden is tossed into Minted Crabmeat Salad, while first-of-season Picholine green olives serve to flavour Steamed Salmon with Warm Lemon Vinaigrette.

MARIA'S GINGER PRAWNS

This dish is an homage to my editor, Maria Guarnaschelli. It's a zesty combination of ginger, garlic and white wine, and one that is full of character and depth, just like dear Maria. I created it one spring Sunday on the way to my Paris market on Rue Poncelet. I had seen giant fresh prawns – gambas – there the day before, and thought of all the flavours I wanted to enjoy for lunch that day. So I combined many of my cherished aromas, ingredients and tastes in a single dish.

At the same time, it seemed that a dish as fragrant as this demanded a perfumed accompaniment, and then I remembered the package of basmati rice that Maria gave me on a recent trip to New York. Quite coincidentally, the contract for this book had just been signed and returned to New York via Federal Express the day before. Well, my husband, Walter and I relished this dish, toasting Maria, only saddened that she wasn't with us to celebrate!

In this recipe, the wine – either a Sauvignon Blanc or a young white Rhône – is slightly reduced, adding depth of flavour as well as character to the sauce.

16 to 20 (about 500 g/1 lb) large raw prawns, shelled and deveined
2 tablespoons extra-virgin olive oil
4 tablespoons grated fresh ginger
7 plump fresh garlic cloves, halved, degermed and slivered
Fine sea salt to taste
500 ml (16 fl oz) dry white wine
4 tablespoons fresh basil leaves, finely sliced
Basmati Rice (page 273)

1. Rinse the prawns and pat them dry. In a frying pan large enough to hold all the prawns in a single layer heat the oil until hot but not smoking. Add 3 tablespoons of the ginger, all the garlic and a pinch of salt. Cook over moderately high heat just until the garlic turns golden but does not brown, 2 to 3 minutes.
2. Pour the wine all over the surface of the pan, bring to a simmer and cook until reduced to 250 ml (8 fl oz), about 8 minutes.
3. Add the prawns in a single layer and cook, stirring occasionally, just until the prawns turn pink throughout, about 4 minutes.
4. Serve the prawns and their juices spooned over basmati rice in shallow bowls. Sprinkle with the remaining ginger and fresh basil.

SERVES 4

WINE SUGGESTIONS: A nicely chilled, floral wine is a great match here: A French or Californian Viognier or a white Châteauneuf-du-Pape are my choices.

SHERRY & GINGER LOBSTER

Inspired by Parisian chef Alain Passard, this recipe suggests a new, modern approach to lobster: Rather than presenting the entire tail in a single piece, the meat is quartered into long strips – still attached to the shell – making for an unusual and elegant presentation. There are also gustative and practical advantages to cutting the tail meat in this manner: The moist strips of meat better absorb the zesty sherry-ginger sauce (so delicious you could drink it alone!), and are less cumbersome to eat. To keep the tail straight as it cooks, a classic French technique is used: A stainless steel spoon is tied to the tail. The lobster is boiled briefly, then the meat is cooked in the oven and warmed in a fragrant, sherry and ginger sauce sweetened with honey. While Passard prepares his sauce with the sherry-like *vin jaune* of the Jura region, as well as hazelnut oil, my version combines a reduction of sherry wine blended with honey, olive oil, and a hint of ginger. For special occasions in Provence, I order live fresh 'blue' lobsters from the Brittany shores and serve this dish as a romantic main dish for two.

Sherry & Ginger Lobster.

(continued on next page)

EQUIPMENT: An immersion mixer

2 live lobsters (500 g/1 lb each)
500 ml (16 fl oz) best-quality Spanish fine dry sherry, such as Gonzalez Byass's
  Tío Pepe or Pedro Domecq's La Ina *fino*
2 tablespoons honey, or to taste
6 tablespoons extra-virgin olive oil
Fine sea salt
½ teaspoon ground ginger, or to taste

1. Prepare the lobsters: Thoroughly rinse the lobsters under cold running water. Bring a large pot of water to a rolling boil over high heat. Hold a lobster by the neck between your thumb and index finger. Place a metal spoon down the length of the interior of the tail. Wrap string around each articulation of the tail, pulling so the string winds around tightly. Tie the string in a secure knot. With scissors, remove the rubber bands restraining the claws. Repeat for the remaining lobster.

2. Cook the lobsters: Plunge the lobsters, head first, into the boiling water. Counting from the time the lobster hits the water, cook for 4 minutes. (The lobsters may be cooked one at a time.) Carefully remove the lobsters from the water, drain and set aside to cool for 10 minutes, to allow the lobster meat to firm up.

3. Preheat the oven to 220°C/425°F/gas mark 7).

4. Place the lobsters in a large, shallow pan with a fitted cover. Place in the centre of the oven and cook for 10 minutes. Remove the pan from the oven and transfer the lobsters to a clean, flat work surface. Strain the juice in the pan through a fine-mesh sieve into a small bowl. Set aside.

5. Prepare the sauce: In a large, nonreactive saucepan, bring the sherry to a boil over high heat. Reduce the heat and simmer until the wine is reduced to about 250 ml (8 fl oz) and all the alcohol has burned off, about 5 minutes. Add the reserved lobster-cooking juices and cook for 2 minutes more. Add the honey and stir to dissolve. Remove from the heat and add 1 tablespoon of olive oil at a time, blending to a thick emulsion with an immersion mixer. (Alternatively, blend in a blender. Return to the saucepan.) Add the ginger, and taste for seasoning. Set aside.

6. Remove the meat from the claws: Twist each large claw off the body of the lobster. Gently crack the shells with a nutcracker or hammer, trying not to damage the meat. Extract the meat with a seafood fork, toothpick or lobster pick: It should come out in a single piece. Set aside. Gently detach the tail from the rest of the body. Remove and reserve the pale green tomalley (liver) from the upper portion of the body cavity. Remove and carefully reserve the deep red coral, if present. (The tomalley and coral will not be used in this recipe. They can be reserved – and frozen – to add to a lobster sauce for another preparation.) Discard the head. Repeat for the remaining lobster.

7. Prepare the tail meat: Remove the spoon and string wrapped around each lobster tail. Place a lobster tail with the interior facing upwards on a flat work surface. With a large, sharp chef's knife, make a cut through the middle down the length of the tail. By applying additional pressure on the knife, you should be able to cut through the outer shell, cutting the lobster tail in half lengthwise. Cut each half in half again so that each tail yields four long strips. (The meat should remain connected to the shell.) Set aside carefully. Repeat for the remaining lobster.

8. To finish: Transfer the sauce to a large, shallow frying pan and warm over moderate heat. Carefully add the strips of lobster and shell in a single layer, along with the claw meat. Roll the pieces around in the sauce to warm them up and finish cooking, 3 to 4 minutes.

9. To serve: Arrange four pieces of tail meat lengthwise in the centre of each warmed dinner plate. Place a claw on both sides of the tail meat. Repeat for the remaining plate. Spoon the sauce between, over and around the pieces of lobster. Serve immediately.

SERVES 2

WINE SUGGESTION: This dish deserves a regal white Burgundy. My preference is for a Chassagne-Montrachet from the house of Olivier Leflaive, a wine that seems to flatter everything with which it comes in contact.

MONKFISH 'CARPACCIO'

I first tasted a version of this dish at Paul Minchelli's extraordinary fish restaurant on Paris's Left Bank. The monkfish is cut into thin horizontal slices, arranged like petals on a large platter atop a drizzle of oil and a sprinkling of fine sea salt, then anointed with another trace of oil. The fish is then passed under the grill rapidly and, before bringing it to the table, sprinkled with a touch of fresh lemon juice and chives. Slip a piece of crusty homemade bread in the toaster as the fish goes in the oven, and you'll have an instant feast. Because the tastiness of the dish depends upon the pure flavour of utterly fresh fish, there are a few caveats. Do not make this dish with anything but the very best ingredients. If you are in doubt, simply ask your fishmonger which is the freshest fish available.

> OPTIONS: Red snapper, sea bass, sea scallops, or cod
>
> 2 tablespoons extra-virgin olive oil
>
> Fine sea salt to taste
>
> 250 g (8 oz) super-fresh monkfish in one piece, membranes removed
>
> 2 teaspoons freshly squeezed lemon juice
>
> 2 tablespoons chives, snipped extra-fine with scissors

1. Preheat the grill.
2. Drizzle a large ovenproof platter with about 1 tablespoon of oil, shifting the plate back and forth so it is evenly coated. Sprinkle parsimoniously with fine sea salt.
3. Using a very sharp knife (a flexible fish boning knife is ideal), cut the fish horizontally into 2-mm (⅛-in) thick slices. (The length and width of the pieces in not important, but the thinness is.) Place the slices of fish side by side, very slightly overlapping, on the oiled platter. Drizzle with the remaining tablespoon of oil.
4. Place the baking dish under the grill, about 5 cm (2 in) from the heat. Grill until the fish turns pearly, opaque and tender, 30 seconds to 1 minute. (The sweet, deliciously milky juice the monkfish exudes will merge into a golden creamy mass as it cooks and combines with the oil.) Remove the platter from the oven. With a slotted spatula or spoon, transfer the pieces of fish in a single layer to warmed, individual dinner plates. Drizzle with lemon juice and sprinkle with chives. Transfer the juices from the platter to a small jug or gravy boat with a pouring spout. Serve immediately, passing the jug of juices and additional oil, salt, and lemon juice, if desired. Serve with crusty grilled bread alongside.

SERVES 4 AS A FIRST COURSE, 2 AS A MAIN COURSE

WINE SUGGESTIONS: The quick grill calls for a lovely white, or even an exceptional rosé, a young and perfumed wine that will pay homage to the fresh fish: My choices include a rosé from Provence, a Sauvignon Blanc from California or Washington, a Pinot Grigio from Italy, or a Muscadet-sur-Lie from France.

Local farm-raised trout for sale at the Vaison market.

◡ **LIKE A CARPACCIO PAINTING** ◡   The legend behind the culinary term 'carpaccio' tells the story of an Italian chef with a small dilemma. Apparently, a certain Contessa, Nagi Mocenigo, a regular customer, was ordered by her doctor to avoid cooked meats. The chef, Giuseppe Cipriani, the original owner of 'Harry's Bar' in Venice, rose to the challenge and crafted the simplest and most delicious of tastes. Supposedly inspired by the painter Carpaccio, famous for his brilliant combination of reds and whites, Cipriani combined thin slices of fresh raw beef drizzled with a translucent white variation of mayonnaise.

The modern interpretation of carpaccio allows it to be applied not only to raw meats, but also to raw and cooked fish, even vegetables. Here, thin slices of fish are layered carpaccio-style on a plate and cooked in just seconds.

BONITO IN PARCHMENT WITH WARM PISTOU

One sunny Provençal Friday just before Christmas, I attended a luncheon spon-sored by olive growers from the region of Les Baux. Each course included the newly pressed oil from one of the mills. My favourite dish of the day was a whole loup de mer – or sea bass – steam-roasted in parchment, accompanied by a basil purée and tomatoes. It may have been winter, but the dish made me feel as though it was a summer day by the sea, bright with the flavours of ripe tomatoes, fresh basil and fra-grant rich olive oil.

Luckily, on returning home, I was able to harvest some pistou from my freezer, the fishmonger turned up a tiny whole bonito, and there were willing guests on hand to share the feast. Other whole fish to use here include mackerel and bluefish. If whole fish are hard to find, this dish could be prepared with a variety of fish and a variety of cuts. Try cooking individual parchment parcels of tuna, dolphin fish (mahi-mahi), or swordfish steaks (placing the pistou and herbs on top of the fish), baking for just 10 minutes each.

> OPTIONS: Whole sea bass, red snapper or bluefish or steaks of tuna, dolphin fish (mahi-mahi) or swordfish
>
> 1 whole bonito (about 750 g/1½ lb), cleaned, but with head and tail on, rinsed, and patted dry
> Sea salt and freshly ground black pepper to taste
> 5 tablespoons Pistou (page 316)
> Large sprig of fresh thyme
> 4 whole fresh bay leaves
> 3 tablespoons extra-virgin olive oil
> 2 medium tomatoes, skinned, cored, deseeded and chopped
> Freshly squeezed lemon juice to taste

1. Preheat the oven to 230°C/450°F/gas mark 8.
2. Cut a sheet of baking parchment large enough comfortably to wrap the fish. Centre it on a baking sheet. Place the fish in the centre of the sheet. Season the fish inside and out with salt and pepper. Fill the cavity of the fish with 3 tablespoons of the pistou. Tuck the thyme and bay leaves inside. Carefully fold the other half of the paper over the fish, clos-ing it like a book. To seal the package, plait or crimp-fold the parchment to form a neat package. Alternatively, double-fold the edges and secure each side with several staples.
3. Place in the centre of the oven and bake for 20 minutes.
4. Meanwhile, just lightly warm the chopped tomatoes with the olive oil and remaining 2 tablespoons of pistou. Taste for seasoning, adding a touch of lemon juice.

(continued on next page)

5. Remove the package from the oven and, with scissors, carefully cut it open: Watch out, there will be plenty of steam. Let it sit for about 3 minutes so the fish firms up and will be easier to fillet.

6. Carefully fillet the fish (see note below) and place a portion on each of 4 warmed dinner plates. Arrange a spoonful of pistou on top of the fish. Spoon the warmed tomato sauce around the fish. Pass with a cruet of olive oil. I first served this with a Celeriac 'Lasagne' (page 124) a vegetable dish that perfectly matches the character of the fish and pistou.

SERVES 4

WINE SUGGESTIONS: The first time I prepared this, we enjoyed it with an aged red Bandol from Domaine Tempier, a wine whose exuberance and sophistication paired beautifully with the sturdy bonito. The dish is also lovely with the lemony flavour of a select white, Viognier: my favourite comes from the Domaine les Gouberts in Gigondas.

❧ THE ART OF FILLETING A WHOLE BAKED FISH ❧   I made my first real attempt to fillet a cooked fish not that long ago, a small task that I always left for my husband, Walter, who is generally more adept than I am. He coached me along as I made the first cuts and gave me a few words of invaluable advice. 'Remember,' he began matter-of-factly, 'a fish is two-dimensional and the same on both sides.' Basic, but invaluable.

The best way to attack a small to medium-sized fish is with an ordinary fork and knife. The 'two-spoon' method is also a possibility, as they do in the fancy fish restaurants in Paris. Lay the fish on its side on a flat surface, and press the back of the fork gently against the top fillet to hold the fish steady. Begin at the head end of the fillet and cut 1 cm (½ in) deep down the length of the back to the tail end. Place the knife around the belly area of the fillet and delicately push the knife further into the fish until the flesh is completely dislodged from the bone. Use the fork to hold up the ventral part that is now separated and run the knife down to the tail so that the bottom half of the fillet is now off the bone. Gently work the knife upwards, lifting the upper half of the fillet off as well. Transfer immediately to a serving platter. For the second fillet, use the tines of the fork gradually to lift the backbone off the second fillet. Begin at the tail end and work upward. The fork does the lifting as the knife gradually elevates and dislodges the bones. The head is removed forcibly when the backbone has been removed. Lay the second fillet next to or on top of the other on the serving dish and enjoy!

NOTE: The removal of skin is important for many varieties of fish, though some can be eaten with the skin intact. As a general rule, remove the skin before removing the fillets from the bone. That way, the fillets will not have to be touched or fiddled with once intact off the bone.

Some varieties of fish can be eaten with the skin. For example, red snapper, sea bass

Local fish merchants Aymar and Eliane Berenger at work outside their village shop.

and salmon all have skin that is delicious as a flavour contrast to the flesh. Some flatfish, such as sole and turbot, are eaten with the black skin removed from one side but the white skin on the underside intact. Other fish, such as bluefish, tuna and skate have edible skin but it can be overpowering and bitter in flavour.

∿ **ON COOKING WITH PARCHMENT** ∿   The virtues of cooking in parchment paper are many. The first and foremost is that it provides moist, perfectly cooked fish. Encasing the fish in a protective layer steams it as it cooks and prevents it from drying out or losing flavour. Cooking *en papillote,* or with parchment, is also an impressive way to present fish to guests. Imagine a simple country restaurant on a cold autumn day. The waiter emerges with the puffed-up paper gift and cuts it open, letting the steaming aroma waft out to tempt the nostrils. It is this steam which accumulates in the paper case as the fish, sauce, and vegetables cook that creates the dramatic result. The steam has no way to escape, so the ingredients have no choice but to mingle and cook together. Cooking in parchment also allows for low-fat cooking that is high in flavour. Whole small fish are very receptive to this method.

STEAMED SALMON WITH WARM LEMON VINAIGRETTE

For all those cooks out there who have a fear of cooking fish – and even those who don't – I advise steaming. It's easier and more precise than poaching and the steam's gentle moist heat is ideal for the delicate flesh of fish. This recipe was devised one winter's day as the fresh local Picholine olives had just been harvested and cured. I love their bright green colour, assertive fennel flavour, and almost slippery feel on the palate. The meaty olives here are paired with the tang of capers, bathed in olive oil, a touch of lemon juice and a shower of dill, making for a quick, easy, delicious dish we savour time and again.

> 125 g (4 oz) green olives, preferably French Picholine (or substitute top-quality Spanish or Greek olives)
> 4 tablespoons capers
> 4 salmon fillets, about 2 cm (¾ in) thick and weighing about 200 g (7 oz) each
> Fine sea salt and freshly ground black pepper to taste
> 4 tablespoons extra-virgin olive oil
> 4 tablespoons freshly squeezed lemon juice
> Fresh fennel fronds or fresh dill, snipped with scissors, for garnish

1. Bring a large pan of water to the boil. Add the olives and blanch in the boiling water for 2 minutes to rid them of excess salt. Drain well and set aside.

2. Drain the capers, rinse well and soak in cold water for 10 minutes to rid them of excess salt. Set aside.

3. Bring 1 litre (1¾ pints) of water to a simmer in the bottom of a steamer. Place the salmon fillets, on the steaming rack. Season very lightly with salt and generously with pepper. Place the rack over simmering water, cover and steam until the salmon is opaque through: 5 to 6 minutes for medium-rare, 6 to 8 minutes for medium. To test the salmon, insert the tip of the blade of a sharp knife into the thickest part of the fish.

4. Meanwhile drain the capers. In a small saucepan combine the olive oil, lemon juice, capers and blanched olives in a small saucepan, stir to blend and warm gently over low heat.

5. To serve, transfer the salmon to 4 individual warmed plates and spoon the sauce on top and around the fish. Sprinkle with fresh fennel fronds or fresh dill. Serve immediately, with steamed potatoes in their jackets.

SERVES 4

WINE SUGGESTIONS: The first time I prepared this we sampled the salmon with a chilled Sablet Blanc from the nearby perched village of Sablet, but any white of character will do fine here. If the budget permits, a good white Burgundy (Meursault or a Chablis Grand Cru) will be a delight, as would an Australian or Californian Chardonnay.

*A friend … showed me into the kitchen of her new home with the words,
'This is my office'. I knew what she meant. This is where I do
the work I want to, the work I like and enjoy.*
SHASHI DESHPANDE

MINTED CRABMEAT SALAD

Crab and mint are lively companions, reminding me of complicity of the garden and the sea. Each ingredient has a sort of proud elegance, a fresh clean taste. This dish, quickly prepared, makes for a lovely main-course lunch or supper dish. Be certain to allow the mint leaves to infuse for a full 30 minutes in the warmed vinaigrette, allowing for a mellow subtle mingling of fresh mint and mellow crab. Slices of freshly toasted Provençal Olive Oil Brioche (page 167) are the perfect accompaniment.

4 tablespoons best-quality cider vinegar
6 tablespoons extra-virgin olive oil
30 g (1 oz) fresh mint leaves, snipped with scissors
500 g (1 lb) fresh crab meat, drained, picked over and flaked into generous bite-sized
    pieces
Fine sea salt and freshly ground black pepper to taste

1. In a small saucepan, combine the cider vinegar with the oil and bring just to the boil over moderate heat. Add half the mint, remove from the heat, cover, and set aside to infuse for 30 minutes. This will allow the mint to flavour the vinaigrette gently.
2. Strain the vinaigrette into a bowl, discarding the mint. Place the crab meat in a bowl, pour the liquid over the crab, add the remaining mint leaves, and toss to blend. Season to taste. (This fresh mint must be added at the very last moment or it may turn brown and, potentially, bitter.)
3. Transfer to four small, chilled salad plates, and serve immediately.

SERVES 4

WINE SUGGESTIONS: If you're in a festive and frivolous mood, serve the salad with flutes of bubbling champagne. Otherwise a chilled white, such as a Sauvignon Blanc a dry Californian or Australian Riesling, a Riesling or Semillon from America's Northwest, a Californian or French Viognier, or a flinty French Pouilly-Fumé from the Loire.

Food can look beautiful, taste exquisite, smell wonderful, make people
feel good, bring them together, inspire romantic feelings....
At its most basic, it is fuel for a hungry machine.

ROSAMOND RICHARDSON

PETITE FRITURE: FRIED BABY FISH

Each Tuesday in the Vaison-la-Romaine market, there are more than half a dozen exquisite fish stalls, not to mention the stand outside my local fishmonger, La Poissonnerie des Voconces. Miniature silvery fish, sold simply as *petite friture,* can be had fresh for a song. The tiny fish, dusted with seasoned flour and fried ever so quickly, have become the centre of our standard after-market lunch, served simply with lemon wedges and plenty of baby-fine sea salt. After much experimentation, I find that the fish taste more of the sea if they are not rinsed first, though I leave that choice up to the individual cook. I love to prepare these as guests gather around, devouring the fish as soon as they are sprinkled with salt.

EQUIPMENT: A deep-fry thermometer

135 g (4½ oz) plain fine flour
Fine sea salt to taste
¼ teaspoon cayenne pepper
1-1.5 litres (1¾-2½ pints vegetable oil (sunflower, soybean, grapeseed, peanut, or a
   blend of oils), for deep-frying
500 g (1 lb) mixed small fish, such as sardines, smelt or whitebait (rinsed and drained,
   if desired)

1. In a plastic bag, combine the flour, ½ teaspoon of salt, and the cayenne pepper. Shake to blend.
2. Preheat the oven to 100°C/200°F/gas mark 1.
3. Pour the oil into a wide 6 litre (10-pint) saucepan, or use a deep-fat fryer. (The oil should be at least 2 cm/2 in deep.) Place a wire skimmer into the oil, so that when you lift the fish from the oil, they will not stick to the skimmer. Place a deep-fry thermometer in the oil. Heat the oil to 190°C/375°F.
4. Dip a handful of fish into the bag of flour and shake to coat with the flour mixture. Transfer the coated fish to a fine-mesh sieve and shake off excess flour. Carefully drop the

(continued on next page)

FACING PHOTOGRAPH: *Fresh baby fish, ready for frying.*

Petite Friture: *Fresh baby fish are dusted with seasoned flour, then quickly deep fried.*

fish by handfuls into the hot oil. Cook until lightly browned, 1 to 2 minutes. With a wire skimmer, lift from the oil, drain and transfer to paper towels. Immediately season with fine sea salt. Place them in the oven – the door slightly ajar – to keep warm. Continue frying until all the fish are cooked, allowing the oil to return to 190°C/375°F each time before adding another batch. Serve immediately, with lemon wedges.

SERVES 6-12 AS AN APPETIZER

🌳 **WINE SUGGESTION:** We enjoy serving this with our local white, a Sablet blanc from the Domaine Les Gouberts in Gigondas. Other light whites that go well with light fried foods include a Sauvignon Blanc, a white Bordeaux, or an Alsatian Riesling.

SEARED PANCETTA-WRAPPED COD

Inspired by London chef Alastair Little – who served me a version of this one winter's evening in his Soho restaurant – this simple, flavourful dish can be prepared in a matter of minutes. Here, fish fillets are given a protective wrapping – either pancetta, ham, or bacon – that add a touch of needed fat and also help create a brilliant contrast of colour and texture. The wrapping acts as a second skin, both protecting and imparting flavour and texture to the final dish. I always keep a piece of Provençal 'pancetta' (peppered rolled pork sold as *poitrine roulé*) on hand, so wrap my fish with paper-thin slices, slicing it thinly without creating pieces of lace! The end result is a lovely blending of the land and the sea, the crunchy and the soft, a splash of red, white and green.

OPTIONS: Monkfish, grouper, striped bass

4 cod fillets, each about 180 g (6 oz)
4 very thin slices of pancetta, unsmoked ham or unsmoked bacon
3 tablespoons capers
6 tablespoons extra-virgin olive oil
2 tablespoons freshly squeezed lemon juice
Freshly ground black pepper
Fresh parsley leaves, snipped with scissors, for garnish

1. Wrap the pieces of fish in pancetta, ham or bacon. Secure with toothpicks at each end.
2. Drain the capers, rinse and soak in cold water for 10 minutes to remove excess salt.
3. In a large non-stick frying pan, heat 2 tablespoons of oil over moderately high heat until hot but not smoking. Sear the wrapped pieces of fish for about 3 minutes on each side, or until the fish is firm and offers little resistance when pressed with the fingertip.
4. While the fish is cooking, warm the sauce. In a small saucepan combine the drained capers, the remaining 4 tablespoons of olive oil and the lemon juice. Stir to blend and warm gently over low heat.
5. To serve, transfer the fish to 4 individual warmed plates, season very generously with freshly ground black pepper and spoon the sauce on top and around the fish. Sprinkle with fresh parsley.

FOUR SERVINGS

WINE SUGGESTION: This dish calls for a rich dry white wine: a Rhône Valley white, such as a Châteauneuf-du-Pape; a Californian or Australian Chardonnay.

WHOLE FISH ROASTED IN A CRUST OF SEA SALT

One New Year's Eve I told my husband, Walter, that I would prepare anything in the world for him for our traditional dinner for two. I anticipated his wish list would include caviar, maybe a lobster or foie gras. But no, his sole request was for my *Bar en croute de sel*. I could not have been a happier cook that evening, enveloping a glistening sea bass, in handfuls of fragrant sea salt from Brittany.

This is, in fact, my preferred method of preparing any fish: roasted whole, encased in fragrant sea salt. Easy, uncomplicated, unfussy, it is a method that allows the fish – cooked whole and on the bone – to preserve its integrity, retaining maximum moistness, flavour, and texture.

The salt, with its high water content, firms up as it bakes, encasing the fish in a clay-like, hermetic package. (Any coarse salt can be used here, with equally good results.) Many varieties of fish can be roasted in this manner, including red snapper, sea bream, or even salmon. Do not scale the fish, for the scales will not only add flavour to the fish and protect it as it cooks, but adhere to the salt, making it easier to fillet after cooking. In Provence, where bay leaves grow in profusion, I usually stick several fresh bay leaves in the cavity of the fish, as well as layer them within the mound of salt to perfume the dish even more. Leftover fish is delicious the next day, served with Pistou (page 316).

EQUIPMENT: One ovenproof baking dish large enough to hold the fish

1 1-kg (2-lb) whole sea bass, gutted, but not scaled, head left on, tail
   and fins trimmed
Several fresh bay leaves (optional)
2 kg (4 lb) coarse sea salt
Extra-virgin olive oil and fresh lemon sections, for garnish

1. Preheat the oven to 230°C/450°F/gas mark 8).
2. Rinse the fish thoroughly inside and out until there is no trace of blood. If the gills have not been removed, do so to avoid bitterness. Pat dry. Season the cavity of the fish with salt and, if desired, tuck in a few bay leaves as well.
3. Evenly spread 250 g (8 oz) of the salt in the bottom of the baking dish. Place the fish on top of the salt, and pour the remaining salt over the fish to completely cover it from head to tail. It should look as though you have a baking dish mounded with nothing but salt. (If the fish is large, there's a chance the tail fin will extend outside the baking dish. That won't alter the baking of the fish.)
4. Place the dish in the centrer of the oven, and bake for 10 minutes per 500 g (1 lb), or minutes for a 1 kg (2 lb) fish. Adjust baking times by 5 minutes either way for each 250 g (8 oz) of fish.

(continued on next page)

5. Remove the dish from the oven. Allow it to sit for 3 minutes to firm up the flesh and make it easier to fillet. Brush away as much salt as possible from the fish, so it will not fall into the flesh when you remove the skin. Using the blade of a sharp knife, gently scrape away and discard the skin from the top fillet of the fish. Remove and discard the bay leaves from the cavity of the fish.

Using the knife, gently trace along the backbone of the fish to divide the top fillet in half. Begin at the head end of the top fillet and cut 1 cm (½ in) deep down the centre, the full length of the fish. Trim off and discard any fat, extraneous flesh and skin from the sides of the fillet. This will make for neater fillets and easier removal. Using two large spoons, gently remove one half of the top fillet in neat pieces and transfer to two warmed dinner plates. Repeat for the other half of the top fillet. With the spoons, carefully remove and discard the centre bone. Repeat for the bottom fillet, dividing it into two and removing the halves of the fillet in pieces. Transfer to two additional warmed dinner plates.

6. Serve immediately, passing a cruet of olive oil and a bowl of lemon wedges for seasoning.

SERVES 4

WINE SUGGESTION: This regal dish demands a regal white, such as a rich, dry Chassagne-Montrachet from Burgundy.

Any variety of fish can be roasted in salt. It is a method that retains maximum moistness, flavour and texture.

GINGER & LIME SEVICHE

Seviche has always seemed to me a miracle. How easy, to toss fresh fish or shellfish with citrus juice, and have the acid actually cook it. In traditional seviche recipes, lime juice is preferred to lemon, since it is usually more flavourful, slightly more fragrant and pairs naturally with any fresh firm white fish or shellfish. I have prepared this recipe with sea scallops and monkfish, as well a Northern-Atlantic fish found in my Paris markets called *beryx* or *bérix*, a fish similar to a sea bream. Be certain to tell your fishmonger you are making a seviche, so he understands you need perfectly fresh fish.

> OPTIONS: Red snapper, sea bass or scallops (avoid cod and other relatives, as they have a higher parasite level in relation to other types of fish)
>
> 250 g (8 oz) super-fresh white fish (see options)
> 4 tablespoons freshly squeezed lime juice
> 1 tablespoon grated fresh ginger
> Fine sea salt to taste

1. Using a very sharp knife (a flexible fish boning knife is ideal), cut the fish horizontally into slices about 2 mm (⅛ in) thick. (The length and width of the pieces is not important, but the thinness is.)
2. Lightly season a large platter. Place the slices of fish side by side, very slightly overlapping, on the platter. Spoon the lime juice over the fish and shower with ginger. Cover and refrigerate for 20 minutes.
3. With a slotted spatula or spoon, transfer the fish to individual chilled dinner plates. Serve with a green salad and plenty of freshly grilled country bread.

SERVES 4 AS A FIRST COURSE, 2 AS A MAIN COURSE

BEVERAGE SUGGESTION: Actually, my choice here is a nice, chilled beer. The acid of the lime is a bit much to compete with a fine wine, but beer can certainly do the trick in quenching one's thirst.

∾ **SEVICHE** ∾ What is it? A dish that has its origins in Chilean or South-American cooking, seviche is more a technique for treating raw fish than a recipe. Essentially, a seviche is a piece of raw fish that is marinated in some form of acid – lemon, lime juice or vinegar – and then served raw. The fish is cooked by the acid, though no heat is involved in the cooking process, much in the way the Japanese dip their raw fish in soy sauce, a seasoning that adds flavour and slightly cooks the fish as well.

If man be sensible and one fine morning, while he is lying in bed,
counts at the tips of his fingers how many things in this life truly will give him enjoyment,
invariably he will find food is the first one.

LIN YUTANG

CATALAN TUNA DAUBE

Tuna is often called the 'pot roast of the sea', since it take so well to long slow cooking, a method that beautifully tenderizes its meaty flesh. This version – a daube that simmers slowly in the oven – takes advantage of many full-flavoured ingredients which combine to make for a dish of very intense, complex flavours.

Here, in a dish I first sampled in Spain, black peppercorns are crushed with garlic, then accented by hints of lemon, anchovy, garlic and caper. I also enjoy the grassy flavours that green peppers impart: With the popularly of red peppers, green peppers have been mistakenly eclipsed in the modern kitchen. Lemon, tomatoes, and wine all work their magic in tenderizing this meaty flavourful fish. The tuna is equally delicious the next day, served cold.

4 flat anchovy fillets in olive oil
4 tablespoons whole milk
1 tablespoon capers
1 medium onion (about 150 g/5 oz), peeled
4 plump fresh garlic cloves, peeled and halved
20 whole black peppercorns
Fine sea salt to taste
3 green sweet peppers
6 tablespoons extra-virgin olive oil
1 kg (2 lb) tuna steaks, cut about 5 cm (2 in) thick
Freshly ground black pepper to taste
Wide strips of zest of 1 lemon
Bouquet garni: Several parsley stems, celery leaves, and sprigs of thyme, wrapped in the green part of a leek and securely fastened
375 ml (13 fl oz) dry white wine (such as a white Rhône, Riesling, Aligoté, or Chenin Blanc)
1 small can (400 g/14½ oz) whole plum tomatoes in juice
½ teaspoon ground cayenne pepper, or to taste

1. Rinse the anchovies, discarding any visible bones. Pat them dry and chop finely. Place in a small bowl with the milk. Set aside for 15 minutes. Drain, discarding the milk. Set aside.

2. Drain the capers, rinse well and soak in cold water for 10 minutes. Drain and set aside.

3. Slice the onion in half lengthwise. Place each half, cut side down, on a cutting board and cut across into very thin slices.

4. In a mortar crush the garlic, peppercorns and ½ teaspoon of salt with a pestle to form a paste. Set aside.

5. Char the skin of the peppers over a gas flame or under the grill. Peel, deseed and cut into strips, reserving as much juice as possible. Set aside.

6. Preheat the oven to 180°C/350°F/gas mark 4.

7. In a large frying pan, heat 2 tablespoons of oil over high heat. When the oil is hot but not smoking, add the tuna, searing over high heat for 2 minutes. Turn the tuna to sear the other side. Season the seared side generously with salt and pepper. Transfer the tuna to a platter, seasoning the second side generously with salt and pepper.

8. In a large, unheated ovenproof casserole, combine the remaining 4 tablespoons of oil, the onion, the crushed garlic and peppercorns, the lemon zest and the bouquet garni. Toss to coat evenly with oil. Cook over moderate heat, until the onions are soft and the mixture is well-blended, about 10 minutes. Add the wine, pouring it all over the surface of the pan. Adjust the heat to bring the liquid to a gentle simmer and cook, uncovered, until the alcohol has cooked off, about 7 minutes from the time the liquid comes to a simmer. Add the seared tuna slices. Add the tomatoes and their juice, the cayenne pepper, the green peppers and their juice, the anchovies, and the capers.

9. Cover the casserole and place in the centre of the oven. Cook until the tuna is very tender, about 1 hour.

10. Remove from the oven. Remove the pieces of tuna from the casserole and discard the skin of the tuna. Place a portion of tuna on a warmed dinner plate and, with a slotted spoon, spoon the solid ingredients over the tuna. Spoon a bit of the sauce over and around the fish. Serve with steamed rice or baked potatoes.

SERVES 6-8

 WINE SUGGESTION: Serve with a hearty red Rhône wine, such as Vacqueyras.

THE VAISON FISHMONGER'S FRESH TUNA CASSEROLE

One Tuesday in March, one of the fishmongers at the local Vaison-la-Romaine market was ecstatic over the arrival of the season's first red tuna from the seaside village of Sete. The fish was gorgeous – rosy and sweet-smelling, you could see the 'marbling' of fat. I asked for a thick steak, and he said 'Of course you'll do it *à la cocotte*.' Then without missing a beat, he quickly reeled off this recipe. The fishmonger advised me *not* to sear the tuna – as is the usual practice – for tuna can easily dry out. With this dish, the tuna cooks quickly in the tomato sauce, just enough to soften the onions and make for a richly flavoured sauce. Later, I thought about how *cocotte* is the word for 'casserole,' but this is a far cry from the canned tuna casserole of my youth, garnished with canned, fried onions rings!

1 small tuna steak, cut about 3.5 cm (1½ in) thick (about 1 kg/2 lb)
Sea salt and freshly ground pepper to taste
4 small onions (about 300 g/10 oz), peeled and quartered
1 small can (400 g/14½ oz) whole plum tomatoes in juice
2 teaspoons capers, rinsed
2 tablespoons extra-virgin olive oil
Bouquet garni: Several parsley stems, celery leaves, and sprigs of thyme, wrapped in
    the green part of a leek and securely fastened
2 teaspoons best-quality red wine vinegar or sherry vinegar

1. Select a frying pan just slightly larger than the tuna. Generously season both sides of the tuna with salt and pepper. Place the tuna in the pan, tuck the onion quarters around the tuna and cover with the tomatoes and their juice. Add the capers, oil and bouquet garni, cover and simmer over low heat just until the tuna is cooked through and flakes with a fork, about 25 minutes.
2. Drizzle the vinegar over the tuna, cover and let rest off the heat for 1 to 2 minutes to allow the fish to absorb the vinegar.
3. To serve, quarter the tuna, remove and discard the skin and the bouquet garni. Serve on warm dinner plates, surrounded by the vegetables.

SERVES 4

WINE SUGGESTIONS: Try this with a medium-bodied red wine, such as a Chinon from the Loire Valley, a Merlot from Bordeaux, or a Santenay from Burgundy.

WALTER'S THANKSGIVING OYSTER CASSEROLE

In the 1970s when I met my husband, Walter, he was a much better cook that I was. At least he had a lot of impressive 'gourmet' gadgetry I hadn't yet collected, like fish poachers, stock pots, sharp knives, and an impressive collection of regional cookbooks, especially those from the South. With our move to Paris in 1980, Walter's cooking career was abruptly halted by the demanding schedule at the *International Herald Tribune.*

Yet each thanksgiving by popular demand he prepares his now-famous oyster casserole. The recipe was adapted from Charleston Receipts, the cookbook published in 1950 by the Charleston Junior League and credited to Miss Jane Christie Hammond. But when Walter decided to put the casserole back on the menu after we moved to France, we found a decided absence of one of the casserole's main ingredients, saltine crackers. Quickly we found that the easy-to-find matzos gave the dish even more texture and flavour. Hardly kosher; even, as the French would say, *pas catholique non plus*!

1 litre (1¾ pints) oysters freshly opened and in their own liquor (2 to 3 dozen)
250 ml (8 fl oz) crème fraîche or sour cream
½ teaspoon mace, freshly ground
125 g (4 oz) unsalted butter
About 125 g (4 oz) medium-coarse cracker crumbs (saltines or matzos)
Sea salt and freshly ground black pepper to taste

1. Preheat the oven to 180°C/350°F/gas mark 4.
2. Drain the oysters. Strain the oyster liquor through dampened cheesecloth and reserve. In a small bowl, combine the crème fraîche and mace. Set aside.
3. In a small saucepan over low heat, melt the butter. Add the cracker crumbs and mix thoroughly. Season to taste with salt and pepper.
4. Spread half the crumbs in the bottom of a baking dish measuring about 30 cm (12 in) square by 5 cm (2 in) deep. Arrange all the oysters on top of the cracker mixture. Add the remaining cracker crumbs. Pour the crème fraîche mixture over all. Drizzle lightly with about 2 tablespoons of the reserved oyster liquor. Place in the centre of the oven and bake until most of the liquid has evaporated and the top is crisp and golden, 20 to 25 minutes. (Take care not to overcook; the oysters should poach until tender and not become rubbery.) Serve as a side dish to roast poultry, or as we do, with the Thanksgiving turkey.

SERVES 6-8

8

POULTRY & GAME

PLUMP CHICKENS AND TURKEYS FROM THE
Bresse region, local pigeon and quail, fresh and
wild rabbit, and moist mallard duck raised by
our very own winemaker make up the family poultry
larder from season to season. Give me a whole
chicken and I'll turn it into a feast, gently coaxing handfuls of herbs beneath the skin, tucking it into the
bread oven to roast to a crispy, golden tenderness.
Rabbits have long been part of the history and lore
of our farmhouse, so naturally they find their way
to the table, with a Provençal version (Chanteduc
Rabbit with Garlic & Preserved Lemons) as well as
one from Italy's Piedmont (Pina's Braised Rabbit.)
My butcher, Roland Henny, adds his expertise, sup-
plying us with his version of Rabbit Bouillabaisse,
while a trip to Switzerland and lunch at grand chef
Fredy Girardet's inspired me to create a new family
favourite, Duck with Lime & Honey.

FACING PHOTOGRAPH: *A corner of the Chanteduc kitchen, with an assortment of wooden kegs for homemade vinegars.*

POULET AUX FINES HERBES:
BUTTER-ROASTED HERBED CHICKEN

Every time I roast a chicken, I learn something new. Perhaps my greatest 'training' came when I was taught the following 'rotation' method by chef Joël Robuchon. By roasting the bird on both sides, then breast side up, then finally breast side down, the bird is evenly, uniformly browned and roasted. I've also added a final step, roasting it breast side down at the end, tail in the air, so the juices begin to run to the breast even as it is still roasting. I also find the bird roasts more evenly if it is set on a rack in the roasting pan, allowing the heat to circulate around the chicken.

In this recipe, I've given the breast – which tends to dry out in roasting – a protective coating of butter, which is slipped with the fingers beneath the skin, creating a stunning presentation and a very moist chicken. Basting is not necessary here: In fact the chicken skin will be crispier if you do not baste at all. This is a good picnic bird, for the dish is truly wonderful served the next day at room temperature.

EQUIPMENT: One oval baking dish, just slightly larger than the chicken (about 23 x 33 cm/ 9 x 13 in) fitted with a roasting rack

1 lemon, preferably organic
Sea salt and freshly ground black pepper to taste
1 free-range roasting chicken (about 2.5 kg/5 lb), with giblets
1 bunch of fresh thyme
5 tablespoons very finely chopped fresh herbs, carefully stemmed, preferably a mix of chervil, tarragon, chives and parsley
75 g (2½ oz) unsalted butter, softened

1. Preheat the oven to 220°C/425°F/gas mark 7.
2. Rinse the lemon in cold water and dry. Soften the lemon by rolling it back and forth along a flat surface. Using a two-pronged fork, a trussing needle or a toothpick, pierce the skin of the lemon at least 20 times, to help the lemon release its juices during roasting. Generously season the cavity of the chicken with salt and pepper. Place the giblets, lemon and bunch of thyme in the cavity. Truss.
3. In a small bowl, combine the finely chopped fresh herbs, ½ teaspoon each of salt and pepper and 60 g (2 oz) butter. Mash with a fork, and blend evenly.
4. Be sure to remove any rings from your fingers, for they might pierce the skin of the chicken. Entering from the neck end of the chicken, push your fingers through the skin over one side of the breast to separate the skin from the flesh. Be gentle, so as not to tear the skin. Working with the tips of your fingers, spread half the butter and herb mixture over one side of the breast meat. Repeat the same process on the other breast side.

Pressing down on the skin from the exterior of the skin, even out the butter mixture and pat the skin back into place. Rub the skin of the chicken with the remaining 15 g (½ oz) butter. Season all over with salt and pepper.

5. Place the chicken on its side on the roasting rack in the baking dish. Place in the centre of the oven and roast, uncovered, for 20 minutes. Turn the chicken to the other side, and roast for 20 minutes more. Turn the chicken breast side up, and roast for 20 minutes more, for a total of 1 hour's roasting time. By this time the skin should be a deep golden colour. Reduce the heat to 190°C/375°F/gas mark 5. Turn the chicken breast side down, at an angle if at all possible, with its head down and tail in the air. (This heightens the flavour by allowing the juices to flow down through the breast meat.) Roast until the juices run clear when you pierce a thigh with a skewer, about 15 minutes more.

6. Remove from the oven and season generously with salt and pepper. Transfer the chicken to a platter and place at an angle against the edge of an overturned plate, with its head down and tail in the air. Cover loosely with foil. Turn off the oven and place the platter in the oven, with the door open. Let rest a minimum of 10 minutes and up to 30 minutes. The chicken will continue to cook during this resting time.

7. Meanwhile, prepare the sauce: place the baking dish over moderate heat, scraping up

(continued on next page)

any bits that cling to the bottom. Cook for 2 to 3 minutes, scraping and stirring until the liquid is almost caramelized. Do not let it burn. Spoon off and discard any excess fat. Add several tablespoons cold water to deglaze (hot water will cloud the sauce). Bring to a boil. Reduce the heat to low and simmer until thickened, about 5 minutes.

8. While the sauce is cooking, carve the chicken and place on a warmed platter.

9. Strain the sauce through a fine-mesh sieve and pour into a sauce boat. Serve immediately, with the chicken. (If serving the chicken at room temperature, use the sauce to prepare a vinaigrette for an accompanying salad.)

SERVES 4-6

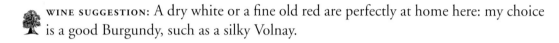 WINE SUGGESTION: A dry white or a fine old red are perfectly at home here: my choice is a good Burgundy, such as a silky Volnay.

TIP: When you don't have time to wait for your oven to warm up, try the cold-start method. Turn the oven to 220°C/425°F/gas mark 7, and follow the recipe below, allowing about 15 additional minutes roasting time. Since some ovens heat up more quickly than others, roasting time may vary.

⌒ HOW'S YOUR HERB AWARENESS? ∾ A little quiz to test your herb awareness: do you know the difference between *herbes de Provence* and *fines herbes*? *Herbes de Provence* is usually a mixture of dried fennel, rosemary, sage, savory and wild or domestic thyme. *Fines herbes* are composed of fresh chervil, tarragon, chives and parsley.

FRENCH COUNTRY GUINEA FOWL & CABBAGE

Few dishes embody classic country French as this warming speciality. It can be prepared with a whole chicken, but a plump and meaty guinea fowl – the domesticated bird that is closest to wild game – is one of the world's great culinary treats.

1 guinea fowl (about 1 kg/2 lb) or substitute chicken

2 shallots, peeled and halved

1 thin slice of smoked ham, finely chopped

Bouquet garni: A generous bunch of flat-leaf parsley, celery leaves, fresh bay leaves, and sprigs of thyme, tied in a bundle with string

90 g (3 oz) unsalted butter

1 onion, finely chopped

1 carrot, finely chopped

500 ml (16 fl oz) chicken stock, preferably homemade (page 322)

1 large green cabbage, quartered lengthwise

1 tablespoon sherry vinegar

Sea salt and freshly ground black pepper to taste

1. Season the exterior and cavity of the bird with salt and pepper. Place the shallots, ham and bouquet garni inside the cavity and sew up the opening. Set aside.

2. In a large covered casserole, melt 15 g (½ oz) butter with the oil over moderate heat until hot but not smoking. Add the guinea fowl and brown it carefully on all sides, about 10 minutes. Transfer the bird to a platter and discard the fat in the pan. Season the exterior generously with salt and pepper. Still over moderate heat, add another 15 g (½ oz) butter to the casserole, scraping up the browned bits that cling to the bottom of the pan. Add the onion and carrot and cook until soft, about 5 minutes. Return the bird to the pan, add the stock, cover and simmer over low heat until the chicken is cooked, about 50 minutes.

3. In a large pan, bring 6 litres (10 pints) of water to a rolling boil. Add 3 tablespoons of salt and the cabbage, and blanch, uncovered, for 5 minutes. Drain and set aside.

4. In a large frying pan, melt the remaining butter over moderate heat. Add the vinegar, cabbage, seasoning, and cook, trying to keep the pieces of cabbage intact and well coated with sauce. Cover and cook over low heat until soft, about 20 minutes. Season to taste.

6. Meanwhile, carve the guinea fowl and arrange the pieces on a warmed serving platter. Spoon the stuffing, sauce and warmed cabbage over the sliced poultry and serve at once.

SERVES 4-6

 WINE SUGGESTION: With this dish, which makes me think of the Alsatian region to the east, I love a nicely chilled Riesling.

CHICKEN WITH TARRAGON & SHERRY VINEGAR

Chicken with vinegar is a classic speciality of France's Bresse region, famous for its pampered poultry, a special breed of bird that sports pure white plumes and amazing blue feet. Chicken with tarragon is another classic Bresse preparation, and in this dish I've combined these national treasures, adding a rich flavour base of onions, shallots and garlic. The sauce is also enriched with reduced stock and a touch of mustard and cream, creating a thick sensuous sauce that matches the simple elegance of this homey chicken dish. Serve with plenty of pasta or rice, to absorb the fragrant sauce.

2 medium onions (about 300 g/10 oz), peeled
1 chicken 1.5-2 kg (3-4 lb), at room temperature, cut into 8 serving pieces
Sea salt and freshly ground black pepper to taste
3 tablespoons extra-virgin olive oil
1 tablespoon unsalted butter
4 shallots, peeled and cut into thin rounds
1 head of plump fresh garlic cloves, peeled but left whole
Bouquet garni: Several generous sprigs of fresh tarragon, fresh parsley and fresh
   rosemary, several bay leaves and several celery leaves, tied in a bundle with string
6 tablespoons best-quality sherry vinegar
500 ml (16 fl oz) chicken stock
1 tablespoon tomato paste
1 tablespoon Dijon mustard
4 tablespoons fresh tarragon leaves, snipped with scissors
100 ml (4 fl oz) crème fraîche or double cream

1. Slice an onion in half lengthwise. Place each half, cut side down, on a cutting board and cut across into very thin slices. Slice the remaining onion in this manner. Set aside.
2. Liberally season the chicken on all sides with salt and pepper. In a large frying pan, combine the oil and butter over high heat. When hot, add several pieces of chicken, skin side down (do not crowd the pan but brown the chicken in several batches) and cook until it turns an even golden brown, about 5 minutes. Turn the pieces and brown them on the other side, 5 minutes more. Carefully regulate the heat to avoid scorching the skin. When all the pieces are browned, use tongs – to avoid piercing the meat – to transfer them to a platter.
3. Pour off and discard all but about 2 tablespoons of fat from the frying pan. Add the onions, shallots, garlic, bouquet garni and season lightly with salt. Sweat – cook over low heat without colouring – for about 5 minutes.
4. Add the chicken pieces. Pour about 3 tablespoons of vinegar over the chicken pieces, and cover. Cook very gently over low heat, stirring to make sure the vegetables do not

burn, until the chicken is cooked through, about 25 minutes. Remove and discard the herb bundle.

5. Transfer the chicken pieces to a warmed platter. Cover with foil, and keep warm in a low oven.

6. There should be a thin film of sauce remaining in the frying pan. Leave the vegetables in the pan. Over moderate heat, slowly add the remaining 3 tablespoons of vinegar, scraping up any bits that stick to the bottom of the frying pan. Add the chicken stock, tomato paste, mustard and half the tarragon. Stir to blend, increase heat to high and bring to the boil. Cook vigorously until the sauce is thick and glossy, about 7 minutes. Off the heat, stir in the cream and stir to blend the ingredients. Return to the heat and over low heat just to heat through. The resulting sauce should be thick, creamy and fragrant. Taste for seasoning.

7. To serve, transfer the chicken pieces to warmed dinner plates. Spoon the sauce and vegetables over and alongside the chicken. Sprinkle with the remaining tarragon. Serve immediately, accompanied by rice or fresh noodles.

SERVES 4-6

WINE SUGGESTION: A light but elegant Bordeaux. I've loved this with a well-aged Pommard.

Happy and successful cooking doesn't rely only on know-how; it comes
from the heart, makes great demands on the palate, and needs
enthusiasm and a great love of food to bring it to life.

GEORGES BLANC

CHICKEN WITH SHALLOTS, LEMON & THYME

Few dishes are as welcoming as a moist whole chicken, browned and then braised in wine in a covered casserole with mountains of herbs and an avalanche of perfectly shaped whole shallots. Here, white wine creates the base of the sauce, adding good balance to the dish. Choose an assertive wine – such as a French or Californian Riesling or a white Burgundy – that will cut through the rich flavours of the cream and eggs.

1 free-range roasting chicken (about 1.5 kg/3 lb), at room temperature

Sea salt and freshly ground black pepper to taste

1 lemon, preferably organic

2 large bunches of fresh thyme

45 g (1½ oz) unsalted butter

2 tablespoons extra-virgin olive oil

750 ml (27 fl oz) white wine (see Wine Suggestions)

Bouquet garni: A generous bunch of fresh tarragon, flat-leaf parsley, celery leaves, fresh bay leaves, and sprigs of thyme, tied in a bundle with string

20 best-quality shallots, peeled but left whole

2 tablespoons crème fraîche or double cream

3 large egg yolks

2 to 3 tablespoons freshly squeezed lemon juice

About ¼ teaspoon freshly grated nutmeg

1 tablespoon fresh thyme leaves, carefully stemmed

1. Generously season the cavity of the chicken with salt and pepper. Scrub the lemon and pierce it with a two-pronged fork about a dozen times. Place the lemon and 1 bunch of thyme inside the cavity of the chicken and, using household string, sew up the opening. Truss. Set aside.

2. In a large covered casserole, melt the butter with the oil over moderate heat until hot but not smoking. Add the chicken and brown carefully on all sides, about 10 minutes. Adjust the heat to avoid scorching the skin. Use tongs to turn the chicken to avoid piercing the skin. Transfer the chicken to a platter and season generously with salt and pepper.

3. Discard the fat in the pan. Still over moderate heat, deglaze the pan with the wine. Bring the wine to a boil and boil vigorously until the alcohol has burned off and there is no alcohol aroma wafting from the casserole (give it a good sniff from time to time!), about 5 minutes.

4. Return the chicken to the pan, breast side up. Surround the chicken with the bouquet garni, the other bunch of thyme and the shallots. Cover and simmer very gently over very low heat, until the chicken is cooked through, 40 to 50 minutes.

5. Meanwhile, in a large bowl, combine the crème fraîche, egg yolks, 2 tablespoons lemon juice and nutmeg. Stir to blend. Set aside.

6. Transfer the chicken and shallots to a warm serving platter, cover with foil and set aside in a warm oven to keep warm. Discard the bouquet garni and thyme. Pass the remaining cooking liquid through a fine-mesh sieve and return to the pan. (It should measure about 375 ml/13 fl oz). Return the pan to the heat and whisk in the crème fraîche and egg yolk mixture. Simmer gently – do not let the sauce boil – whisking regularly for about 5 minutes, until the sauce begins to thicken slightly. Taste for seasoning, adding additional lemon juice if desired. Strain the sauce through a fine-mesh sieve into a bowl.

7. Carve the chicken and transfer the pieces to a large warmed serving platter. Arrange the shallots alongside. Drizzle about half the sauce over the chicken and shallots. Sprinkle with fresh thyme leaves. Serve warm, with Basmati Rice (page 273), passing the remaining sauce.

SERVES 4-6

WINE SUGGESTIONS: The choice of cooking and drinking wines here is endless. I am partial to the fragrant whites of the Rhône, where the vines share the soil with such wild natural herbs as rosemary and thyme, and pair so well with their pungent flavours and aromas. Any wine with a nice balanced acidity here is good: A French Riesling, a white Burgundy, a not-too-oaky Californian Chardonnay, a Rhône Valley Viognier or simple Côtes-du-Rhône blanc de blanc.

↔ THE LOVE OF THYME ↭ If I had only one herb to grow in the garden, it would be thyme. In Provence, where it also grows wild at will, the herb is called *farigoule*. Sometimes, when I run in the warm summer mornings, the surrounding woods around Chanteduc smell like grilled thyme. The herb will grow in almost no soil at all, and the leaves fall from the stems as it soon as is picked. In the intense summer heat of Provence, fresh thyme becomes almost dried.

*In light of what Proust wrote with so mild a stimulus, it is the world's loss
that he did not have a heartier appetite. On a dozen Gardiner's Island oysters, a bowl of
clam chowder, a peck of steamers, some bay scallops, three sautéed soft-shell crabs, a few ears
of fresh-picked corn, a thin swordfish steak of generous area, a pair of lobsters,
and a Long Island duck, he might have written a masterpiece.*

A.J.LEIBLING

THE WINEMAKER'S DUCK WITH OLIVES & ARTICHOKES

A few days before Christmas our winemaker, Daniel Combe telephoned to say casually that some of his barnyard poultry was ready for the table: He suggested a duck, a goose or a chicken. What an embarrassment of riches! I hadn't cooked a duck in a long time, so that was my choice. I quickly scanned a stack of old Provençal cookbooks, and adapted a recipe for duck with olives and artichokes, two of my favourite ingredients. That duck was the best I'd ever tasted – we cooked it in the bread oven in our courtyard, and you could hear the sizzling of the fat against the brick oven walls all the way to the kitchen. For months to come, the fat I collected from the duck that day was used to prepare the most delicious golden sautéed potatoes.

4 globe artichokes (see Note page 95) or two 270-g (9-oz) packets of frozen artichoke hearts, defrosted

4 tablespoons freshly squeezed lemon juice

4 tablespoons extra-virgin olive oil

About 125 g (4 oz) best-quality black olives, (such as French Nyons olives), drained and stoned

About 125 g (4 oz) best-quality green olives, (such as French Picholine olives), drained and stoned

1 duck (about 2.25 kg/5 lb), liver reserved, trimmings (neck, heart, wing tips) chopped

Sea salt and freshly ground white pepper to taste

Bouquet garni: Generous branch of fresh tarragon, thyme, rosemary and parsley, secured with string

3 plump fresh garlic cloves, peeled and halved

1 small carrot, cut into thick diagonal slices

1 small onion, cut into thick slices

(continued on next page)

1. Preheat the oven to 220°C/425°F/gas mark 7.

2. In a small bowl, combine the artichoke hearts, lemon juice, olive oil and olives and stir to blend. Set aside.

3. Liberally season the exterior of the duck on all sides, as well as the cavity, with salt and pepper. Place the duck liver, the chopped trimmings, bouquet garni and garlic, carrot and onion in the cavity. Truss.

4. Place the duck on its side on a roasting rack in the roasting pan. Place in the oven with the fullest part of the duck – the breast portion – toward the back of the oven. Roast, uncovered, for 10 minutes. Turn the duck on the other side and roast for 10 minutes more. (If the duck releases great quantities of fat, pour off and discard about two-thirds of it). Turn the duck on its back – breast side up – and roast for 10 minutes more. Remove from the oven and surround the duck with the olives and artichokes. Baste with the cooking juices 3 or 4 times so that it will remain moist as it continues to roast. Remove the trussing string from the bird and season the legs with salt. (At this point, the bird will hold its shape on its own. By removing the string, the legs will cook more evenly.) Return to the oven to roast for a total of 13 to 15 minutes per 500 g (1 lb). (If there is not enough fat to keep the trimmings from browning too much, add a few tablespoons of cold water.) Roasting time will vary according to the size of the duck, and your flavour preference. Select the shorter roasting time per 500 g (1 lb) for a large duck, the longer time for a smaller duck. (Thus, total roasting time for a 1.25 kg/2½ lb duck would be about 38 minutes, a 2.5 kg/5 lb duck would be 1 hour and 5 minutes.)

5. Remove the duck from the oven and, *once again, season generously.* Transfer to a platter and place at an angle against the edge of a baking dish, with its head down and tail in the air. This heightens the flavour by allowing the juices to flow down through to the breast meat. Cover with foil. Turn off the oven and place the duck in the oven, with the door slightly ajar. At the same time, transfer the olive and artichoke mixture to a pan. Cover and place in the oven with the duck. Let the duck rest a minimum of 20 minutes and up to 1 hour. The duck will continue to cook during the resting time.

6. To serve: Carve the duck, and arrange in the centre of the platter. Arrange the olives and artichokes around the duck. Serve immediately.

SERVES 4-6

WINE SUGGESTION: This festive dish makes me want to take out a festive local wine, such as a heady Gigondas, one that sings of the thyme-flecked hills of Provence.

DUCK WITH LIME & HONEY

On assignment in Switzerland, I found myself without a dining partner for a few days, and admit I didn't look forward to sitting alone at the table of one of the world's greatest restaurants, Fredy Girardet's in Crissier. Of course one sip of his house champagne and my mood changed – suddenly I felt like a queen, with a bevy of footman. I chatted with the waiters and sommeliers, and relished the regal feast.

When a whole duck arrived, I almost gasped, realizing this extraordinary chef had cooked a whole duck, just for me. I thought about that duck for weeks. Girardet has a great affection for lime, and uses it liberally throughout his repertoire. I let the dish dance around in my head for a while, then I came up with a combination of whole lime, lime zest, a touch of honey and vinegar, and a whisper of tarragon.

Since poultry meat readily absorbs the flavours placed in the cavity of the bird, here the whole pierced limes exude their juices as the duck roasts. When the lime juice, tarragon and moist duck meat converge, the flavours taste faintly Oriental, yet distinctly French. Whenever I prepare this dish, people walk into the kitchen and exclaim, 'It smells like a Chinese restaurant in here.' Serve this with a simple green salad.

4 whole limes (preferably organic)
1 duck 1.25-2 kg (2½-lb), liver reserved, trimmings (neck, heart, wing tips), chopped (see Note)
Sea salt and freshly ground white pepper to taste
Generous branch of fresh tarragon
3 plump fresh garlic cloves, peeled and halved
1 small carrot, cut into thick diagonal slices
1 small onion, cut into thick slices
1 generous sprig of fresh thyme
1 tablespoon creamy honey, or to taste
4-5 tablespoons best-quality sherry or red wine vinegar
45 g (1½ oz) unsalted butter

1. Preheat the oven to 220°C/425°F/gas mark 7.
2. Rinse the limes in cold water and dry. Soften 2 of the limes by rolling them back and forth along a flat surface. Using a two-pronged fork, a trussing needle or a toothpick, pierce the skin of these 2 limes at least 20 times, to help release the juice. Season the duck, inside and out, with salt and pepper. Place the duck liver, the 2 prepared limes and the tarragon in the cavity – they will serve to enrich the final flavour of the meat. Truss.
3. Zest the 2 remaining limes. Juice the limes and set aside in a separate bowl.
4. Place the duck on its side on a roasting rack in the roasting pan. Place in the oven with the fullest part of the duck – the breast portion – toward the back of the oven. Roast,

(continued on next page)

uncovered, for 10 minutes. Turn the duck on the other side and roast for 10 minutes more. (If the duck releases quantities of fat, pour off and discard about two-thirds of the fat). Turn the duck on its back – breast side up – and roast for 10 minutes more. Remove from the oven and surround the duck with chopped trimmings: garlic, carrots, onion and thyme. Baste with the lime juice and spoon the cooking juices over the duck 3 or 4 times so that it will remain moist as it continues to roast. Remove the trussing string from the bird and season the legs with salt. (By this point, the bird will hold its shape on its own. By removing the string, the legs will cook more evenly.) Return to the oven to roast for a total of 13 to 15 minutes per 500 g (1 lb). (If there is not enough fat to keep the trimmings from browning too much, add a few tablespoons of cold water.) Roasting time will vary according to the size of the duck, and your flavour preference. Select the shorter roasting time per 500 g (1 lb) for a large duck, the longer time for a smaller duck. (Thus, total roasting time for a 1.25 kg/2½ lb duck would be about 38 minutes, a 2.5 kg/5 lb duck would be 1 hour and 5 minutes.)

4. Meanwhile, prepare the zest: Bring a medium-size saucepan of water to a boil. Place the zest in a fine-mesh sieve and submerge in the boiling water for 2 minutes to blanch. Rinse under cold running water. Drain. Set aside.

5. Remove the duck from the oven and, *once again, season generously.* Transfer to a platter and place at an angle against the edge of a baking dish, with its head down and tail in the air. This heightens the flavour by allowing the juices to flow down through to the breast meat. Cover loosely with foil. Turn off the oven and place the duck in the oven, with the door slightly ajar. Let rest a minimum of 20 minutes and up to 1 hour. The duck will continue to cook during the resting time.

6. Meanwhile, prepare the sauce: Place the roasting pan with the trimmings over high heat. Cook until the trimmings are nicely browned, 1 to 2 minutes. Drain and discard all the liquid in the pan, for it will be mostly fat. (Do not omit this step, or you will have a fat, greasy, inedible sauce.) Add the honey, stir, and cook 1 to 2 minutes more. Deglaze with several tablespoons of vinegar and cook for 1 minute. Add about 125 ml (4 fl oz) water (or enough to make a rich sauce) and simmer for 5 minutes more.

7. Strain the sauce through a fine-mesh sieve placed over a clean frying pan, pressing down on the trimmings to extract as much juice flavour as possible. To this, add any cooking juices that have drained from the duck as it rests. Bring the sauce to a boil over high heat. Taste and, if necessary, add another teaspoon or two of vinegar. Remove the pan from the heat and add the butter, a few pieces at a time, whisking constantly after each addition, until thoroughly incorporated. Stir in the reserved zest.

8. To serve: Carve the duck, discarding the whole limes, and arrange in the centre of the platter. Spoon about half the sauce over the duck. Pour the reserved sauce into a warmed sauce boat and serve immediately.

SERVES 4

WINE SUGGESTIONS: This duck is ideal with a robust wine of France's southwest. Try to lay your hands on a top-grade Madiran, such as Château Montus, from the duck-raising department of the Gers. It's a wine that will echo the density and richness of the duck, a wine and food marriage made in heaven. I have also loved this with a lemon-zesty Viognier, a grape that's newly fashionable to Provence and California.

⌣ TECHNIQUE FOR CARVING A DUCK ⌣   When the duck has had ample time 'to rest' after cooking and all of the juices have settled into place, it is ready to be carved for the table. Begin with the wing bone – locate the shoulder joint that holds the wing in place and pierce the skin with a sharp knife at this point. Press heavily on the knife, the pressure will be needed to cut through the joint and free the wing. This will make it easier to carve the leg, since there will be more free space for removal. Cut through the skin around the joint between the leg and the thigh in a semi-circular shape, beginning the semi-circle on the underside of the duck and finishing at the top outside. With a little pressure on the bone and a cut into the joint, the thigh is easily detached.

Now the breast is all that remains to be removed: Cut down the middle of the bird, being sure to keep each breast piece intact. Once this initial cut has been made, slice deeply along the breast bone in order to free each side of the breast meat. When both sides of the breast have been removed, place each on the cutting board and cut them at an angle into lengthways slices.

⌣ A TRUSSING TIP ⌣   A handy tip when trussing a duck or any other bird for roasting: When tying the knots to secure the different parts of the duck, tie a regular knot but loop the string an extra time through the knot before pulling it taut. This extra step will keep the knot tighter and the bird in better shape for even roasting.

A FLAVOUR BONUS: To extract the maximum flavour from all poultry trimmings – such as the neck, heart and wing tips – chop them with a cleaver, as finely as possible. For a quick and delicious sauce, sauté them quickly in fat, add aromatics such as carrots, onions, garlic and thyme, then deglaze with a bit of water or wine. Over low heat, reduce for 4 to 5 minutes, then strain.

Even were a cook to cook a fly, he would keep the breast for himself.
POLISH PROVERB

CUMIN-RUBBED GRILLED QUAIL

I love the fragrant, slightly exotic essence of freshly toasted cumin. Here, I use it to infuse quality meat, then enhance it with even more flavour, with a 'dipping' mix of coarse salt, lemon zest, fresh leaf coriander and more ground cumin. I serve both grilled quail and pigeon often, since they cook up quickly and make for elegant individual portions. This dish is equally good hot or at room temperature. I often prepare a huge batch of grilled quail as part of a large buffet. Note that although the bird is split down the back to flatten it for grilling, it remains whole in a single piece.

> 4 large fresh quail (each about 180 g/6 oz)
> 2 tablespoon cumin seeds, roasted and freshly ground (see Note)
> 3 tablespoons extra-virgin olive oil
> Sea salt to taste

GARNISH:
> About 4 tablespoons fresh coriander leaves, snipped with scissors
> Grated zest of 1 lemon, preferably organic
> Coarse sea salt

1. Place the quail breast side down on a flat surface. With a pair of poultry shears, split the bird lengthwise along the backbone. Open it flat, and press down with the heel of your hand to flatten completely. Turn quail skin side up, press down once more to flatten. With a sharp knife, make tiny slits in the skin near the tip of each drumstick. Tuck the opposite drumstick through the slit, to cross the bird's legs. The bird should be as flat as possible, to ensure even cooking. Set aside.

2. In a small bowl, combine 1 tablespoon of toasted ground cumin with the oil and stir to form a wet paste. With a pastry brush, brush the paste evenly over all sides of the quail. Cover loosely with film and set aside to marinate for about 30 minutes.

3. Preheat the grill or prepare a wood or charcoal barbecue. The barbecue is ready when the coals glow red and are covered with ash.

4. Season the quail generously with salt. With the skin side toward the heat, place beneath the grill or on the barbecue about 12.5 cm (5 in) from the heat so that the quail cooks evenly without burning. Cook until the skin is evenly browned, about 5 minutes.

Using tongs so you do not pierce the meat, turn and cook the other side, about 5 more minutes. Continue cooking and turning until the juices run clear when the thigh is pierced with a skewer, for about 15 minutes' total cooking.

5.   Remove the quail from the heat and season once more with salt. Cover loosely with foil and let rest – breast down and tail in the air – for at least 5 minutes.

6. To serve, arrange a whole quail on each of four warmed dinner plates. Arrange tiny mounds of coarse salt, the remaining ground cumin, finely chopped lemon zest and fresh coriander alongside. Invite guests to dip small pieces of the quail in one or more of the garnishes with each bite. Be sure to provide good steak knives. Offer finger bowls and a fresh napkin for each guest.

NOTE: TO ROAST CUMIN SEEDS: Heat a small heavy-duty frying pan over medium heat for 2 minutes. Add the cumin and roast over medium heat, stirring and shaking the pan constantly in order to prevent burning. For the first minute or two the cumin will give up its liquid and it will appear that nothing is happening. Watch carefully, for the cumin will brown quickly. (Reduce heat if the cumin appears to be browning too quickly.) Roast just until the cumin fills the kitchen with its fragrance and turns dark brown, about 4 minutes total time. Immediately transfer the cumin to a plate to cool.

To grind, place the cooled spice in a clean coffee grinder, spice mill, or electric blender and grind to a fine powder.

SERVES 4

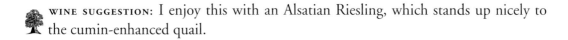 **WINE SUGGESTION:** I enjoy this with an Alsatian Riesling, which stands up nicely to the cumin-enhanced quail.

᙮ **DON'T FORGET THE FINGER BOWLS!** ᙮   I think that we all love permission to eat with our fingers, especially to savour every nugget of flavour of poultry and meats cooked on the bone. When serving foods that will be picked up and eaten with one's fingers, be sure to provide finger bowls, small vessels of tepid water to which you've added a slice of fresh lemon. Out of consideration, also provide a second fresh napkin for each diner.

*When I asked the charismatic chef Gigi what exactly it consisted of,
he replied, 'Don't worry, you going to "ave eet."' And 'ave eet,' indeed I did.*

GILLIAN BEAL

MONSIEUR HENNY'S RABBIT BOUILLABAISSE

One spring morning I was standing in line at my village butcher shop, and as soon as the owner – Monsieur Roland Henny – spied me, he ushered me upstairs to his kitchen. Monsieur Henny was so proud on his latest creation, he not only had me taste the rabbit bouillabaisse, but insisted I 'write it down'. He knew this was a dish after my own heart. Who could resist a combination of tender rabbit, colourful saffron, fragrant fennel, laced with a spicy garlic aïoli? 'Print it!' my editor husband said as he tasted the dish, and so we did. The dish could also be prepared just as successfully with chicken.

1 whole fresh rabbit (about 1.5 kg/3 lb), cut into serving pieces
Sea salt and freshly ground black pepper
3 tablespoons extra-virgin olive oil
1 head of plump fresh garlic, cloves separated and peeled
Pinch of saffron threads
1 teaspoon fennel seeds
Several sprigs of fresh thyme
4 fresh bay leaves
2 tablespoons tomato paste
2 tablespoons anise liqueur or Pastis
750 ml (27 fl oz) water
250 ml (8 fl oz) dry white wine (such as a Riesling, a white Burgundy, a not-too-oaky Californian Chardonnay or white Côtes-du-Rhône)
500 g (1 lb) small, yellow-fleshed potatoes, peeled and thinly sliced
1 recipe Rouille (page 315), prepared and set aside covered

1. Generously season the rabbit pieces with salt and pepper. In a large, deep-sided frying pan, heat 3 tablespoons of oil over moderately high heat. When hot but not smoking, add the rabbit pieces. Reduce the heat immediately to low (to keep the rabbit meat from drying out), cover, and cook lightly until the rabbit is tender but still moist, shaking the pan from time to time, about 5 minutes per side. (Cooking time will vary according to

(continued on next page)

FACING PHOTOGRAPH: *Roland Henny, the model village butcher.*

the size of the pieces.) With tongs, transfer the rabbit to a platter, cover with foil and set aside.

2. To the frying pan with the oil, add the garlic, saffron, fennel, thyme, bay leaves, tomato paste, Pastis, water and wine, scraping up any browned bits that cling to the bottom of the pan. Cover and simmer for 30 minutes. Remove and discard the bay leaves and thyme. Purée in batches in a blender or food processor.

3. Return the rabbit to the frying pan. Add the potatoes, cover and simmer very gently for 25 minutes. Taste for seasoning. The liquid should be soup-like and tinged with colours or saffron-orange.

4. To serve, transfer portions of the rabbit and potatoes into warmed shallow soup bowls. Spoon the sauce over the rabbit. Pass the spicy rouille, allowing guests to swirl in a few spoonfuls to thicken and season their soup. Serve with plenty of toasted homemade bread.

SERVES 4

 WINE SUGGESTION: Serve this with a chilled Bandol rosé, from Domaine Tempier.

∿ TIPS ON COOKING WITH RABBIT ∿ Although rabbit can successfully be replaced by chicken in most recipes, it should not be cooked in exactly the same manner. While chicken benefits from a good browning or searing before cooking, rabbit has no skin or covering of fat to protect its tender meat. Rather, begin cooking rabbit over low heat, then cover it, to assure moist, evenly cooked meat.

I hate people who are not serious about their meals.
OSCAR WILDE

PINA'S BRAISED RABBIT

Close your eyes and imagine yourself in a trattoria in the Piedmont: there's no sign, just a double wooden door covered with immaculate white curtains. There's no menu, just a series of staunchly traditional Piedmontese specialities, prepared with love. A single room, a menu that changes little from day to day, season to season. The food? Flavours at once rich and intense, all subtle, simple, dishes that come from the kitchen of a remarkable cook, Pina Bongiovanni, at the Osteria dell'Unione in Tresio, near Alba.

Pina's favourite dish is also her best, an exquisite platter of rabbit braised in Barolo with sweet red peppers spiked with cloves and cinnamon, a dish for cooks short on money, rich on time. The rabbit meat all but falls off the bone, the sauce nearly reduces to a thick syrup, the spice reminiscent of deep, dark game dishes of days long past. What's amazing here is the depth of flavour Pina achieves with so few ingredients.

For best results, be certain to use a wine that is rather high in alcohol, 13 or 14 per cent. The brief marinade tenderizes the meat without robbing the rabbit of its delicate flavours. The red wine also gives what no other liquid in the world could: flavour, acidity, colour and richness.

> 1 whole fresh rabbit (about 1.5 kg/3 lb), cut into serving pieces
> 500 ml (16 fl oz) tannic red wine, such as Barolo, Barbera or Côtes-du-Rhône
> 3 tablespoons extra-virgin olive oil
> Bouquet garni: 2 fresh bay leaves and a large bunch of thyme, fastened with
>   string
> 1 cinnamon stick, halved
> 2 whole cloves
> 1 onion, peeled and halved
> 2 large red sweet peppers
> Sea salt and freshly ground black pepper to taste

1. In a large shallow bowl, combine the rabbit, wine, 2 tablespoons of the olive oil, the bouquet garni and cinnamon stick. Stick a clove into each of the onion halves and add to the bowl. Cover and marinate at room temperature for 1 to 2 hours. Turn the rabbit from time to time, making sure the pieces evenly absorb the marinade.

(continued on next page)

2. Meanwhile, roast the peppers directly over a gas flame or under a grill, as close to the heat as possible, turning often, until charred all over. Transfer to a sealed plastic bag and let steam for 10 minutes. Scrape off and discard the blackened skins and remove and discard the stems, seeds and ribs. Cut the pepper flesh into thin strips. Set aside.

3. In a large covered casserole, heat the remaining olive oil over moderately high heat. Remove the individual rabbit pieces from the marinade and pat them dry. When the oil is hot but not smoking, add the rabbit. Reduce the heat immediately to low (to keep the rabbit meat from drying out), cover, and cook lightly until the rabbit is tender but still moist, shaking the casserole from time to time, about 5 minutes per side. Do not crowd the casserole; this may have to be done in batches. (Cooking time will vary according to the size of the pieces.) As each piece of rabbit is cooked, transfer to a platter and season lightly with salt and pepper.

4. Return all the cooked rabbit pieces to the casserole and add the marinade ingredients and red pepper strips to the casserole. Bring just to a simmer, then reduce heat to very low. Simmer gently, covered, turning the meat from time to time, cooking until the rabbit is fork-tender, about 1 hour.

5. With a slotted spoon, transfer the rabbit and the pepper strips to a platter and cover to keep warm. Strain the sauce (discarding the bouquet garni, cinnamon sticks and onions) and wipe out the casserole. Return the sauce to the casserole and boil over high heat until thick and glossy. Return the rabbit and peppers to the casserole, cover and cook over low heat, turning once or twice, until heated through, about 5 minutes. Taste for seasoning. Serve immediately, on warmed dinner plates, accompanied by Creamy Semolina with Bay Leaf & Parmesan (page 243).

SERVES 4-6

WINE SUGGESTION: We sampled this with a local Barbaresco, a wine with a perfect acid balance, custom-made for a region like the Piedmont in Italy, where food is earthy and plentiful.

CUTTING UP A RABBIT   To cut up a whole rabbit for cooking: Place the rabbit, belly-side-down on a clean work surface. Trim the flaps of skin, tops of the forelegs and any excess bone. Reserve. With a cleaver or a heavy-duty knife, divide the carcass across into three sections: hind legs, saddle, and forelegs, including the rib cage. Cut between the hind legs to separate them into two pieces. Split the front carcass into two pieces to separate the forelegs. Split the saddle across into three even pieces.

CREAMY SEMOLINA WITH BAY LEAF *&* PARMESAN

If you love polenta but don't love the labour-intensive, long stirring, then you'll love this creamy semolina, which cooks in less than 5 minutes. I cook it in whole milk scented with bay leaf, then flavour the delicate creamy grains with a touch of freshly grated nutmeg and Parmesan. I think of it as grown-up's nursery food. I love to serve this with both *La Broufade*, Beef & White Wine Daube from Arles (page 256), and Pina's Braised Rabbit (page 241). Any leftover semolina can be smoothed into a gratin dish, dotted with butter and additional cheese, then placed under a grill to brown. In this recipe, either fine semolina or semolina flour for preparing pasta can be used.

    1 litre (1¾ pints) whole milk
    2 fresh or dried bay leaves
    2 teaspoons fine sea salt
    170 g (5½ oz) fine semolina
    60 g (2 oz) freshly grated Parmigiano-Reggiano cheese
    Freshly grated nutmeg

1. In a large saucepan, combine the milk and bay leaves, and bring to the boil over moderate heat. Remove from the heat, cover and let steep for 1 hour.
2. Bring the milk back to simmer over moderate heat. Add the salt and very slowly add the semolina in a thin steady stream, stirring constantly with a wooden spoon to prevent lumping. (Should any lumps form, press them against the side of the pan and they will disappear.) Once all the semolina has been added, adjust the heat so that the mixture bubbles. Stir constantly, until the mixture forms a mass that cleanly pulls away from the sides of the pan, 3 to 5 minutes. (The mixture should resemble a very elegant potato purée).
3. Add the cheese and a sprinkling of nutmeg and stir to blend. Remove the bay leaves, taste for seasoning, and serve. (The mixture will harden up as it cools, but can be softened by reheating.)

SERVES 6-8

NOTE: If you can't spare the extra moments to infuse the milk with bay leaf, simply add the bay leaf to the milk as it is simmering, removing the bay leaf once the semolina is cooked.

*In my experience it is the countryman who is the real gourmet and
for good reason: It is he who has cultivated, raised, hunted, or fished
the raw materials and has made the wine himself.*

PENELOPE GRAY

CHANTEDUC RABBIT
WITH GARLIC & PRESERVED LEMONS

Rabbits have long been a part of the culture at Chanteduc. Through the years, successive generations of farmers who lived on the property raised rabbits, walking down the hill once a week to sell them at the Tuesday market. When we moved to the farm in 1984, the farmer's son, Yves Reynaud, regularly came around, hunting the rabbits and wild hare that raced through the vineyards, or the ducks, geese and wild boar found in the woodland. Yves always shared his bounty, and so Walter and I were well supplied with wild game for our table. One autumn he presented me with a rabbit the day before I was leaving to return to Paris. There wasn't going to be time to prepare or eat it, so I cut it up to freeze. I was alone in the house on that rainy evening, and just as I was preparing the rabbit a mouse appeared from behind a shelf. I nearly lost my cool that evening: This was a lot more of the rustic life than I had bargained for!

I created this recipe as a special springtime dish, designed for when the season's first heads of garlic show up in the market around the middle of April. The garlic is cooked whole – just the very top third of the head is trimmed off and discarded. As the garlic cooks cut side down in an aromatic blend of white wine, rabbit braising liquid, preserved lemons and the juice in which they are preserved, it takes on a biting, deep flavour. The rabbit itself stays decidedly tender, as the preserved lemons blend completely into the sauce. I prepare many variations of this dish, adding quartered new potatoes, or stoned black olives, or both. I like to accompany it with Couscous My Way (page 247 below) or Creamy Semolina with Bay Leaf & Parmesan (page 243).

6 plump fresh whole heads of garlic

3 tablespoons extra-virgin olive oil

1 whole fresh rabbit (about 1.5 kg/3 lb), cut into serving pieces (or substitute chicken)

Bouquet garni: 2 fresh bay leaves and a large bunch of thyme, fastened with string

12 slices of Preserved Lemons (page 319), plus 4 tablespoons liquid from the jar of
    preserved lemons

250 ml (8 fl oz) dry white wine (see Wine Suggestions)

Sea salt and freshly ground black pepper to taste

(continued on next page)

1. Trim and discard the top third of each head of garlic. Set aside.

2. In a large covered casserole, heat the olive oil over moderately high heat. When the oil is hot but not smoking, add the rabbit. Reduce the heat immediately to low (to keep the rabbit meat from drying out), cover and cook lightly until the rabbit is tender but still moist, shaking the pan from time to time, about 5 minutes per side. This may have to be done in batches. (Cooking time will vary according to the size of the pieces.) As each batch of rabbit pieces are cooked, transfer them to a platter and season lightly with salt and pepper.

3. In the fat that remains in the casserole, brown the trimmed heads of garlic, cut side down, until they are toasty brown, 2 to 3 minutes.

4. Return the rabbit to the casserole, along with the bouquet garni, preserved lemons and their liquid, and the wine. Cover and reduce heat to very low, allowing the liquid to simmer very gently. Stir from time to time. Braise until the rabbit is cooked through, but still soft and moist, about 1 hour. The sauce should be thick and glossy. Taste for seasoning.

5. To serve, arrange portions of rabbit and garlic on warmed, individual dinner plates, spooning the sauce over it all.

SERVES 4-6

WINE SUGGESTIONS: Serve this with a gentle white: I like it with a floral white from the Rhône, such as a Sablet blanc de blanc. Other worthy contenders include a young Italian white Pinot Bianco, with its flowery fragrance and crisp acidity, or a Californian Sauvignon Blanc, a wine grape that loves garlic.

COUSCOUS MY WAY

I prepare couscous almost as often as rice or pasta, since it's a quick ideal accompaniment to some of my favourite poultry and fish dishes. This is my favourite way to prepare couscous: It is all but foolproof, demands little time and results in a perfectly seasoned couscous that is ultimately fine, with no lumps. The secret is the microwave oven, which steams the grain to perfection. Serve this with Rabbit with Garlic & Preserved Lemons (page 245).

180 g (6 oz) quick-cooking couscous
¾ teaspoon fine sea salt
3 tablespoons extra-virgin olive oil
300 ml (½ pint) water or stock

1. In a large shallow bowl, combine the couscous and salt and toss with a large two-pronged carving fork to blend. Add the oil and fluff until the grains are evenly separated and coated with oil. Add the liquid and continue to fluff. Set aside for 15 minutes, continuing to fluff and toss the grains until all the liquid has been absorbed.
2. Cover with plastic film and place in the centre of a microwave oven. Cook for 2 minutes on high. Remove from the oven, fluff once more and serve immediately. (Leftover couscous can easily be reheated in the microwave. Just be sure to continue to fluff the grains to avoid lumps.)

SERVES 4-6

᷎ WHAT IS THIS THING CALLED COUSCOUS? ᷎ Couscous is often mistakenly called a pasta, but it is actually a refreshingly light and crunchy grain, made from coarsely ground hard durum wheat. It is packaged in both traditional and pre-cooked varieties. Couscous is the traditional dish of the North-African countries of Morocco, Algeria, and Tunisia, where it is eaten almost daily in some form. A nutritional powerhouse, couscous contains 13% vegetable protein, and is highly digestible.

The Chanteduc dining room, ready for a feast.

9

MEAT

EVER SINCE MY EARLIEST DAYS IN PROVENCE, my local butcher, Roland Henny, has played a major role in our lives. The freshest local lamb, pedigreed beef from award-winning cattle in the Auvergne, deliciously moist pork, and delicate veal grace our table, thanks to his attention to quality and extraordinary skills. Ask for a leg of lamb, and out of the cooler comes an entire baby lamb, to be butchered with the skill of a surgeon. The pork roast doesn't come ready cut, but will be fashioned from just the right portion of the pig, then tied with the virtuosity of a fine craftsman. And along with each cut will come a recipe filled with invaluable tips. He'll share the secrets of a perfect Provençal beef daube (use several cuts of meat and lace it with strips of pork rind, or *couenne*). He'll decorate the leg of lamb with artistry and flourish, and even run to his *atelier* upstairs, to share his special curry when he hears that Curry d'Agneau is on the menu tonight.

Cookery means … English thoroughness, French art, and Arabian hospitality;
it means the knowledge of all fruits and herbs and balms and spices;
it means carefulness, inventiveness, and watchfulness.

JOHN RUSKIN

DAUBE OF VEAL, WINE *&* GREEN OLIVES

In France, one of the most popular cuts of veal for long slow cooking is *tendron*, the portion of the breast that contains the cartilaginous rib-like portions that visually resemble pork spare ribs when cooked. *Tendrons* are delicious, full of body and flavour, slightly gelatinous and chewy. For this recipe, you can choose from any number of good cuts of stewing veal, including the breast, the short ribs, veal shoulder and shoulder chops, or the knuckle. This is the sort of dish that reminds you that it is always better to cook meat, fish or poultry on the bone, for it will always guarantee greater flavour. To avoid the dish from tasting fatty or greasy at the end, be sure to carefully trim as much fat as possible from the veal before cooking it.

> 4 tablespoons extra-virgin olive oil
> 1.5 kg (3 lb) breast of veal with the bone (ask your butcher to cut across the lower breast portion to make several strips of equal width)
> 3 medium onions, halved and thinly sliced
> Sea salt and freshly ground black pepper to taste
> 500 ml (16 fl oz) white wine, such as a Chardonnay
> Bouquet garni: large bunch of fresh thyme and several fresh bay leaves, tied in a bundle with string
> 1 small can (400 g/14½ oz) whole plum tomatoes in juice, drained
> 300 g (10 oz) stoned green olives

1. In a large covered casserole, heat 3 tablespoons of the oil over moderate heat. When the oil is hot, begin to brown the veal, carefully regulating the heat to avoid scorching the meat. Do not crowd the pan and be patient: Good browning is essential, so the veal retains all of its flavour. The meat should be browned on all sides in several batches, taking about 10 minutes to brown each batch thoroughly. As each batch is browned, use tongs – to avoid piercing the meat – to transfer the veal to a platter. Immediately season generously with salt and freshly ground black pepper.

2. In the same casserole with the remaining fat in the pan, use a spatula to scrape up any browned bits that stick to the bottom of the pan. (This will help enrich the final sauce.) Add the onions and a pinch of fine sea salt and cook over moderate heat until the onions

are soft and translucent, about 10 minutes. Add the wine, bouqet garni and tomatoes, and crush the tomatoes with a wooden spoon. Bring to the boil and cook for 2 to 3 minutes.

3. Return all the veal and any juices the meat has released to the casserole and bring just to a simmer over low heat. Cover and simmer gently – turning the veal to coat it evenly with the sauce – until the meat is very tender almost falling off the bone, about 2 hours.

4. Meanwhile, bring a large pan of water to the boil. Add the olives and blanch in the boiling water for 2 minutes. Drain well and add to the casserole. Taste the sauce for seasoning. Simmer over very low heat for 30 minutes more.

5. Transfer the pieces of veal to warmed shallow soup bowls. Reduce the sauce over high heat until lightly thickened. Pour the sauce over the meat. Serve with Creamy Semolina with Bay Leaf & Parmesan (page 243). (The daube can be prepared 1 to 2 days in advance. If so, allow the daube to cool thoroughly at room temperature, then cover and refrigerate until serving time. To serve, remove and discard any fat that has risen to the top of the daube. Gently reheat.)

SERVES 6-8

WINE SUGGESTION: This is a quiet, subtle dish, calling for a wine of like personality: I enjoy this with an older red that has toned down with age, or a young Burgundy, such as a Savigny-les-Beaune from the house of Tollot-Beaut.

ROASTING TIPS

• Place meat fat side up, so that as the fat melts, it bastes, seasons and tenderizes the meat.
• Always be sure to remove the meat from the refrigerator several hours before roasting. Even an entire day is not too much: The meat must be at room temperature when placed in the oven, otherwise it will steam and not roast evenly.
• Plan on 1 kg (2 lb) of beef rib for 4 people. For a crowd, roast several steaks.
• Do not season meat before roasting: Salt tends to draw juices, and flavour from the meat. Do season generously immediately after removing from the oven: This will give the steak a well-seasoned flavour.
• Let it rest: The meat continues to cook during the resting period. During this time, the juices retreat back into the meat, making for a juicy steak with richer flavour.

ON BLANCHING OLIVES It's a tiny step, but one that can make all the difference between a dish that's refined, elegant, finished, and one that is simply awkward. Green olives can impart a very strong, even sometimes bitter flavour when cooked. By blanching them for just 1 or 2 minutes in boiling water, you rid them of excess salt and potential bitterness.

MONSIEUR HENNY'S THREE-BEEF DAUBE

This is the richest, most sublime daube recipe I know. And one of the prettiest. During my earliest weeks of cooking school, our butcher, Roland Henny, put on a stunning show, demonstrating how to cut up rabbits, truss chickens, and select meat for a proper Provençal daube. He advises using at least three cuts of beef from different parts of the animal, thus some (such as short ribs or *plats de côtes*) enhance flavour with their cartilaginous bones, others (such as topside or *tende de tranche*) provide purer meat with little muscle separation, while still others (the chuck or *paleron*) add both meat and muscle for added texture. The addition of both cloves and nutmeg here is his small touch of genius: They serve to perfume the dish, but also bring out the sheer animal essence of the beef. Mr. Henny adds both marrow bones and thick strips of pork rind or *couenne de porc* to his daube, ingredients that provide additional fragrance, texture, and flavour. He enhances the Provençal accent of the dish by embellishing it with the sweet and bitter touch of orange zest and the salty pungency of black olives. Mr. Henny's daube glistens like a jewel and the sauce has a hauntingly rich texture, so smooth you want to coat everything in sight with it – the meat, a slice of bread, toss it with pasta, spoon it into your mouth all on its own. The ideal vessel for preparing the daube is a pot-bellied earthenware *daubière,* a well-designed piece of kitchen equipment that reduces the amount of surface exposed, minimizing the evaporation of precious juices. The shape also makes it easier to skim off any fat that rises to the surface.

6 medium onions, peeled

6 cloves

2.5 kg (5 lb) stewing beef, preferably two or three different cuts, choosing from topside, back and top rib, and chuck

2 bottles (75 cl each) sturdy red wine, such as a Côtes du Rhône

A handful of fresh thyme

5 bay leaves, preferably fresh

1½ teaspoons freshly grated nutmeg

3 tablespoons extra-virgin olive oil

Sea salt and freshly ground black pepper

3 tablespoons tomato paste

1 kg (2 lb) carrots, peeled and sliced into thin rounds

One 480-g (16-oz) can peeled Italian plum tomatoes in juice

4 beef marrow bones, cut into 5 cm (2 in) lengths

90 g (3 oz) pork rind, cut into thin strips

Grated zest of 1 orange, preferably organic, or a strip of dried orange peel

125 g (4 oz) black olives (such as French Nyons), drained and stoned

(continued on next page)

1. Slice an onion in half lengthwise. Place it cut side down on a cutting board, and slice crosswise into very thin slices. Slice four more onions in this manner. Halve the remaining onion and insert three cloves into each half.

2. In a large nonreactive vessel, combine the meat, onions, wine, thyme, bay leaves, and nutmeg. Cover and set aside to marinate at room temperature for 24 hours.

3. The next day, strain out and separate the onions and meat. Reserve the marinade liquid. In a large, covered casserole, heat the oil over moderate heat until hot but not smoking. Add the onions, reduce heat to low, and gently brown the onions, 4 to 5 minutes. With a slotted spoon, transfer the onions to a platter. In the remaining fat, begin to brown the beef, carefully regulating the heat to avoid scorching the meat. Do not crowd the pan, and be patient: Good browning is essential, so the beef retains all of its flavour. The meat should be browned on all sides in several batches, taking about 10 minutes to thoroughly brown each batch. As each batch is browned, use tongs – to avoid piercing the meat – to transfer the beef to a platter. Immediately season generously with salt and freshly ground black pepper.

4. Once all the meat is browned, return it to the casserole, along with the browned onions, tomato paste, and marinade liquid. Season with salt and pepper. Bring to a bare simmer and cook, covered, for 1 hour. Add the carrots, tomatoes, marrow bones, and pork rind and stir to evenly distribute the ingredients. Return to a bare simmer and cook, covered, for 2 hours more. Taste for seasoning. Test the meat for tenderness: If necessary, allow the daube to simmer for 1 hour more, or until the beef is fully tender. During the last 30 minutes of cooking, add the orange zest and black olives.

5. The daube will be more flavourful and less fatty if it is allowed to rest for 24 hours before serving. Allow the daube to cool thoroughly at room temperature, then cover and refrigerate until serving time. To serve, scrape off and discard all the fat that has solidified on the surface of the daube. Gently reheat and serve in warmed shallow soup bowls.

SERVES 8-10

WINE SUGGESTIONS: Any lusty, full-flavoured red would be at home with this daube: Try a young Côtes du Rhône, a Corbières from France's Midi, a California Zinfandel, or an Australian Shiraz.

18-MINUTE CITY STEAK

Côte de boeuf, or a thick single prime rib of beef, is one of France's favourite cuts of meat. Beautifully marbled, cooked to a rare tenderness, it is the quickest way I know to satisfy a craving for a pure and simple roast.

Since I cook in the city as well as the country, I devised this 'city steak' for those who don't have access to a real grill. The method is classically French: the beef rib is set atop a bed of salt (which serves as a flavourful cushion as well a delicate seasoning) and roasted in a very hot oven for about 18 minutes for a 2-lb (1-kg) steak. The resulting flavour is a cross between a roasted prime rib roast and a perfectly grilled steak.

As a sauce, I simply serve the juices that drip from the beef as it rests, accompanied by Fake *Frites* (page 137) and Cheesemaker's Salad (page 75).

> 375 g (12 oz) coarse sea salt
> 1 prime rib of beef (about 1 kg/2 lb), at room temperature, trimmed of excess fat
> 1 teaspoon extra-virgin olive oil
> Sea salt to taste
> Coarsely ground black pepper to taste

1. Preheat the oven to 250°C/475°F/gas mark 9.
2. Place the salt in a thin even layer on a baking sheet. Lightly brush the beef on both sides with oil. Place the beef, fattest side up, on the bed of salt. Place in the lower portion of the oven and roast until the skin is crackling and brown, and the meat begins to exude fat and juices, about 18 minutes. To test for doneness, insert an instant meat thermometer into the thickest part of the steak for at least 15 seconds. At 50°C (120°F) the steak is rare; at 55°C (130°F) it is medium rare.
3. Remove from the oven. Remove the beef from the bed of salt. Season generously with salt and coarsely ground pepper on both sides. Place the beef on a rack set over a pan or a platter to catch the drippings. Loosely tent with foil and set aside to rest at least 15 minutes in a warm place to allow the meat to absorb the juices uniformly.
4. To serve: With a large carving knife and fork, cut the meat away from the bone, following the contours of the bone. Slice the beef into thick diagonal slices. Transfer to a warmed platter. Place the juices collected during the resting period in a sauce boat. Serve.

SERVES 4

WINE SUGGESTION: The simplicity of this roast allows you to pull out a great bottle of red: I look for one of my oldest vintage Châteauneuf-du-Pape, preferably from Château du Beaucastel.

LA BROUFADE: BEEF *&* WHITE WINE DAUBE FROM ARLES

One cool, but sunny, afternoon in Arles, I sat on the narrow first-floor terrace of Les Vaccarès, overlooking the plane trees and an oversized statue of the Provençal poet, Fréderic Mistral. It was the first time I had sampled this wonderfully fragrant and tender Provençal daube, thin slices of beef cooked with some of my favourite ingredients: white wine, capers, anchovies, garlic, onions and tomatoes. The daube, also known as *broufaddo,* is an ancient one. It was a favourite with boatmen who worked on barges on the Rhône River, men who would be away from home for days at a time. It is a satisfying dish that takes well to reheating, and tastes even better the second or third day.

2 whole anchovies in salt or 4 anchovy fillets in salt
4 tablespoons whole milk
2 tablespoon capers
2 medium onions
10 plump fresh garlic cloves, peeled and halved
One 765-g (28-oz) can of peeled plum tomatoes in juice, drained (juice can be
    reserved for sauces, soups or stocks)
6 small French gherkins or cornichons, thinly sliced
Sea salt to taste
1 bottle (75 cl) white wine, preferably from the Rhône Valley
1 fresh bay leaf
Several sprigs of fresh thyme, wrapped and tied in a cheesecloth bundle
1 kg (2 lb) boneless braising beef in a single piece (such as beef shoulder, chuck,
    blade, neck, rump or brisket), cut against the grain into six 3-cm (1½-in) thick
    slices and trimmed of most of its fat
Freshly ground black pepper to taste

1. Rinse the anchovies and fillet them if necessary. Soak the anchovies in the milk and set aside for 10 minutes to soften and remove any excess salt.

2. Drain the capers, rinse well and soak in cold water for 10 minutes to remove any excess salt.

3. Slice an onion in half lengthwise. Place the flat cut side on a cutting board cut across into very thin slices. Slice the second onion in this manner. Place in a large bowl. Add to the bowl the garlic, drained tomatoes and cornichons. Rinse the anchovies (discarding the milk) and the capers and add to the bowl. Add 1 teaspoon fine sea salt and toss to blend, slightly breaking the tomatoes up with the back of a spoon.

4. Cook the alcohol off the wine: Place the wine in a large saucepan, bring to a simmer, and simmer gently until no alcohol aroma wafts from the pan, about 10 minutes. Set aside.

5. In a large heavy-bottomed casserole, place about one-third of the tomato/onion mixture on the bottom of the casserole. Add the bay leaf and thyme bundle. Top with a layer

of beef, lightly seasoning each slice of beef with salt and pepper. Continue with two additional alternating layers of the tomato/onion mixture and the beef. Add enough wine just barely to cover the mixture. Cover and bring just to a simmer over moderately low heat. Simmer gently until the meat is very tender, about 4 hours. There should be plenty of rosy, thick sauce. Check the daube from time to time, stirring up ingredients and making sure they are well distributed and the meat is largely submerged. Do not let the mixture boil. Taste for seasoning. Remove and discard the bay leaf and thyme.

6. The daube can be served immediately, or may be prepared 1 to 2 days in advance. If so, allow the daube to cool thoroughly at room temperature, then cover and refrigerate until serving time. To serve, scrape off and discard all the fat that has solidified on the surface of the daube. Gently reheat and serve in warmed shallow soup bowls. Serve with Brown Rice from the Camargue (page 272) or Creamy Semolina with Bay Leaf & Parmesan (page 243).

SERVES 4-6

WINE SUGGESTIONS: Although one always thinks of red wine with beef, the white wine used to prepare this daube would be an ideal accompaniment. For whites, choose a white Rhône, or even a white Hermitage. Otherwise, serve a young red, such as a Côtes-du-Rhône.

Clos Chanteduc, the wine from the Wells property.

⌣: WHAT'S IN A DAUBE? :⌣ You could call it a stew, but that would only be half the story. The daube is one of many French dishes that fall into the category of *la cuisine mijotée*, earthy, soul-satisfying preparations that simmer slowly in a tightly enclosed vessel. Unlike other stews or one-dish meals that are bound with thickening agents – such as *boeuf bourguigon*, thickened with flour and butter, or a *blanquette*, thickened with egg yolks – a proper daube focuses not on the accompanying sauce or vegetables but the meat, fish or poultry that is slowly simmered to created a potful of complex concentrated flavours. The most traditional daubes come from Provence, historically a region where meat, usually came in a dish prepared with the most inexpensive cuts, generally lamb, mutton, or beef. Cooked in a well-seasoned *daubière* – a large rotund earthenware casserole, with a long narrow neck designed to minimize evaporation – the daube might be coaxed along over an open fire, in a brick oven or on top of a stove

BEEF DAUBE WITH MUSTARD, HERBS & WHITE WINE

I can guess why a daube might have earned a reputation as hearty, sometimes heavy, fare. The wrong mix of hefty ingredients and you've got a dish that makes your cheeks bulge and your digestive system demand a rebate. Over years of preparing these long-simmering favourites, I've developed a way to make a light, very digestible daube, essentially a dish that comes to equal more than the sum of its parts.

The key is a careful balance of flavours, of acids, of herbs. This recipe, to my mind, has it all. A rather tough cut of beef is teamed up with light, acerbic ingredients such as white wine, mustard and a tangy dose of herbs, all of which serve to tame, tenderize and perfume the pieces of meat that are ready to absorb such pungent flavours.

I think of this as a springtime daube, for days when the heartiness of beef and a warm bowl of stew is what you want, yet nothing too overwhelming. Be sure to give the bouquet garni an extra little potion of tarragon – its flavour marries beautifully with the mustard and white wine. Incredibly simple, incredibly delicious, the daube is a perfect match for the gentle sweetness of the Onion-Parmesan Gratin (page 128). Note that the chunks of meat here may seem large at first, but the meat shrinks in size at it cooks.

3 medium onions, peeled
3 tablespoons extra-virgin olive oil
1 kg (2 lb) boneless braising beef (such as beef shoulder, chuck, blade, neck, rump or
   brisket), cut into 7.5-cm (3-in) cubes
Sea salt and freshly ground black pepper to taste
1 bottle (75 cl) dry white wine, such a Chardonnay
2 tablespoons Dijon mustard
One 480-g (16-oz) can of whole plum tomatoes in juice
3 garlic cloves, peeled and halved
Bouquet garni: Several sprigs of flat-leaf parsley, thyme, tarragon and fresh bay leaves
   tied in a bundle with string

1. Slice an onion in half lengthwise. Place cut side down on a cutting board and slice across into very thin slices. Slice the remaining onions in this manner. Set aside.

2. In a large covered casserole, heat the 3 tablespoons of oil over moderate heat. When the oil is hot, begin to brown the beef, carefully regulating the heat to avoid scorching the meat. Do not crowd the pan, and be patient: Good browning is essential, so the beef retains all of its flavour. The meat should be browned on all sides in several batches, taking about 10 minutes to brown each batch thoroughly. As each batch is browned, use tongs – to avoid piercing the meat – to transfer the beef to a platter. Immediately season generously with salt and freshly ground black pepper.

3. Only a thin film of fat should remain in the bottom of the casserole. (Should there be an excess of fat, pour off and discard it.) Add the wine, pouring it all over the surface of

the pan and scraping up any browned bits from the bottom of the casserole. Adjust heat to bring the liquid to a gentle simmer and cook, uncovered, until most of the wine – and alcohol – have cooked off, about 7 minutes from the time the liquid comes to a simmer. Add the mustard and whisk to blend.

4. Return the beef, and any juices it has released, to the casserole. Add the tomatoes and their liquid, the onions, garlic and bouquet garni. Cover and simmer over low heat until the beef is fork-tender, 2 to 3 hours.

5. Remove and discard the bouquet garni. With a slotted spoon, transfer the beef, onions and tomatoes to a platter. Boil the sauce over high heat until reduced by about one-third, about 10 minutes. Return the solids to the sauce, reheat gently, and serve in warmed shallow soup bowls. (The daube can be prepared 1 to 2 days in advance. If so, allow the daube to cool thoroughly at room temperature, then cover and refrigerate until serving time. To serve, scrape off and discard all the fat that has solidified on the surface of the daube. Gently reheat and serve in warmed shallow soup bowls.)

SERVES 4-6

WINE SUGGESTIONS: The last time I prepared this daube, I rummaged around in my wine cellar and came up with a 1982 white Hermitage for Gérard Chave. I was certain the wine would be past its prime, but it wasn't at all. Other favourite wines for this dish include a white Savennières from the Loire valley, or a Mâcon-Villages from Burgundy.

A WORD ON BRAISING What's the difference between a stew and a braise? When dealing with mental images, one imagines a stew as a hearty and substantial one-dish meal. Braising has a sexy quality to it, as if the meat is obliged to go through many rites of passage before it can be officially dubbed 'braised'. In reality, stewing usually means that the meat is cut into pieces and is completely submerged in liquid as it cooks. Braising usually calls for a whole piece of meat and the quantity of cooking liquid is diminished considerably in relation to the meat.

I love braising, for it coaxes the optimum flavour from the meat in two phases. Initially, the meat is coloured on all sides, giving it a wonderful brown 'crust' without allowing the flavour of the meat to escape. This step also creates pan juices that enrich the sauce. Before the meat can become any tougher, it is bathed in cooking liquid and cooked, with a cover. This second phase steams the meat and gradually tenderizes it, breaking down the tough and fibrous qualities characteristic of tastier but tough cuts.

EAT YOUR CURRY, AND BE BRILLIANT!
Why should I make the effort to try something new when I already like the food I eat?
Part of the answer lies in the Indian belief that eating more complex and subtly flavored foods
exercises the brain, making it better at understanding and appreciating
and surviving the subtle complexities of life.

THE SPICE HOUSE CATALOG, ON CURRY POWDERS

SPICY LAMB CURRY WITH YOGURT & APPLES

Lamb curry – or *curry d'agneau* – is one of France's classic bistro dishes. I've always loved the idea of this spicy warming dish, but in many bistros the curry is prepared with strong-flavoured mutton rather than lamb, and the seasoning tends to be bland. So, I make it at home, with fresh spices from my own pantry.

While a classical curry needs an acid base – such as tomatoes – to balance the dish, this version uses a touch of yogurt and grated apple, refreshing additions. Be certain to remove as much fat as possible from the lamb, to make for a lighter, more flavourful dish. And don't rummage around your spice cabinet for old bottles of stale spices. Invest in a few new bottles – for I'm sure you'll make this often. The spice level suggested here makes for a fairly hot curry. If a more subtle flavour is desired, reduce or eliminate the cayenne pepper.

6 tablespoons extra-virgin olive oil
1 lamb shoulder, about 1.5 kg (3 lb), bone reserved and meat cut into 5-cm (2-in)
    cubes, excess fat removed
Sea salt and freshly ground black pepper to taste
4 medium onions, halved lengthwise and thinly sliced
One 60-g (2-oz) piece of fresh ginger, finely chopped
4 plump fresh garlic cloves, finely chopped
1 tablespoon cumin seeds, freshly ground
2 tablespoons coriander seeds, freshly ground
1 tablespoon ground turmeric
1 teaspoon ground cayenne pepper
250 ml (8 fl oz) whole-milk yogurt
1 firm acidic apple, such as a Granny Smith, grated

1. In a large covered casserole, heat 3 tablespoons of the oil over moderate heat. When the oil is hot, begin to brown the lamb, carefully regulating the heat to avoid scorching

the meat. Do not crowd the pan, and be patient: Good browning is essential, so the lamb retains all of its flavour. The meat should be browned on all sides in several batches, taking about 10 minutes to brown each batch thoroughly. As each batch is browned, use tongs – to avoid piercing the meat – to transfer the lamb to a platter. Immediately season generously with salt and freshly ground black pepper.

2. In the same casserole with the remaining fat in the pan, use a spatula to scrape up any browned bits that stick to the bottom of the pan. (This will help enrich the final sauce.) Add the onions and a pinch of fine sea salt and cook over moderate heat until the onions are soft and golden brown, about 15 minutes. Add the ginger and garlic and cook 1 minute more. Add the ground cumin, coriander, turmeric and cayenne and cook until the spices are fragrant, about 15 seconds more.

3. Add the lamb, and any juices the meat has released, to the casserole, along with the yogurt, grated apple and 250 ml (8 fl oz) hot water. Stir to blend. The liquid should just barely cover the meat. Cover and simmer gently – turning the lamb regularly to evenly coat it with the sauce – until the meat is very tender, about 1½ hours. The sauce should be fragrant and fairly thick. Taste for seasoning. Remove and discard the bone. (The lamb can be prepared in advance. If so, cool in the casserole and refrigerate up to 1 day. If desired, scrape off any fat that has risen to the surface. At serving time, return to a simmer over low heat. Taste for seasoning.)

4. To serve, transfer the curry to warmed dinner plates. Serve boiled basmati rice alongside.

SERVES 4-6

WINE SUGGESTIONS: One could choose wines of two different kinds here: A rich round tannic red wine, such as a well-aged Gigondas from the Côtes-du-Rhône region would stand up well to the spice. Equally interesting and compatible would be a choice of a spicy white wine, such as a Güwîrztraminer, a floral white such as a Viognier, or a Bandol rosé, filled with floral spicy flavours.

There is no sight on Earth more appealing than
the sight of a woman making dinner for someone she loves.
THOMAS WOLFE

LEMON-THYME LAMB CHOPS

Dry cooking over high heat produces meat with a crisply golden and crusty exterior, and a tender melting interior. For this style of dry cooking, you need tender meat, such as top-quality lamb chops or slices of leg of lamb. To keep the interior of the meat moist while cooking (and to keep if from sticking to the unoiled pan or grill) the meat is first marinated in a classic mixture of the very best olive oil and freshly squeezed lemon juice. Do not salt the meat, or it will draw out the flavourful juices. These thin and dainty lamb chops are meant to be eaten with the fingers or, if you can find them, special silver lamb-chop holders sold in some antique shops in France.

> 8 single-rib lamb chops, partially boned (about 1 cm/½ in thick; 180-270 g/6-9 oz per chop)
> 3 tablespoons freshly squeezed lemon juice
> 3 tablespoons extra-virgin olive oil
> 1 teaspoon fresh lemon-thyme leaves or thyme leaves
> Fine sea salt and freshly ground black pepper to taste

1. Place the lamb chops, lemon juice, oil and thyme in a large, shallow dish. Cover with plastic wrap and marinate at room temperature for 20 minutes, turning the chops over once or twice.

2. Preheat a heavy-duty cast iron frying pan or ridged pan over high heat for 5 minutes. Or prepare a wood or charcoal fire. The fire is ready when the coals glow red and are covered with ash.

3. If cooking in a frying pan, reduce the heat to moderate, add the lamb chops and cook until nicely browned, about 2 minutes per side for rare, seasoning each side with salt and pepper after cooking.If cooking over a wood or charcoal fire, cook about 2 minutes per side for rare, seasoning each side with salt and pepper after cooking. (To test for doneness, press the meat with the tip of your finger. If the meat is very soft, the lamb chops are rare. If the meat is medium-soft, the lamb chops are medium-rare. If the meat is very firm, the lamb chops are well-done.)

4. To serve, pour any liquid remaining from the marinade over the lamb chops, or use the liquid as a vinaigrette for an accompanying salad. Serve immediately.

SERVES 4

🌳 **WINE SUGGESTION:** Certainly the most traditional combination is lamb and a lovely red Bordeaux. Other choices are Cabernet equivalents from Australia, New Zealand or California, or a fine Rioja Reserva.

~ **SALT OF THE EARTH** ~ My favourite salt, the *sel gris de Guérande* is a totally unrefined salt gathered along the Guérande peninsula of Brittany, near the villages of Batz-sur-Mer, Kervalet, Saillé and Guérande. Working by hand, from May to September, the salt workers, or *paludiers* trap the sea water in shallow beds, allow it to evaporate in the sun and the wind and then rake the salt into gigantic mounds. This is why they like to call it 'the fruit of the ocean, the sun and the wind'.

The colour is naturally just a slightly pale grey, thus the name *sel gris*. Most of the salt is sold in this state, with a bit a moisture still clinging to the grains of salt. Other varieties are simply dried slightly with very faint electrical power, reducing the water content by about 8 per cent. The salt is then ground with a stone mill for a finer grain.

On the very top surface of the evaporating beds, a very thin layer of even finer salt casts a veil, and this – called the *fleur de sel*, literally the 'flower of the salt' – is the caviar of the sea salt world. With a very faint perfume of violets, this very fine-grained salt is favoured by bakers and chefs, used sparingly as a table salt and a special final seasoning.

~ **THOUGHTS ON LAMB** ~ The term 'spring lamb' is often bandied about without much thought to its meaning. Originally, spring lamb described a young lamb, born in the early months of the year and slaughtered in the spring months. Since cross-breeding of different species enables the ewe to give birth all year round, the term has come to describe any tender lamb that is less than a year old and slaughtered in the spring or summer months.

Other descriptive terms, such as milk-fed lamb, generally mean the lamb has been fed on nothing but mother's milk and is sold under the age of ten weeks. Since these lamb are so young, they are smaller in size, weighing anywhere from 9-13.5 kg (20-30 lb). Even as the lamb grows older, to approximately 6 months, and is 22.5-27 kg (50-60 lb) in weight, it can still be considered young lamb.

LEG OF LAMB ON A BED OF ARTICHOKES, POTATOES & HERBS

This recipe originated one Christmas week when we had a houseful of guests begging for lamb. Potatoes and artichokes are a brilliant combination, especially when enhanced by the drippings from roasting lamb. The final touch of fresh herbs from a bouquet garni perfume both your kitchen and the dish as the lamb roasts.

EQUIPMENT: One oval baking dish just slightly larger than the lamb (about 23x33 cm/ 9x13 in)

4 globe artichokes (see Note, page 95) or two 250-g (9-oz) packets of frozen artichoke hearts, defrosted
1 kg (2 lb) medium-sized yellow-fleshed potatoes (such as Estima), peeled and quartered
1 tablespoon fresh thyme leaves, carefully destemmed
2 plump fresh heads of garlic, cloves peeled but left whole
3 tablespoons extra-virgin olive oil
2 tablespoons freshly squeezed lemon juice
4 large bouquets garnis: each made up of several sprigs of parsley, several sprigs of thyme, summer savory, rosemary and several fresh bay leaves, securely fastened with string
Sea salt and freshly ground black pepper to taste
1 leg of lamb, with bone (about 2.5 kg/5 lb), carefully trimmed of fat and tied (ask your butcher to do this for you)

1. Preheat the oven to 220°C/425°F/gas mark 7.
2. In a large bowl, combine the artichokes, potatoes, thyme leaves, garlic, 2 tablespoons of oil and the lemon juice. Toss to coat evenly with the oil. Arrange two bouquets garnis on the bottom of the baking dish. Add the artichoke-potato mixture and season generously with salt and pepper. Top with the remaining bouquets garnis.
3. Place a small metal roasting rack on top of the baking dish. Rub the lamb all over with the remaining tablespoon of oil. Season generously all over with salt and pepper. Place the lamb on top of the rack, so it will roast evenly and not steam. Place the baking dish in the oven and roast, allowing 10 to 12 minutes per 500 g (1 lb) for medium rare, 15 minutes for medium. Turn the lamb several times during cooking and baste occasionally.
4. Remove the lamb from the oven and once again season generously on all sides with salt and pepper. On a large carving board, place a salad plate upside down on a dinner plate. Transfer the lamb, exposed bone in the air, at an angle on the upside-down plate. Cover loosely with foil. Let rest for at least 25 minutes and up to 1 hour.

5. Meanwhile, test the vegetables in the roasting pan for doneness. Continue roasting if necessary. Once completely roasted, taste for seasoning. Discard the bouquets garnis. Transfer the vegetables to a large platter, leaving the juices in the pan. Cover and keep warm in a low oven until the lamb is ready.

6. Place the roasting pan with cooking juices over moderate heat, cook to caramelize the juices, 2 to 3 minutes. Be careful not to burn them. Spoon off any excess fat, and add several tablespoons of cold water to deglaze the pan, scraping up any bits that cling to the bottom. Reduce the heat to low and simmer until reduced by half, 5 to 7 minutes. Strain through a fine-mesh sieve. Taste for seasoning and pour into a warmed sauce boat. Set aside and keep warm.

7. To serve, carve the lamb into very thin slices. Add any juices the meat releases to the sauce boat. Arrange the lamb alongside the vegetables on the platter. Serve, passing the sauce.

SERVES 10-12

WINE SUGGESTIONS: While a Cabernet is traditional with lamb, the acidity of the potato-artichoke mixture calls for a more acidic, floral white: I enjoy a white Côtes-du-Rhône, or if I'm feeling in a festive mood, a white Châteauneuf-du-Pape or Hermitage. For a red, I would pick a young Côtes-du-Rhône.

It is not really an exaggeration to say that peace and happiness begin,
geographically, where garlic is used in cooking.
MARCEL BOULESTIN

GIGOT PROVENÇAL: OVEN-ROASTED LEG OF LAMB

Our Provençal butcher, Monsieur Roland Henny, sells the finest local lamb; tender meat that has a mild delicate flavour, just faintly perfumed with the wild thyme and rosemary of the land on which the animals graze. I roast it ever so simply, adding a healthy touch of garlic, roasted whole in its skin, making for a meltingly tender dish.

> 6 plump fresh whole heads of garlic
> 2 large bouquets garnis: Each made up of several sprigs of parsley, several sprigs of thyme, summer savory, rosemary and several fresh bay leaves, securely fastened with string
> About 2 tablespoons extra-virgin olive oil
> 1 leg of lamb, with bone (about 2.5 kg/5 lb), carefully trimmed of fat and tied (ask your butcher to do this for you)
> Sea salt and freshly ground black pepper to taste

1. Preheat the oven to 220°C/425°F/gas mark 7.
2. Trim and discard the top third of each head of garlic. Place cut side up on the baking dish and drizzle with oil. Arrange the bouquets garni around the garlic. Place a small metal roasting rack on top of the baking dish. Rub the lamb all with olive oil. Season the lamb generously with salt and pepper. Place the lamb on top of the rack. (This will allow the lamb to roast evenly, and not steam.) Place the baking dish in the oven and roast, allowing 10 to 12 minutes per 500 g (1 lb) for medium rare, 15 minutes for medium. Turn the lamb several times during cooking.
3. Remove the lamb from the oven and once again season generously. On a large carving board, place a salad plate upside down on a dinner plate. Transfer the lamb, exposed bone in the air, at an angle on the upside-down plate. Tent with foil and let rest for at least 25 minutes and up to 1 hour. Discard the bouquets garnis. Cover and keep warm in a low oven until the lamb is ready.
4. Meanwhile, prepare the sauce: Place the roasting pan dish over moderate heat, scraping up any bits that cling to the bottom. Cook for 2 to 3 minutes, scraping and stirring

(continued on next page)

LEFT: *Patricia removes the lamb from the bread oven before letting it rest.*
RIGHT: *Walter, the family meat carver, at work on a freshly roasted leg of lamb.*

until the liquid is almost caramelized. Do not let it burn. Spoon off and discard any excess fat. Add several tablespoons of cold water to deglaze (hot water would cloud the sauce). Bring to the boil. Reduce the heat to low and simmer until thickened, about 5 minutes.

5. Strain the sauce through a fine-mesh sieve and pour into a sauce boat. Carve the lamb into very thin slices. Arrange on a large warm serving platter, surrounded by the garlic.

SERVES 10-12

🌳 **WINE SUGGESTION:** A good Bordeaux, preferably from the Paulliac region, is the classic French choice. In our region, we are more likely to drink a peppery full-bodied red, such as one from the village of Gigondas.

I pray that death may strike me in the middle of a large meal.
I wish to be buried under the tablecloth between four large dishes.

MARC DESUAGIERS

SPIT-ROASTED BRINE-CURED PORK

George Germon and Johanne Killeen are neighbours of ours in Provence, and besides sharing a passion for cooking and hearty eating, we also share a love for cooking with a live fire. George is particularly adept at fire-building and rôtisserie cooking, and when a roast such as this spit-roasted, brine-cured pork is on the menu, I let him take charge, firing up the waist-high fireplace we installed as a centrepiece of our kitchen. George's special cure uses many of the herbs and spices found on our property, including the juniper berries that grow wild in the oak and pine woods, and the fennel grains we gather from plants once they have gone to seed.

Be sure to choose a pork roast that is not completely devoid of fat: The fat will melt and circle the pork as it roasts, keeping the pork moist and delicious. Excess fat will fall into the drip pan to season vegetables resting below. For those who do not have access to a rotisserie, oven directions are included.

> 90 g (3 oz) sugar
> 150 g (5 oz) coarse sea salt
> 15 peppercorns
> 8 juniper berries
> 2 tablespoons fennel seeds
> 10 sprigs of fresh rosemary
> 10 sprigs of fresh thyme
> 6 fresh bay leaves
> 1.5-2 kg (3-4 lb) boneless pork loin, rolled and tied with string at 3-cm (1½-in)
>   intervals

GARNISH:

> 8 carrots, trimmed and peeled
> 4 plump fresh heads garlic, top third trimmed and discarded

1. In a large non-metallic container, combine the sugar, salt, peppercorns, juniper berries, fennel seeds, 5 sprigs of rosemary and 5 sprigs of thyme, and the bay leaves. Add 1 litre (1¾ pints) of boiling water, stirring to dissolve the sugar and salt completely. Add 3 litres (5 pints) of cold water to cool the brine.
2. Place the pork in the brine, making sure it is completely submerged. If the meat floats

(continued on next page)

to the surface, weight it down with a plate. Cover and refrigerate. Allow the pork to cure for at least 24 hours and up to 48 hours, depending upon how much of a cured flavour you want the meat to acquire. The brine will draw out moisture from the meat and accentuate its natural sweet flavour. A longer curing process will produce a saltier and more pronounced taste from the brine.

3. Several hours before roasting, remove the pork from the brine and place it on a rack to drain. Allow the meat to come to room temperature. Remember to reserve some of the brine for basting the meat.

4. With paper towels, completely dry the pork. Lace the remaining sprigs of rosemary and thyme under the string.

FOR OPEN FIRE ROASTING: Build a hot fire with aromatic woods. Place a rôtisserie in front of the fire with a drip pan underneath. Make certain your spit is either chrome-plated or made of stainless steel. Other metals could taint the flavour of the meat. Spit the roast through the centre of the meat so it will be properly balanced as it turns. Take your time at this point: If the spit does not turn smoothly, excess strain will be put on the rôtisserie and the meat may cook unevenly. The distance between the fire and the rôtisserie will determine the intensity of the heat.

Place the spit on its rack, with the meat about 15 cm (6 in) in front of the fire. Arrange the vegetables in the drip pan. After about 20 minutes the fat on the outside of the pork should melt and begin to self-baste the meat. If this has not happened after 30 minutes, move the spit closer to the fire. (On the other hand, should the roast begin to brown too quickly, move the spit further from the heat.) Keep in mind that although you are cooking with a live fire, the heat should not be extreme. It is the residual heat of the flame that will slow-roast the pork, and it should take about the same time as conventional oven roasting. Do not worry if the herbs singe and smoke a bit: This is how they impart their heady fragrance to the meat. Maintain the heat of the fire by adding logs as necessary.

Cook the pork until it reaches an internal temperature of 65°C (150°F). (Pork is safe to eat at 60°C/140°F.) Total roasting time should be 1 to 2 hours, depending upon the intensity of the fire. Remove the spit from its rack, remove the spit from the roast, and place the roast on a cooling rack over a pan or a plate to catch the drippings.

FOR OVEN ROASTING:
Preheat the oven to 220°C/425°F/gas mark 7.

Place the pork on a roasting rack in a roasting pan. (The rack will prevent the pork from sticking to the pan and will allow it to roast more evenly.) Place in the centre of the oven and roast until the skin is crackling and brown, and the meat begins to exude fat and juices, 20 to 30 minutes.

Reduce heat to 180°C/350°F/gas mark 4 and baste with the juices from the pan, adding brine liquid if necessary – about 125 ml (4 fl oz) at a time – to maintain a thin layer of liquid in the pan at all times. Arrange the vegetables around the pork.

Roast for about 25 minutes per 500 g (1 lb), or until the pork reaches an internal temperature of 65°C (150°F). Baste at 20-minute intervals. Remove from the oven. Place the roast on a cooling rack over a pan or a plate to catch the drippings.

5. Loosely tent with foil and set aside to rest about 20 minutes in a warm place. To serve, remove and discard the string and the herbs. Cut the pork into thick slices and place on a warmed platter, along with the carrots and garlic. Drizzle with drippings collected during the resting period and serve.

SERVES 12

WINE SUGGESTIONS: A light red, a rich white or even beer are good choices here: try a nicely chilled Alsatian Riesling, a Californian Zinfandel or an Italian Dolcetto d'Alba.

BROWN RICE FROM THE CAMARGUE

The Camargue is France's marshy rice-growing region just south of Arles, the city made most famous by Van Gogh. Here farmers produce a uniquely nutty, fragrant brown rice known as *ris de camargue*. The grains – so the growers claim – take on a special richness, for they're air-dried by the mighty Provençal wind, the Mistral. But there's more than folklore to the flavour! Any excellent brown rice can be used here. In this recipe, the rice is 'toasted' in the oil before the liquid is added, to intensify the nutty essence of the grain.

2 tablespoons extra-virgin olive oil
200 g (7 oz) best-quality brown rice
1 teaspoon fine sea salt
Bouquet garni: generous bunch of parsley stems, fresh bay leaves, basil leaves, rosemary leaves, celery leaves and sprigs of thyme, wrapped in the green part of a leek and securely fastened
500 ml (16 fl oz) water, homemade Potager Stock (page 321) or Chicken Stock (page 322)

1. In a large heavy-duty saucepan, combine the oil and rice and toss to coat. Cook over low heat, stirring with a wooden spoon, until the rice begins to crackle and a lightly toasted aroma wafts through the kitchen, 2 to 3 minutes.
2. Add the salt, bouquet garni and water or stock. Stir and bring to the boil over high heat. Cover, reduce heat to low and cook, without stirring, for 30 to 35 minutes. Once cooked, the rice should be firm to the bite, and not mushy.
3. Remove and discard the bouquet garni, and serve.

SERVES 6

⌁ **ON STORING RICE** ∾ Remember that rice can turn rancid over time, and should not be considered a 'for life' pantry item. Buy in small quantities and date your packages. Try to keep grains such as brown rice in the refrigerator, and store for no more than six months.

⌁ **THE BOUQUET GARNI** ∾ A bouquet garni is a simple way to infuse almost any soup, stock or grain with the subtle perfumes of herbs and spices. The classic bouquet garni consists of parsley, thyme, bay leaf and a few peppercorns. But use your imagination: rice is particularly happy with basil, juniper berries, rosemary and thyme.

BASMATI RICE

Indian basmati rice – 'basmati' translates as 'queen of fragrance' – wins me over on aroma alone. Grown along the foothills of the Himalayas, basmati is a long-grain rice, that I think of as feminine, almost flirtatious in its delicacy and tenderness. If you have a choice of varieties, select the highest grade Dehradun. In this recipe, I don't embellish the rice at all, simply boil it in the traditional manner, in lightly salted water. For a fluffier, more tender result, the rice can be soaked in cold water for 1 hour to soften the grains. When pressed for time, I simply give it a quick wash in cold water. Because the grains of basmati rice are small and light, they cook quickly, an additional plus when time is of the essence. Note that cooking times for rice are not constant: Time will vary according to the freshness of the rice, the pan in which it is cooked, and the exact degree of heat.

> 175 g (6½ oz) basmati rice
> 325 ml (11 fl oz) water
> ¾ teaspoon fine sea salt

1. Pour the rice into a large bowl and cover with cold water. Swish the grains around with your fingers to allow any impurities to float to the top. Carefully pour off and discard the water. Set aside.
2. In a medium-size saucepan with a tight-fitting lid, bring the water to a rolling boil over high heat. Add the rice and salt, and stir. Once the water boils, stir again to make sure the rice does not stick to the bottom of the pan. Reduce heat to very low, cover and cook until the rice is tender and has absorbed all of the water, 10 to 15 minutes. Do not stir.
3. Remove the pan from the heat and allow the rice to relax, covered, for up to 15 minutes. Fluff the rice with two forks, and serve.

SERVES 4

10
DESSERTS

WITH ORCHARDS OF CHERRIES, WILD as well as greengage plums, green and purple figs, three varieties of pears, one wild peach, a trio of apricots, a pair of almond trees, and a fledgling hazelnut, it's no wonder that fruit and nut desserts feature prominently on the Chanteduc dessert menu. From May to December the harvest supplies the makings of Cherry-Almond Tart, Cherry & Goats' Cheese Gratin, Provençal Honey-Almond Cookies, and our ever-favourite Apricot-Honey-Almond Tart. Come autumn, the last grapes on the vines star in the Winemaker's Grape Cake, while our single wild apple tree supplies fruit for Eli's Apple Crisp. Even the herb garden plays a role, flavouring the delicate Fresh Lemon Verbena Ice Cream, and come autumn, I gather every bit of fruit I can to create our bread oven favourite, Baked Fruit & Honey with Beaumes de Venise.

FACING PHOTOGRAPH: *A view from the courtyard at Chanteduc, looking up to the windows of the Pigeonnier, where the farmers once raised pigeons. Walter carved a heart into a door leading to a storage area for clay garden pots and tools.*

WINEMAKER'S GRAPE CAKE

Come September, I prepare this cake often, taking advantage of whatever clusters of grapes I can find on our vines after harvesting. At Chanteduc, we grow a mixture of Grenache, Syrah and Morvèdre grapes, each of which contributes its own personality to the wine and to this cake. I love the rustic crunch seeded grapes impart, and so also recommend trying Zinfandel, Corinth or Cabernet grapes. For seedless grapes, try Red Flame. The original recipe was given to me by Rolando Beramendi at Italy's fine Tuscan estate, Capezzana, where this intriguing not-too-sweet cake appears frequently at the table during the autumn harvest. Note that the cake is prepared with equal parts butter and olive oil, producing an unusually light and moist cake.

EQUIPMENT: One 23-cm (9-in) springform cake tin

> Butter and flour for preparing cake tin
> 2 large eggs, at room temperature
> 150 g (5 oz) sugar
> 4 tablespoons extra-virgin olive oil
> 60 g (2 oz) unsalted butter, melted
> 5 tablespoons whole milk
> ½ teaspoon pure vanilla extract
> 200 g (7 oz) plain flour
> ¾ teaspoon baking powder
> Pinch of sea salt
> Grated zest of 1 lemon
> Grated zest of 1 orange
> 300 g (10 oz) small fresh purple grapes (see above for varieties)
> Icing sugar, for decoration

1. Preheat the oven to 180°C/350°F/gas mark 4.
2. Generously butter and flour a 23-cm (9-in) springform cake tin, tapping out any excess flour. Set aside.
3. In the bowl of an electric mixer fitted with a whisk, beat the eggs and sugar until thick and lemon-coloured, about 3 minutes. Add the oil, butter, milk and vanilla extract, and mix to blend.
4. Sift the flour, baking powder and salt into a large bowl. Add the lemon and orange zest and toss to coat the citrus zest with flour. Spoon the mixture into the bowl of batter and stir with a wooden spoon until thoroughly blended. Scrape down the sides of the bowl and mix once more. Set aside for 10 minutes, to allow the flour to absorb the liquids.
5. Stir about three-quarters of the grapes into the batter to blend. Spoon the batter into the prepared cake tin, smoothing out the top with a spatula.

(continued on next page)

6. Place the tin in the centre of the oven. Bake for 15 minutes, then sprinkle the top of the cake with the remaining grapes. Bake until the top is a deep golden brown and the cake feels quite firm when pressed with a fingertip, about 40 minutes more, for a total baking time of 55 minutes. Remove to a baking rack to cool. After 10 minutes, run a knife along the sides of the tin. Release and remove the side of the springform tin, leaving the cake on the tin's base. Sprinkle with icing sugar just before serving. Serve at room temperature, cutting into thin wedges.

SERVES 8-12

 WINE SUGGESTIONS: Grape cake is an ideal match for *vin santo*, the rich smooth aromatic sweet wine prepared in small quantities on many Italian estates.

ᴗ: IN A PURPLE HAZE :ᴗ   Over time, I have identified the mystery that discourages many shoppers from buying grapes: the inevitable hazy white film. Though one might understandably assume it's due to a spray of pesticide, the film is in fact a natural substance produced by the grape. It acts as a protective covering to prevent moisture from penetrating the fruit. It also keeps the skin from cracking when the grape loses moisture. Even better, the film contains nothing toxic! You will find the same harmless film on plums.

A selection of grapes from the Vaison market.

LAVENDER HONEY ICE CREAM

Honey-making is a thriving cottage industry in my corner of Provence, where independent honey makers are about as numerous as independent cheese makers. At the weekly market in Vaison, it seems that every other stall sells either cheese or honey. I have a favourite, sold at the stand right in front of the post office. Since adding local honey to my pantry, I find I often substitute it for sugar in any recipe where it makes sense. This one was inspired by chef-proprietor Charles Mouret, at the family-run restaurant Saint-Hubert in the nearby village of Entrechaux. One evening, when I declined dessert, Madame Mouret insisted I try their lavender honey ice cream. I never regretted it! If you can't find lavender honey, choose a first-rate fresh honey with a strong bouquet, preferably one that is not more than year old. It should still be fragrant and it should not be too dark. You want the cream to turn the colour of a pale egg shell.

EQUIPMENT: One 1-litre (1¾-pint) capacity ice cream maker

2 teaspoons top-quality pure vanilla extract
6 large egg yolks
650 g (22 oz) creamy lavender honey or other good fresh honey
500 ml (16 fl oz) whole milk
250 ml (8 fl oz) crème fraîche or double cream

1. In the bowl of an electric mixer, beat the vanilla extract, egg yolks and honey at high speed until thick and lemon-coloured, about 1 minute. Set aside.

2. In a large saucepan, heat the milk over moderate heat just until tiny bubbles form around the edges of the pan. Gradually pour one-third of the boiling milk into the egg yolk mixture, whisking constantly. Return this milk and egg yolk mixture to the remaining milk in the saucepan. Reduce the heat to low and, keeping the custard below the simmering point, stir constantly with a wooden spoon in a figure-of-eight motion, until the mixture reaches the thickness of double cream, or 75°C (165°F) on a sugar thermometer. Do not let it boil. For a visual test, run your finger down the back of the spoon: If the mark holds, the mixture is sufficiently cooked. The process should take about 5 minutes.

3. Remove the custard from the heat and immediately stir in the crème fraîche to stop the cooking. To achieve a perfectly smooth texture, strain the mixture through a fine-mesh sieve. Cool completely before placing the mixture in an ice cream maker. (To speed cooling, transfer to a large chilled bowl placed inside a slightly larger bowl filled with ice cubes and water. Stir occasionally. To test the temperature, dip your fingers into the mixture. The cream should feel cold to the touch. The process should take about 30 minutes.)

4. When thoroughly cooled, transfer to an ice cream maker and freeze according to manufacturer's instructions.

MAKES ABOUT 1 LITRE (1¾ PINTS) ICE CREAM

APRICOT∗HONEY∗ALMOND TART

For the past 10 years, this has been, hands down, my most successful dessert. I love to make it and I love to eat it. It's one of those homey tarts that is so dazzling to look at, your guests will be incredulous, exclaiming '*You* made that?' when you bring it to the table. And the recipe, from start to finish, is child's play. The pastry is simply patted into the tin, and it's foolproof. So much so that during the sizzling summer months I often get up very early and bake the tart first thing, before the idea of lighting an oven strikes me as a criminal act.

The purely Provençal combination of apricots, almonds and honey seem to have been made in heaven, for when apricots are at their peak, they virtually drip with the intense flavours of honey and of almonds. When apricots are out of season, I use fresh purple figs, halved lengthwise and arranged in an attractive pattern on top of the pastry shell. Plums – or a combination of fruits such as peaches, apricots and nectarines – are also favourites. Whenever using stoned fruits, be sure to cut them in half and bake them cut side up, so the juices will reduce and intensify during baking. Baked this way, there is also less of a tendency for the juices to leak into the crust.

EQUIPMENT: One 23-cm (9-in) fluted tart tin with removable bottom

THE CRUST

Unsalted butter for preparing the tart tin
125 g (4 oz) unsalted butter, melted and cooled
90 g (3 oz) sugar
⅛ teaspoon pure almond extract
⅛ teaspoon pure vanilla extract
Pinch of fine sea salt
180 g (6 oz) plain all-purpose flour
2 tablespoons finely ground unblanched almonds

THE CREAM

100 ml (4 fl oz) double cream
1 large egg, lightly beaten
½ teaspoon pure almond extract
½ teaspoon pure vanilla extract
2 tablespoons raw full-flavoured honey, such as lavender
1 tablespoon plain flour

About 750 g (1½ lb) fresh apricots, stoned and halved (do not peel)
Icing sugar, for decoration

(continued on next page)

FACING PHOTOGRAPH: *Variations on a theme: Raspberry Tart and Apricot-Honey-Almond Tart.*

1. Preheat the oven to 180°C/350°F/gas mark 4.

2. Butter the bottom and sides of the tart tin with removable bottom. Set aside.

3. In a large bowl, combine the butter and sugar and stir to blend with a wooden spoon. Add the remaining ingredients and stir to form a soft, biscuit-like dough. Do not let it form a ball. Transfer the dough to the centre of the buttered tin. Using the tips of your fingers, evenly press the pastry along the bottom and sides of the tin. The dough will be quite thin.

4. Place the tin in the centre of the oven and bake until the dough is slightly puffy and set, about 12 to 15 minutes. Sprinkle the almonds over the bottom of the crust. (This will prevent the crust from becoming soggy).

5. Meanwhile, in a medium-size bowl, combine the cream, egg, extracts and honey and whisk to blend. Whisk in the flour. Starting just inside the edge of the prebaked pastry, neatly overlap the halved apricots, cut side up, at a slight angle, into two or three concentric circles, working toward the centre. Fill in the centre with the remaining apricots. Pour the cream evenly over the fruit. Place in the centre of the oven and bake until the filling is firm and the pastry a deep golden brown, 50 to 60 minutes. The apricots will shrivel slightly. Remove to a rack to cool. Sprinkle with icing sugar just before serving.

SERVES 8

VARIATION: To prepare this same tart with fresh raspberries, prebake the dough as directed, add the cream and bake until the filling is firm and the pastry a deep golden brown, about 10 minutes. Remove from the oven and allow to cool. At serving time arrange a single layer of raspberries (you will need about 375 g/12 oz berries) on top of the filling. Sprinkle with icing sugar just before serving.

A tart variation prepared with fresh purple figs.

FIADONE: CORSICAN CHEESECAKE

Light, fluffy and with a tinge of lemon, this cheesecake might well be considered Corsica's flagship dessert. It would be hard to spend a day on this sunny Mediterranean island without encountering some version of what the Corsicans call *fiadone*. I first sampled these tiny individual cheesecakes at a village café deep in the centre of the island, where they served individual lemony cheesecakes along with a zesty lemon soda, perfect for a blazing hot July afternoon. You will find this cake much lighter than a traditional cheesecake, and far more delicate.

EQUIPMENT: One 23-cm (9-in) springform cake tin

Unsalted butter and flour for preparing the cake tin
2 teaspoons pure vanilla extract
6 large eggs, separated
125 g (4 oz) sugar
1 kg (2 lb) whole-milk ricotta (or two 425-g/15-oz tubs)
Grated zest of 2 lemons, blanched and refreshed
Icing sugar, for decoration

1. Preheat the oven to 160°C/325°F/gas mark 3.
2. Generously butter and flour the tin, tapping out any excess flour. Set aside.
3. In the bowl of an electric mixer fitted with a whisk, beat the vanilla extract, egg yolks and sugar at high speed until thick and lemon-coloured, about 3 minutes. At low speed, gradually incorporate the cheese and the lemon zest. Beat until smooth.
4. In the bowl of an electric mixer fitted with a whisk, beat the egg whites at top speed until stiff but not dry. Whisk one-third of the egg whites into the cheese mixture and combine thoroughly. With a rubber spatula, gently fold in the remaining whites. Do this slowly and patiently. Do not overmix, but be sure that the mixture is well blended and no streaks of white remain.
5. Pour the batter into the prepared cake tin. Place the tin in the centre of the oven and bake until the cheesecake is a deep golden-brown, fairly firm in the centre, pulls away from the sides of the pan and a toothpick inserted in the centre comes out clean, about 1½ hours.
6. Transfer to a baking rack to cool. Once cooled, cover the cheesecake with plastic wrap and refrigerate until serving time. (The cake can be made 1 day in advance.) To serve, release the sides of the springform tin, leaving the cheesecake on the pan base. Sprinkle the top generously with icing sugar and serve, cut into very thin wedges.

SERVES 16-20

CROQUETTES: PROVENÇAL HONEY=ALMOND COOKIES

Croquettes, or firm dry cookies perfumed with the almonds and honey of Provence, can be found at nearly every pastry shop in the region. Recipes vary from baker to baker, but these crunchy biscuits, which closely resemble the Italian *biscotti*, are dear to the Provençal heart. I consider my friend Rita Kramer the ultimate cookie sleuth: she will spend days perusing pastry windows, examining displays and sampling sweets before delivering her careful judgement. These are my interpretation of the pure-honey *croquettes* she judged best in our village, those found at a small bakery off Place Montfort. Like many bakers, I often add a touch of fragrant orange flower water to the dough, though it is optional. When *croquettes* are carefully stored in an airtight container, they remain fresh for weeks. They are a fine accompaniment to a cup of coffee or tea, are ideal with Lavender Honey Ice Cream (page 279) or for dipping into homemade orange liqueur, '44', (page 337).

Almonds in many stages: fresh from the tree,
dried in their shells, and freshly cracked.

3 large eggs

250 g (8 oz) honey

½ teaspoon pure vanilla extract

½ teaspoon almond extract

2 teaspoons orange flower water (optional)

A pinch of salt

300 g (10 oz) whole unblanched almonds

300-335 g (10-11 oz) plain flour

1. Preheat the oven to 180°C/350°F/gas mark 4.

2. In the bowl of an electric mixer fitted with a whisk, whisk the eggs, honey, extracts, orange flower water if using, and salt at medium speed until thoroughly blended, about 2 minutes. With a wooden spoon, stir in the almonds. Gradually incorporate enough flour, spoonful by spoonful, to form a soft dough.

3. Thoroughly flour your hands, and roughly divide the dough into four pieces. The dough will be very soft and sticky. With your hands, form each piece of dough into logs about 7.5 cm (3 in) wide and 27.5 cm (11 in) long. Place on a non-stick baking sheet.

4. Place the baking sheet in the centre of the oven and bake until the dough is an even light golden-brown, 25 to 30 minutes. Remove the baking sheet from the oven and transfer the logs to a rack to cool for about for 10 minutes. Do not turn off the oven.

5. Transfer each log to a cutting board and, with a sharp knife, cut into 1-cm (½-in) thick diagonal slices. Stand the slices upright on the baking sheet. Return the baking sheet to the centre of the oven and bake until the croquettes are a deep golden-brown, 10 to 15 minutes more. Remove from the oven and transfer the croquettes to a rack to cool. They should be dry and crisp. (Once cooled, the croquettes can be stored in an airtight container for up to 1 month.)

MAKES ABOUT 60 COOKIES

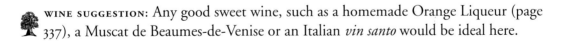 **WINE SUGGESTION:** Any good sweet wine, such as a homemade Orange Liqueur (page 337), a Muscat de Beaumes-de-Venise or an Italian *vin santo* would be ideal here.

COOK'S NOTE: When using honey in place of sugar in a recipe, the ratio of the substitution is 1 to 1.

What is a roofless cathedral compared to a well-built pie?
WILLIAM MAGINN

CHERRY‑ALMOND TART

Cherries and almonds are natural partners, and this is one dish that heads my hit-parade of desserts in May and June, when there is an abundance of the fruit on our trees and at the market. Serve this with fresh Vanilla Bean Ice Cream (page 289) and watch your guests swoon.

EQUIPMENT: One 23-cm (9-in) fluted tart tin with removable bottom

Unsalted butter for preparing the tart pan
125 g (4 oz) unsalted butter, melted and cooled
100 g (3½ oz) sugar
Pinch of fine sea salt
⅛ teaspoon pure almond extract
⅛ teaspoon pure vanilla extract
2 tablespoons finely ground blanched almonds
180 g (6 oz) plain

THE FILLING
5 tablespoons double cream
1 large egg, lightly beaten
½ teaspoon pure almond extract
½ teaspoon pure vanilla extract
60 g (2 oz) sugar
1 tablespoon plain flour
4 tablespoons finely ground blanched almonds
1 tablespoon cherry eau-de-vie or Kirsch
500 g (1 lb) fresh cherries, stoned
Icing sugar, for decoration

1. Preheat the oven to 180°C/350°F/gas mark 4.
2. Butter the bottom and sides of the tart tin. Set aside.

(continued on next page)

3. In a medium-size bowl, combine the butter and sugar, salt, extracts and almonds. Stir with a spoon to blend. Gradually incorporate enough flour to form a smooth soft dough. (The dough should resemble soft biscuit dough.) Place the dough in the centre of the buttered tin. With the tips of your fingers, evenly press the pastry along the bottom and sides of the tin. The dough will be quite thin. (You do not need to weight or prick the shell.)

4. Place the lined tart tin in the centre of the oven and bake until the dough is just slightly puffy and turns a very pale brown, about 10 minutes. Remove from the oven and set aside. Do not turn off the oven.

5. Meanwhile, in a small bowl, combine the cream, egg, and extracts and whisk to blend. Stir in the sugar, flour, ground almonds, and eau-de-vie or Kirsch.

6. Sprinkle 2 tablespoons of ground almonds on top of the prebaked pastry. (They will help absorb some of the cherry juice and deter it from soaking into the pastry.)

7. Arrange the cherries in a single layer in the pastry shell. Pour the filling over the cherries. Sprinkle with the remaining ground almonds. Place in the centre of the oven and bake until the filling is firm and the pastry a deep golden-brown, about 45 minutes. Remove to a rack to cool. Sprinkle with icing sugar just before serving.

SERVES 8

꙳ ON ALMONDS ꙳ The almond is actually a close relative of the peach, plum and apricot, so it is no surprise that the trees grow harmoniously in our small orchard. The almond belongs to the rose family, and the nut is actually the seed of a fruit that has both a sweet edible and a hard stony layer. Essentially, almonds fall into two categories – 'bitter' almonds which can be toxic if eaten in quantities and are primarily reserved for the production of almond extract. The other type of almond is the one we enjoy in tarts, pastries, and savoury dishes.

As far back as the Middle Ages, almonds were in great demand for making such stylish foods as marzipan and 'almond milk' a mixture of water and ground almonds. The most delicate variety of almonds sold for eating are 'jordan' almonds. Long and thin in shape, the name is a variation of the French word *jardin*, or garden.

VANILLA-BEAN ICE CREAM WITH FRESH CHERRIES

When it comes to cooking, sometimes it's fun to gild the lily. This is that leaf of gold created to stand on its own or to embellish a fresh Cherry-Almond Tart (page 287). I love replacing cream with thick crème fraîche, making for a tart, puckery ice cream – a dramatic match with cherries.

EQUIPMENT: One 1-litre (1¾-pint) capacity ice cream maker

> 4 plump moist vanilla beans
> 500 ml (16 fl oz) whole milk
> 6 large egg yolks
> 150 g (5 oz) sugar
> 250 ml (8 fl oz) crème fraîche or double cream
> 500 g (1 lb) fresh cherries, stoned and quartered

1. Flatten the vanilla beans and cut them in half lengthwise. With a demitasse (coffee) spoon or small knife, scrape out the seeds and place them in a bowl. Reserve the pods.
2. In a large saucepan, combine the milk and vanilla pods over high heat. Bring just to the boil and remove from the heat. Cover and set aside to infuse for 15 minutes.
3. In the bowl of an electric mixer fitted with a whisk, beat the vanilla seeds, egg yolks and sugar until thick and lemon-coloured, about 3 minutes. Set aside.
4. Strain the milk with the vanilla pods through a fine-mesh sieve into a large saucepan. Pour the milk into another saucepan and place over moderate heat just until tiny bubbles form around the edges of the pan. Gradually pour one-third of the boiling milk into the egg yolk mixture, whisking constantly. Return this milk and egg yolk mixture to the milk in the saucepan. Reduce the heat to low and, keeping the custard below the simmering point, stir constantly with a wooden spoon in a figure-of-eight motion, until the mixture reaches the thickness of double cream, or 75°C (165°F) on a sugar thermometer. Do not let it boil. For a visual test, run your finger down the back of the spoon: If the mark holds, the mixture is sufficiently cooked. The whole process should take about 5 minutes.
5. Remove the custard from the heat and immediately stir in the crème fraîche to stop the cooking. To achieve a perfectly smooth texture, strain the mixture through a fine-mesh sieve. Cool completely before placing the mixture in an ice cream maker. (To speed cooling, transfer the cream to a large chilled bowl. Place that bowl inside a slightly larger bowl filled with ice cubes and water. Stir occasionally. To test the temperature, dip your fingers into the mixture. The cream should feel cold to the touch. The process should take about 30 minutes.)
6. When thoroughly cooled, stir in the cherries. Transfer to an ice cream maker and freeze according to manufacturer's instructions.

MAKES ABOUT ONE LITRE (1¾ PINTS) ICE CREAM

CHERRY & GOAT CHEESE GRATIN

The old saying 'necessity is the mother of invention' proved true with this recipe. One afternoon I was 'trapped' at home, waiting for a delivery man to show up. I'd intended to make this gratin with fresh cream, but discovered I had none on hand. The only possible substitutes were yoghurt and a very fresh young goats' cheese. I gambled on the goats' cheese and won. My guests were delighted, and so was I, for I had a new creation, with a myriad possibilities.

Try this with cherries, a mix of berries, peaches, or raspberries, or just with apricots, a personal favourite. The slight tartness of the goats' cheese goes well with this, as does the flavour surprise once cooked. And while some cooks commonly think of a 'gratin' as something with a cheese topping, in French cooking a 'gratin' can be anything baked in a round vessel, or gratin dish.

EQUIPMENT: One 27-cm (10½-in) round baking dish

Unsalted butter for preparing the baking dish
750 g (1½ lb) cherries, stoned
125 g (4 oz) very fresh moist goats' cheese
65 g (2¼ oz) sugar
2 large eggs
90 g (3 oz) finely ground blanched almonds
Pinch of fine sea salt
½ teaspoon pure vanilla extract
½ teaspoon pure almond extract
Icing sugar, for decoration

1. Preheat the oven to 190°C/375°F/gas mark 5.
2. Butter the baking dish. Arrange the cherries in it in a single layer.
3. In the bowl of a food processor, combine the remaining ingredients and process to blend. Pour the mixture over the cherries.
4. Place the baking dish in the centre of the oven. Bake until the gratin is firm and a deep golden-brown, about 30 minutes. Remove to a rack to cool. Dust lightly with icing sugar, and serve in wedges.

SERVES 6-8

CHANTEDUC CLAFOUTIS

In the summer months, our property in Provence, as well as the market, is alive with a great mix of last-of-season cherries with first-of-season fresh raspberries, redcurrants, blueberries from the Auvergne, and wild blackberries from our fields. The more berries you mix here, the more complex flavours you will achieve, the more potential applause! When preparing this with mixed fruits, I do stone the cherries for a more elegant – and less dangerous – dessert. This clafoutis should be served at room temperature, but serve it the same day you prepare it, for maximum flavour.

EQUIPMENT: One 27-cm (10½-in) round porcelain baking dish

2 tablespoons Kirsch (cherry eau-de-vie)
100 g (3½ oz) plus 2 tablespoons granulated sugar
1 kg (2 lb) mix of berries and other fruit, such as stoned cherries, raspberries, blackberries, blueberries and currants
2 large eggs
6 tablespoons crème fraîche or double cream
6 tablespoons whole milk
Icing sugar, for decoration

1. Preheat the oven to 220°C/425°/gas mark 7.

2. In a small bowl, combine 1 tablespoon Kirsch and 2 tablespoons of sugar and stir to dissolve the sugar. Add the berries and toss to blend. Transfer the mixture to the baking dish. Place in the centre of the oven and bake until the fruit is hot and steaming, about 10 minutes. (The pre-baking will help the fruits give up excess liquid that might make the clafoutis watery.)

3. Transfer the fruits to a colander to drain. (Reserve the juice to flavour the baked clafoutis, whipped cream, iced teas or mineral water.) Set aside to cool, about 5 minutes.

4. Reduce the oven heat to 180°C/350°F/gas mark 4.

5. In the bowl of an electric mixer, whisk the eggs at high speed until frothy, 1 to 2 minutes. Add the remaining sugar and whisk until well blended, 1 to 2 minutes more. Add the crème fraîche or cream, milk and remaining 1 tablespoon Kirsch. Beat until well blended and set aside.

6. Transfer the drained fruits to the baking dish, arranging them in a single layer. Carefully pour the batter over the fruits, filling just to the top. (You may have an excess of batter. If so, fill to the top, place the pan in the centre of the oven and bake for 5 minutes. Then add the remaining batter. This will avoid the problem of the batter spilling over on the floor of the oven.) Continue baking until the batter is golden and set, 35 to 40 minutes. Transfer to a rack to cool.

(continued on next page)

7. Preheat the grill.

8. When the clafoutis is cool, place on a baking sheet. Sprinkle the top evenly and generously with icing sugar. Place under the grill, about 2.5 cm (1 in) from the heat. Grill until the sugar is caramelized and golden, about 1 minute. Transfer to a rack to cool.

9. Serve at room temperature, with whipped cream flavoured with a touch of Kirsch, with the berry cooking juices or with Vanilla Bean Ice Cream (page 289).

SERVES 8

 WINE SUGGESTION: A festive aperitif, such as a pink champagne

∴ CLAFOUTIS ∿ The classical definition of a *clafoutis* is a flan or thick crêpe baked in the oven with dark cherries. The cherry stones are left intact to impart their own flavour to the thick batter as it bakes. A dish native to the Limousin region of France, it is a rustic dessert shared on the family table, as a simple yet hearty and fulfilling end to a meal.

LEMON LOVER'S TART

Hands down, lemon and chocolate are my preferred winter dessert flavours. I created this rich creamy tart one Christmas in Provence, where it was the perfect ending to a festive family turkey dinner. Lemon curd – a puckery blend of eggs, butter, sugar and lemon which thickens slowly on top of the stove – offers an incomparably pure lemon flavour and a silky smooth texture. This is a cold weather recipe, for days when you will welcome the warmth of steam and the stove. You may initially find the long hand-beating a bit tedious, but once you sample the results, you will not be disappointed. The tart can be prepared several hours in advance, and requires no last-minute preparation, making it ideal for entertaining

> 1 prebaked Lemon Pastry Shell (page 296)
> 2 large eggs, plus 3 large eggs yolks, at room temperature
> 200 g (7 oz) sugar
> 125 g (4 oz) unsalted butter, at room temperature, cut into 8 pieces
> Zest of 2 lemons, preferably organic, blanched and refreshed
> 125 ml (4 fl oz) freshly squeezed lemon juice, strained (the juice of 3-4 lemons)

1. In the top of a double boiler set over, but not touching, simmering water, combine the eggs, egg yolks, and sugar. Whisk frequently until the curd is thick and pale-lemon coloured, about 10 minutes.

2. Add the butter, tablespoon by tablespoon, allowing each spoonful to melt before adding the next. Add the zest and lemon juice, whisking frequently over simmering water, until thick and custard-like and the first bubbles appear on the surface, about 10 minutes. The mixture should not boil.

3. Pour the curd into the prebaked and cooled pastry shell. Even out with the spatula, and set aside to set, about 30 minutes. To serve, cut into thin wedges.

SERVES 8

LEMON PASTRY SHELL

Pat-in-the-pan pastry shells are quick, easy, foolproof and have long been a part of my everyday repertoire. This one, lightened with icing sugar and touched with a hint of lemon, is delicious as the base of my Lemon Lover's Tart (page 295). Note that the dough is delicate and fragile, so be cautious once the shell is baked.

EQUIPMENT: One 23-cm (9-in) fluted tart tin with removable bottom

Unsalted butter for buttering the tart tin
125 g (4 oz) unsalted butter, melted and cooled
¼ teaspoon pure vanilla extract
⅛ teaspoon pure almond extract
Grated zest of 1 lemon, blanched and refreshed
30 g (1 oz) icing sugar
Pinch of fine sea salt
180 g (6 oz) plain flour

1. Preheat the oven to 180°C/350°F/gas mark 4.
2. Butter the bottom and sides of the tart tin. Set aside.
3. In a medium-size bowl, combine the butter, extracts, grated zest, sugar and salt, and stir with a spoon to blend. Gradually incorporate enough flour to form a smooth soft dough. (The dough should resemble soft cookie dough.) Place the dough in the centre of the buttered tin. With the tips of your fingers, evenly press the pastry along the bottom and sides of the tin. The dough will be quite thin. You do not need to weight or prick the shell.) Place in the centre of the oven and bake just until the dough is firm and lightly browned, 12 to 15 minutes. Remove from the oven and set aside to cool for at least 10 minutes before filling. Do not remove from the tin.

MAKES ONE 23-CM (9-INCH) PASTRY SHELL

Food is, delightfully, an area of licensed sensuality, of physical delight which will,
with luck and enduring taste buds, last our life long.

ANTONIA TILL

LEMON *POTS DE CRÈME*

Smooth, airy and with a gentle pucker of lemon, these golden individual lemon creams make a delightfully light dessert, delicious with crunchy *Croquettes*: Provençal Almond Cookies (page 284).

EQUIPMENT: Eight 125-ml (4-fl oz) ovenproof ramekins, custard cups, or *petit pots*

125 ml (4 fl oz) lemon juice (about 4 lemons)
100 g (3½ oz) sugar
6 large egg yolks
375 ml (13 fl oz) double cream

1. Preheat the oven to 160°C/325°F/gas mark 3.
2. In a small bowl, combine the lemon juice and sugar and stir to dissolve thoroughly. In a large bowl, gently whisk the egg yolks, then whisk in the cream. Whisk in the lemon juice and sugar, combining thoroughly. Strain through a fine-mesh sieve or several layers of cheesecloth. Let stand for 2 to 3 minutes, then remove any foam that rises to the top.
3. Place the moulds in a baking pan large enough to hold them generously. Divide the cream evenly among the individual moulds, filling each about half full. Add enough hot tap water to reach about half the depth of the moulds. Cover the pan loosely with foil to prevent a skin from forming. Place in the centre of the oven and bake until the creams are just set around the edges, but still trembling in the centre, 30 to 35 minutes.
4. Remove the pan from the oven and carefully remove the moulds from the water. Refrigerate, loosely covered, for at least 2 hours and up to 24 hours. Serve the *pots de crème* chilled, without unmoulding.

SERVES 8

WINE SUGGESTION: A lemony Gewurztraminer *selection de grains noble*, served lightly chilled.

SCHAUM TORTE: MERINGUES FOR THE MONTH OF MAY

These individual meringue shells are one of the fondest memories of my Wisconsin upbringing. *Schaum Torte* is a Memorial Day speciality created to greet the season's first crop of strawberries. This 'torte' is really a series of individual meringue kisses: slice off the top, fill the meringue with strawberries and cream, replace the top and dig in! My recipe is lighter than the traditional version, which includes a layer of ice cream between the layers of meringue. I prefer the simplicity of a meringue, fresh fruit, and a dollop of freshly whipped cream.

Schaum Torte: *Meringues for the Month of May.*

4 large egg whites, at room temperature
½ teaspoon cream of tartar (optional)
1 teaspoon pure vanilla extract
200 g (7 oz) caster sugar
1 kg (2 lb) fresh strawberries (or mixed berries)
1 tablespoon sugar
175 ml (6 fl oz) double cream

1. Preheat the oven to 110°C/230°F/gas mark ¼. Line a baking sheet with foil or a non-stick liner. (Do not use parchment or a greased and floured baking sheet, for meringues tend to stick to them.)

2. In a heavy-duty mixer fitted with a whisk, beat the egg whites, cream of tartar, if using, and vanilla extract at medium-low speed until small bubbles appear and the surface is frothy, about 45 seconds. Increase the speed to medium and gradually add half of the caster sugar, whisking until soft peaks form, about 45 seconds. Increase the speed to high and whisk until thick, stiff, glossy white peaks form, about 2 minutes more. Remove the bowl from the mixer. Sprinkle the rest of the caster sugar over the mixture and, with a large spatula, quickly and gently fold it in, working the egg whites as little as possible.

3. Using a large serving spoon, ladle six large round dollops of meringue on the prepared baking sheet. Work as quickly as possible so as not to deflate the whites. Place the baking sheet in the centre of the oven and bake until crisp and dry but not yet beginning to colour, about 2 hours.

4. Remove the baking sheet from the oven and, with a spatula carefully transfer the meringues to a wire rack to cool. If they stick to the foil, they haven't sufficiently dried out: If this happens, return them to the oven to dry thoroughly. (The meringues can be prepared several days in advance: if so, store fully cooled meringues in a dry, airtight container.)

5. About 2 hours before serving the meringues, rinse and stem the strawberries. Cut lengthwise into thin slices. Toss with the sugar and set aside at room temperature.

6. In a heavy-duty mixer fitted with a whisk, beat the cream until it forms soft peaks.

7. Using a sharp serrated knife, slice the top quarter from each meringue. (The meringues may chip or break off, but try to avoid transforming them to bits.) Place each meringue on a dessert plate. Spoon the strawberries into the shell, allowing fruit to overflow on to the plate. Top the berries with the whipped cream. Place the meringue caps on top of the whipping cream and serve immediately.

SERVES 6

 WINE SUGGESTION: Try this with a young Sauternes or a sweet Vouvray Moelleux, from the Loire.

CHOCOLATE GOURMANDISE

When one food trend fades from fashion, the void is always filled by a slight variation. You may have ended your love affair with chocolate soufflés, but this creamy warm chocolate dessert – a cross between a soufflé and chocolate mousse – will step in to steal your heart away. The recipe comes from Claude Udron, former chef and co-owner of the Paris restaurant Pile ou Face. It was the finale to nearly every meal I savoured in that extraordinary restaurant. While the dessert must be baked at the very last minute, it can be prepared several hours in advance, making for minimal last-minute work.

EQUIPMENT: Four 250-ml (8 fl oz) ovenproof ramekins

125 g (4 oz) bittersweet chocolate, preferably Lindt Excellence, grated or finely chopped
125 g (4 oz) unsalted butter
3 large eggs
150 g (5 oz) sugar
35 g (1¼ oz) plain white flour
Butter and flour for preparing ramekins

1. In the top of a double boiler set over, but not touching, simmering water, combine the chocolate and butter. Whisk until melted. Set aside.
2. In the bowl of an electric mixer fitted with a whisk, gently whisk together the eggs, sugar, and flour, mixing just to blend. Gradually whisk in the melted chocolate and butter. Set aside to rest for 1 hour, to allow flavours to mellow.
3. Preheat the oven to 200°C/400°F/gas mark 6.
4. Generously butter and flour the ramekins. Place on a baking sheet. Carefully pour the mixture into the ramekins. Place the baking sheet in the centre of the oven and bake just until the edges are set and the interior is still a bit liquid, 10 to 12 minutes. Transfer the ramekins to four dessert plates and serve immediately. (Like individual soufflés, these are eaten directly from the baking dishes.)

SERVES 4

WINE SUGGESTIONS: Chocolate and certain sweet wines are perfect partners: I enjoy this with a slightly chilled red Rasteau *vin doux naturel* from neighbour André Romero at the Domaine de la Soumade, the intensely fruity, cherry-like wine cries out for a match with chocolate. Other good choices are a Muscat de Beaumes-de-Venise, Maury Vintage from Mas Amiel in the Roussillon, a Californian Muscat, or a sip of good rum.

CHOCOLATE-HONEY MOUSSE

In the winter months, when most of the best fruits are out of season, I turn to chocolate for solace. This is a variation on a chocolate mousse created at restaurant El Olivo in Madrid, where it was served rather festively and generously out of a large bowl. Each guest was handed a silver spoon and encouraged to help themselves. The dessert is a cinch to make, and should of course be prepared ahead of time. I often serve it in antique stemmed champagne glasses, or *coupes*, making for a dramatic, old-fashioned presentation.

> 500 ml (16 fl oz) double cream
> 250 g (8 oz) bittersweet chocolate, preferably Lindt Excellence, finely chopped
> 1 tablespoon raw honey, such as lavender
> 4 large egg whites

1. Pour half the cream into a medium saucepan and bring to a simmer over moderate heat. Remove the pan from the heat, add the chocolate, and stir until the chocolate is thoroughly melted and the mixture is well blended.
2. Transfer to a large bowl. Add the honey, and stir to blend. Set aside to cool to lukewarm.
3. In the bowl of a heavy-duty mixer fitted with a whisk, whisk the egg whites until stiff but not dry. Set aside.
4. In another bowl of a heavy-duty mixer fitted with a whisk, beat the remaining cream, whisking at medium speed, gradually increasing to high speed, until the cream is lightly whipped and stiff peaks form when the whisk is lifted. Set aside.
5. Add one-third of the beaten egg whites to the chocolate batter. Mix vigorously. With a large spatula, gently fold in the remaining whites. Do this slowly and patiently. Do not overmix, but be sure that the mixture is well blended and that no streaks of white remain. Add the whipped cream and fold it into the egg and chocolate mixture.
6. Spoon the mousse into a large soufflé dish or attractive serving bowl, into individual ramekins or small bowls. Cover with plastic wrap and refrigerate until firm, around 4 hours.
7. Serve chilled, with *Croquettes*: Provençal Honey-Almond Cookies (page 284).

SERVES 6-8

WINE SUGGESTION: Try this with a distinctive sweet dessert wine, such as a well-aged Spanish Málaga.

GINGERED CONFIT OF APPLES & PEARS

I have always had a fascination for espaliered fruits. So once we began expanding the orchard at Chanteduc, the first fruits I added were three espaliered pear trees, each shaped into a compact, well-trained 'W'. The three French varieties – Comice, Poire William's and Beurré Hardy – ripen at different times and in good years provide plenty of fruit for the table and for cooking.

One of my preferred ways to use them is in this old-fashioned confit, a golden dessert of softened pears and apples bathed in a thick transparent syrup. It is great served warm with a dollop of cream, or at room temperature as a sweet finale to a meal. The cooking procedure is typical of all confits: the juices of the fruits are first released, then gradually reabsorbed by the fruit, which plump up during the long, slow cooking process.

> 250 g (8 oz) sugar
> Zest of 2 lemons, blanched and refreshed
> Zest of 2 oranges, blanched and refreshed
> 500 g (1 lb) cooking pears, preferably a range of varieties
> 2.5 kg (5 lb) cooking apples, preferably a range of varieties
> A walnut-sized knob of ginger and 10 cloves wrapped in a cheesecloth bag
> 1 teaspoon vanilla extract
> 3 tablespoons Poire William's (pear eau-de-vie)

1. Place the sugar, lemon zest and orange zest in a large shallow bowl. Peel, quarter and core the fruit, adding each piece of fruit to the mixture in the bowl as it is prepared. With your fingers, toss to coat the fruit evenly with the sugar mixture.
2. Transfer the coated fruits, sugar and zest to a large heavy-bottomed saucepan. Cook over the lowest possible heat until the sugar has dissolved into a clear liquid, about 20 minutes. Stir from time to time.
3. Add the cheesecloth bag with the ginger and cloves. Cook, uncovered, over the lowest possible heat until the liquid is very thick and syrupy, but the fruit still holds its form, about 3 hours. (The fruit will first release a great deal of liquid. The long slow cooking process is necessary to permit the juices to reduce, intensify and thicken.) Stir from time to time and keep the heat as low as possible to avoid scorching the fruit.
4. Remove and discard the cheesecloth. Stir in the vanilla extract and the pear eau-de-vie. Serve warm, with a touch of fresh cream. (The compote may be stored up to 1 month, covered and refrigerated.)

SERVES 10-12

Local pears, ready for preserving or for eating out of hand.

◡ **PLANT PEARS FOR YOUR HEIRS** ∿ The expression refers to the fact that it can take a pear tree up to 9 years to bear fruit. Patience, patience!

◡ **ON APPLES AND PEARS** ∿ Once you come to know the different varieties of apples and pears, you will have a sense of how they behave when cooked. Golden Delicious, Granny Smith and Discovery are firm-fleshed varieties that offer an intense apple flavour and a pleasant tang. They also hold their shape when cooked. McIntosh tend to fall apart, but a few can be tossed into a mixture of firm-fleshed varieties to add dimension to the flavour. For pears, the Bartlett and Bosc are the most versatile: they not only hold their shape during cooking, they impart a distinctive flavour. The Anjou, though less firm, provides plenty of sweet juice for pies and tarts.

◡ **A TEST FOR RIPENESS** ∿ What's the best way to tell if a pear is ripe? We tend to poke at the fruit, seeking in the flesh a tender spot, a softness. This softness, however, can most often mean that it's already too late. Instead, pull on the stem of the pear. When ripe, the stem should provide little resistance to pressure.

ELI'S APPLE CRISP

Early one November my friend Eli Zabar brought over a crate full of different varieties of apples from his orchard in Provence. The sky that day was a brilliant blue, a few golden leaves were still clinging to the vines in our vineyards and the scent of a warming apple dessert wafting through my kitchen seemed like an ideal way to end a perfect autumn Saturday.

Prepare this with a good tangy cooking apple, and if possible, combine several varieties – such as Granny Smith, McIntosh and Fuji – for a more complex depth of flavour and texture. This is a quick easy appealing and inexpensive dessert, and you don't have to make pastry!

EQUIPMENT: One 27-cm (10½-in) baking dish

Unsalted butter for preparing the baking dish
45 g (1½ oz) unsalted butter
1 kg (2 lb) cooking apples, peeled, cored and cut lengthwise into 8 even wedges
2 tablespoons freshly squeezed lemon juice
½ teaspoon ground cinnamon
1½ teaspoons pure vanilla extract
2 large eggs, at room temperature
75 g (2½ oz) sugar
250 ml (8 fl oz) crème fraîche or double cream

1. Preheat the oven to 200°C/400°F/gas mark 6.
2. Generously butter the bottom and sides of the baking dish. Set aside.
3. In a large frying pan, combine the butter, apples, lemon juice and ¼ teaspoon cinnamon and cook just until soft, about 7 minutes. Stir in ½ teaspoon of vanilla extract.
4. Transfer the apples to the baking dish, evening them into a single layer with a spatula.
5. In a large bowl, combine the eggs and sugar and whisk until well blended. Add the cream, the remaining vanilla extract and cinnamon. Whisk to blend and pour over the apples in the baking dish.
6. Place the baking dish in the centre of the oven and bake until the top is a deep golden-brown, 30 to 45 minutes. Do not underbake, or the results will be soggy, rather than crisp.
7. Serve cut into wedges, accompanied by a dollop of crème fraîche. The dessert is best served the day it is made, as the delicate flavours will fade.

SERVES 8

FRESH LEMON VERBENA ICE CREAM

One of the earliest signs of spring at Chanteduc is the sight of the first bright green shoots of lemon verbena – or verveine – sprouting from this hearty perennial's stalky frame. Within weeks they grow into long pointed rough-textured leaves with an intense, lemony perfume. Throughout the spring and summer, I use lemon verbena leaves liberally, preparing refreshing and lightly sedative herbal teas, or infusions, as well as this popular summer ice cream. The dessert is also delicious prepared with fresh mint, or with less traditional 'sweet' herbs, such as thyme or rosemary.

500 ml (16 fl oz) double cream
250 ml (8 fl oz) whole milk
125 g (4 oz) sugar
60 fresh lemon verbena leaves

1. In a large saucepan, combine the cream, milk, sugar and verbena leaves and place over moderate heat just until tiny bubbles form around the edges of the pan. Remove from the heat, cover and let steep for 1 hour.
2. Strain through a fine-mesh sieve, discarding the verbena. Refrigerate until thoroughly chilled.
3. Transfer to an ice cream maker and freeze according to manufacturer's instructions.
4. Serve with *Croquettes*: Provençal Almond Cookies (page 284).

SERVES 4

FRESH CHEESE WITH PINE NUTS & HONEY

Soft fresh cheese drizzled with honey and sprinkled with pine nuts make a popular Mediterranean dessert. The sweet honey counters the saltiness of cheese and the meaty flavour and crunch of pine nuts add depth and texture.

At Chanteduc, I always have a variety of honeys on hand, and the market provides fresh goats'- and sheep's-milk cheese all year round. While our giant umbrella pines could supply us with tiny meaty pine nuts, I gave up after one laborious attempt to extract the tiny nuts from the cones. I decided it was a lot less bothersome simply to purchase pine nuts in town! If you don't have time to make the cheese, buy a fresh ricotta or a fresh mild goats' cheese.

EQUIPMENT: One 1.5-litre (2½-pint) perforated mould, such as a porcelain *coeur à la crème* mould, or large sieve

THE CHEESE

500 ml (16 fl oz) small-curd whole milk cottage cheese
500 ml (16 fl oz) whole-milk yogurt

GARNISH

About 125 ml (4 fl oz) strong-flavoured raw honey, such as chestnut or buckwheat
4 tablespoons pine nuts, lightly toasted and cooled

1. The day before, or early in the morning of the day you plan to serve the dessert, combine the cottage cheese and yogurt in the bowl of a food processor. Purée until completely smooth. Scoop the mixture into a the cheesecloth-lined mould or sieve set over a bowl. Cover loosely with a cloth. Set aside to drain at room temperature, until the cheese becomes dry and firm, about 12 hours. (Do not be surprised at the quantity of liquid the cheese will release.) It is ready when no more liquid drips from it. With the back of a spoon, carefully smooth out the top of the cheese. Cover and refrigerate until ready to use. (The cheese will benefit from a day's curing, to allow the flavours to develop and mellow.)

2. To serve: If you made the cheese in a perforated mould, unmould it on a chilled serving platter. If you prepared it in a cheesecloth-lined sieve, spoon the cheese into a decorative bowl. Pass honey and pine nuts, letting your guests drizzle their own toppings.

SERVES 6-8

11

PANTRY

ONE SIMPLY CAN'T HAVE AN ACTIVE COUN-
try house without a successful personal
pantry, there to draw upon throughout the
year, to season, to flavour, to embellish. Always, we
have on hand huge crocks filled with our home-
grown ripe olives, some cured simply with salt and
herbs, others immersed in brine, for longer keeping.
Preserved lemons – cured in salt, bay leaves, and
olive oil – are a newer entry, a result of the Moroccan influence on French cuisine. Salt-cured
anchovies rest secure in huge glass jars, and will be
used to flavour appetizers, soups, daubes of tuna as
well as beef. There's the Italian-inspired Mostarda:
Fig & Prune Chutney – designed for the cheese
course, and our favorite *Pili Pili:* Spicy Herb Oil for
anointing pasta, breads, soups, and vegetables.
Chantal's Bachelor's Confiture – pitted fruits preserved in syrup and alcohol – saves the day when we
haven't had time to prepare a serious dessert but want
to end the evening with a sweet finale. And, of
course, there's a selection of homemade liqueurs,
with Fresh Cherry Wine leading the pack.

PILI-PILI: SPICY HERB OIL

Just about every pizzeria table in Provence features a huge bottle of spicy oil, a popular condiment known as *pili-pili*. The oil, seasoned with a variety of herbs and hot pepper, is used to give a touch of fire to pizzas, while at home I also drizzle it over platters of fresh tomatoes and herbs.

When preparing the oil in Provence we use little *piment langue d'oiseau* or bird's tongue peppers, tiny peppers that grow in the tropics. They're fiery hot, much like the *tien tsin* chilli peppers used in Oriental cooking. Crushed red peppers are the most available substitute. Since the oil is going to be overwhelmed by the spice, there is no need to use extra-virgin olive oil here.

The word *pili-pili* actually comes from the Swahili for hot pepper, though the African-Provençal connection is not an obvious one.

> 1 tablespoon dried oregano
> 2 teaspoons crushed red peppers (hot red pepper flakes), or to taste (or substitute about 12 of your favourite dried red peppers)
> 1 teaspoon fennel seeds
> 4 sprigs of fresh thyme
> 4 sprigs of fresh rosemary
> 4 fresh bay leaves
> 250 ml (8 fl oz) olive oil

1. In a sterilized bottle (preferably one that you can discard once you use up the oil), layer the oregano, peppers and fennel seeds. Stick the sprigs of herbs and the bay leaves into the bottle. Cover with oil and close securely. Set aside to mature for at least 1 week.
2. Taste, and, if desired, add additional peppers to taste. Drizzle on pizzas, fresh or grilled vegetables, grilled meats, vegetables or poultry.

MAKES ABOUT 250 ML (8 FL OZ) SPICY OIL

VARIATION: The same flavouring mixture can be added to red wine vinegar to make a perky vinegar for dressing raw sliced tomatoes, cucumbers, or for deglazing Provençal Roast Tomatoes (page 113).

FACING PHOTOGRAPH: Pili Pili *is the spicy herbal oil used to season pizzas, meats, pastas, and cheese.*

'There is no such thing as a little garlic.'
ALFRED BAER

AÏOLI: GARLIC MAYONNAISE

Aïoli is a staple of Provençal cuisine: this golden sauce is used to enrich fish soup, enliven boiled vegetables, in place of a classic mayonnaise on sandwiches, or simply spread on toast to accompany a green salad.

Preferably, garlic mayonnaise should be made by hand with a mortar and pestle: Aïoli made with a blender or a food processor will be glue-like. Alternatively, you can crush the garlic and salt together to a paste with the flat side of a knife, then prepare the mayonnaise with a whisk or a hand-held electric mixer. For best results, be sure that all ingredients are at room temperature.

6 plump fresh garlic cloves
½ teaspoon fine sea salt
2 large egg yolks, at room temperature
250 ml (8 fl oz) extra-virgin olive oil

1. Degerm the garlic: peel and cut the garlic in half. If there is a green, sprout-like 'germ' running through the centre of the garlic, remove and discard it. Finely chop the garlic.
2. Pour boiling water into a large mortar to warm it; discard the water and dry the mortar. Place the garlic and salt in the mortar and mash together evenly with a pestle to form as smooth a paste as possible. (The fresher the garlic, the easier it will be to crush.)
3. Add the egg yolks. Stir, pressing slowly and evenly with the pestle, always in the same direction, to blend the garlic and yolks thoroughly. Continue stirring, gradually adding just a few drops of the oil, whisking until thoroughly incorporated. Do not add too much oil at the beginning or the mixture will not emulsify. As soon as the mixture begins to thicken, add the remaining oil in a slow and steady stream, whisking constantly. Taste for seasoning.
4. Transfer to a bowl and serve immediately. The sauce can be refrigerated, well sealed, for up to 2 days. To serve, bring to room temperature and stir once again.

MAKES ABOUT 250 ML (8 FL OZ) MAYONNAISE

Garlic is the ketchup of intellectuals.
UNKNOWN

ROUILLE: GARLIC, SAFFRON & RED PEPPER MAYONNAISE

Rouille is simply a spicy sibling of aïoli, or garlic mayonnaise. Most of us first tasted this saffron-red sauce as an accompaniment to bouillabaisse, the classic fish soup of the Mediterranean. There are many versions of rouille – some include potato or bread as a thickener, some add white wine for a tangy tartness, but my favourite is a classic aïoli embellished with a hint of saffron and a generous hit of spicy red pepper. Stir a spoonful of this into Monsieur Henny's Rabbit Bouillabaisse (page 239), and you're firmly on the soil of Provence.

6 plump fresh garlic cloves
½ teaspoon sea salt
2 large egg yolks, at room temperature
250 ml (8 fl oz) extra-virgin olive oil
¼ teaspoon saffron threads
¼ teaspoon cayenne pepper (or to taste)

1. Degerm the garlic: peel and cut the garlic in half. If there is a green, sprout-like 'germ' running through the centre of the garlic, remove and discard it. Finely chop the garlic.
2. Pour boiling water into a large mortar to warm it. Discard the water and dry the mortar. Place the garlic and salt in the mortar and mash with a pestle to form as smooth a paste as possible. (The fresher the garlic, the easier it will be to crush.)
3. Add the egg yolks. Stir, pressing slowly and evenly with the pestle, always in the same direction, to blend the garlic and yolks thoroughly.
4. Very slowly add a few tablespoons of oil, drop by drop, stirring until the mixture thickens. This forms the base of the emulsion. Stir in the saffron threads and cayenne pepper. Once this mixture has thickened, you can add the remaining oil in a slow thin stream with less fear of the emulsion breaking. Continue stirring until the sauce is thickened to a mayonnaise consistency. Taste for seasoning.
5. The sauce can be refrigerated, well sealed, for up to 2 days. Bring to room temperature to serve.

MAKES ABOUT 250 ML (8 FL OZ) MAYONNAISE

PISTOU: OLIVE OIL, BASIL & GARLIC SAUCE

Pistou comes from the Provençal word *pista*, which means to *broyer, piler et excraser*, or grind, pound and crush, which is what one does with this universally loved garden-fresh sauce that combines olive oil, garlic, basil and a touch of salt. Pistou is an essential accompaniment to the Provençal vegetable soup of the same name, and does double duty as a perfect sauce for fresh homemade pasta or as a sauce for flavouring whole roasted fish. Unlike the Italian pesto, this sauce does not contain pine nuts or cheese. Each summer I make sure that my garden's basil crop is abundant and bottle that summertime flavour, I always keep small containers of this simple sauce in the freezer. Pistou can be prepared in the food processor, but the sauce will be superior in texture and flavour if prepared by hand.

> 4 plump fresh garlic cloves, halved, germ removed, and finely chopped
> Fine sea salt to taste
> 2 large bunches of fresh basil leaves and flowers
> 125 ml (4 fl oz) extra-virgin olive oil

1. Degerm the garlic: peel and cut the garlic in half. If there is a green, sprout-like 'germ' running through the centre of the garlic, remove and discard it. Finely chop the garlic.

BY HAND: Place the garlic and salt in a mortar and mash with a pestle to form a paste. Add the basil little by little, pounding and turning the pestle with a grinding motion to form a paste. Slowly add the oil, drop by drop, until all the oil has been used and the paste is homogeneous. Taste for seasoning. Stir again before serving.

IN A FOOD PROCESSOR: Place the finely chopped garlic, salt and basil in the bowl of a food processor and process to a paste. Add the oil, and process again. Taste for seasoning. Stir again before serving.

2. Transfer to a small bowl. Serve immediately. (The sauce can be stored, covered and refrigerated, for 1 day or frozen for up to 6 months.) Bring to room temperature, and stir again before serving.

MAKES ABOUT 175 ML (6 FL OZ) SAUCE

I used to love the way everyone talked about food as if it were
one of the most important things in life. And, of course, it is. Without it we would die.
Each of us eats about one thousand meals a year. It is my belief that we should try
and make as many of these meals as we can truly memorable.

ROBERT CARRIER

FRESH HERB SAUCE FOR
MEATS, POULTRY, FISH & VEGETABLES

Fresh herb sauce, or *sauce verte*, is a versatile blend of fresh herbs enhanced with the tang of capers, vinegar and mustard, and the lemony fresh flavour of extra-virgin olive oil. For oil, I prefer one of the fine offerings from the region of Les Baux, near Arles, such as the incomparable oil from the Coopérative Oleicole de la Vallée des Baux in Mausanne-les-Alpilles. I use *sauce verte* as I would mayonnaise, over poached or roasted fish, or leftover roast chicken, lamb, or beef.

2 tablespoons sherry vinegar
Fine sea salt to taste
2 tablespoons Dijon mustard
Small handful of mixed fresh herbs and greens, such as sorrel, parsley, rocket, mint
  and tarragon (carefully destemmed)
6 tablespoons extra-virgin olive oil
2 tablespoons capers, finely chopped

1. In a small bowl, whisk together the vinegar, salt and mustard. Set aside.
2. Using sharp scissors or a large chef's knife, finely chop the leaves of the herbs. Set aside.
3. In the bowl of a food processor, combine all the ingredients and process until well blended. Taste for seasoning. Transfer to a small bowl. Serve immediately. (The sauce can be refrigerated, well sealed, for up to 2 days. To serve, bring to room temperature and stir once again.)

MAKES ABOUT 250 ML (8 FL OZ) SAUCE

DOUBLE VINEGAR VINAIGRETTE

Few sauces I make inspire more compliments than my vinaigrette, a recipe that's certainly proves that less is more. The use of two different kinds of vinegar produces a rich well-rounded flavour. Red wine vinegar contributes colour and robustness. Sherry vinegar adds finesse, perfume and a certain lightness. A vinaigrette of one part vinegar and four parts olive oil, seasoned judiciously with salt and pepper, works magic.

> 2 tablespoons best-quality red wine vinegar
> 2 tablespoons best-quality sherry vinegar
> Fine sea salt to taste
> 250 ml (8 fl oz) extra-virgin olive oil
> Freshly ground black pepper to taste

1. Place the vinegars and salt in a bottle. Cover and shake to blend.
2. Add the oil and shake to blend. Taste for seasoning.
3. The vinaigrette can be stored at room temperature or in the refrigerator up to one week. Shake again at serving time.

MAKES ABOUT 250 ML (8 FL OZ) VINAIGRETTE

∽ AS OIL AND VINEGAR BATTLE IT OUT ∾ A vinaigrette is actually a 'short-term' emulsion, and hence a cousin of such celebrated sauces as béarnaise, hollandaise and its counterpart, mayonnaise, which is always served cold. It is short-term because if left to stand for a period of time, the oil and vinegar will separate. That's logical, since the basic principle linking these sauces is their dependence on a blending of substances that normally 'repel' one another. The easiest example, in the case of the vinaigrette, is oil and water (the vinegar). Even the expression 'they go together like oil and water', to denote two people or things that don't go well together, gives an idea of what kind of relationship must be established.

Classically, the ratios for vinaigrette are comparable to that of mayonnaise, meaning one part vinegar to three of oil. When the oil and vinegar are shaken together, the emulsion holds, but only temporarily. But it does not result in a thick vinaigrette that bathes salad greens in flavour and glossy shine. In fact, it is the addition of other ingredients, namely garlic or other onion flavourings, or mustard to the equation that create a thicker vinaigrette. Chemically, the onions separate the oil and make it a weaker opponent for the vinegar. This leaves more freedom in deciding which ratios of oil to vinegar make the most agreeable tasting vinaigrette. For instance, in my Chanteduc Winter Salad (page 56) I've created a special vinaigrette of equal parts of oil and lemon to be blended into a salad of chicory and Parmesan. I especially like the tanginess of lemon to balance the creamy smoothness of the olive oil.

PRESERVED LEMONS

Preserved lemons are a staple of North-African cuisine, where cooks from Morocco, Tunisia and Algeria use the soft tangy fruit in *tagines*, lamb and chicken dishes. In Provence, where the North-African population is substantial, everything from preserved lemons to couscous and giant bundles of fresh coriander can readily be found at local markets.

The process of preserving a lemon transforms the texture so it is soft and yielding. Even more amazing is the change in taste: pure lemon, removed of any bitter or acrid flavouring, with the added dimension of a pickled flavour. Probably the most vital aspect of properly preserved lemons is to take care to submerge them fully in the oil before storing. Though the initial week of marinating in salt and juices does radically transform the lemon, the period afterwards will mellow and define the final result.

I keep the lemons on hand to chop them finely and toss with couscous, to slip inside a whole roasted fish, and to flavour Chanteduc Rabbit with Garlic & Preserved Lemons (page 245). Any of the distinctive full-flavoured preserving liquid that remains in the jar can be used to flavour olives (page 46), to add sparingly to vinaigrettes, or in place of oil in seasoning fish or poultry.

2 lemons, preferably organic
75 g (2½ oz) coarse sea salt
125 ml (4 fl oz) freshly squeezed lemon juice
About 125 ml (4 fl oz) extra-virgin olive oil

1. Scrub the lemons and dry them well. Cut each lemon lengthwise into 8 wedges.
2. In a bowl, toss the lemon wedges, salt and lemon juice to coat the fruit evenly. Transfer to 500 ml (16 fl oz) glass container with a non-metal lid. Close the container tightly and let the lemons ripen at room temperature for 7 days. Shake daily to distribute the salt and juices evenly.
3. To store, add olive oil to cover and refrigerate for up to 6 months. To use, bring to room temperature.

MAKES ABOUT 500 ML (16 FL OZ) PRESERVED LEMONS

HARISSA: SPICY RED PEPPER SAUCE

Very spicy and highly aromatic, *harissa* is a popular North-African relish that is used to season olives, can be thinned with olive oil and lemon juice to flavour couscous, or can be used to brush on meats or poultry for grilling. Today, *harissa* shows up on some of the finest menus in France: Parisian chef Joël Robuchon prepares a spicy coating for roast lamb, while chef Alain Passard serves a dab of it with his roasted baby pig. In Provence, *harissa* appears everywhere: markets sell a particularly spicy cayenne pepper *piment pour harissa* and the relish can easily be found in supermarkets sold by the tube, much like tomato concentrate. Recipes for *harissa* vary from country to country – some add coriander or caraway, others create a blend of garlic, red pepper, basil, and oil. Some mix only coriander and cumin. My favorite is a simple blend of chilli peppers, cumin, oil, and a touch of salt. I don't store it as a relish, but prepare it fresh each time I serve it.

EQUIPMENT: An electric spice mill

3 tablespoons cumin seeds
2 tablespoons cayenne pepper
Fine sea salt to taste
2 tablespoons extra-virgin olive oil

Place the cumin in a spice mill and grind to a fine powder. In a small bowl combine the cumin, cayenne, and a pinch of salt. Toss to blend evenly. Slowly add the olive oil and whisk to blend. Taste for seasoning. Use to season couscous, brush on grilled meats or poultry, or to season olives.

ABOUT 6 TABLESPOONS SAUCE

POTAGER STOCK

While I always have chicken stock on hand, I also like to make a herbal stock from the garden during the warmer months. The stock is lighter than chicken stock and full of the varied herbal flavours of the garden. I use it as I would any poultry stock, as an ideal base for soups.

4 leeks, cleaned and chopped
4 carrots, scrubbed and chopped
4 turnips, scrubbed and chopped
4 celery stalks, cleaned and chopped
4 onions, halved but not peeled
1 head of garlic, halved but not peeled
2 tomatoes, halved and seeded
2 large bunches of flat-leaf parsley
1 large bunch of thyme
1 large bunch of rosemary
2 bay leaves
6 black peppercorns
4 litres (7 pints) water

1. In an 8 litre (14 pint) stock pot, combine all the ingredients. Bring to the boil, reduce the heat and simmer, uncovered, for 1½ hours.
2. Strain the stock, pressing out as much moisture as possible from the vegetables. Discard the vegetables and herbs.
3. The stock may be refrigerated, covered, for 2 to 3 days or frozen up to 2 months.

MAKES ABOUT 2.5 LITRES (4¼ PINTS)

KEEP THE SKIN ON! When I saw my first batch of stock bubbling way in one of Paris's finer restaurants, I was shocked to see a few onion halves floating around the top. Actually, it wasn't the onions that shocked me, any good stock has to begin with an array of fresh aromatic vegetables and flavourings. What surprised me was the skin still intact on the onions. Thinking it impossible that a French cook would have accidentally or, God forbid, carelessly, thrown the onions in with the stock, I had to ask. In fact, as was explained to me, the skin imparts its colour to the stock as it cooks without adding any bitterness. The purpose of the onion, therefore, is actually twofold, the flesh perfumes the stock while the skin adds richness to the colour. To make a stock that has a lighter flavour of onion, halve the onions (skin and all) and sweat them before adding to the stock. Pre-cooking them will take out some of the strong flavour.

CHICKEN STOCK

This is my light freshly flavoured chicken stock, which I always have to hand in the freezer. It is a way to cut down on cooking time and to enrich my larder, enlarging my repertoire on days I don't have much time to cook. And I adore the way my house smells when the stock is simmering away. Remember not to peel the onion: the onion skin will impart a pleasant colour to the stock.

2 kg (4 lb) chicken parts (necks, wings and feet), rinsed
Sea salt to taste
1 large onion, unpeeled but halved, each half stuck with a clove
3 plump fresh garlic cloves
Bouquet garni: Several parsley stems, celery leaves, bay leaves and sprigs of thyme, wrapped in the green part of a leek, tied in a bundle with string
4 large carrots, peeled
4 leeks, white and tender green part, trimmed, well rinsed
4 whole black peppercorns

1. In the base of a large pasta pot with a built-in colander, combine the chicken parts, 1 tablespoon of salt and cold water to cover. Bring to the boil over high heat, skimming off any impurities that rise to the surface. With a slotted spoon, transfer the trimming to a large sieve. Rinse, drain and set aside. Discard the blanching liquid.

2. Rinse out the pot. Place the colander in the pot. Add the blanched trimmings and all the remaining ingredients. Add cold water to cover and, uncovered, bring just to a simmer over moderately high heat. Skim off any impurities that rise to the surface. Cook at the gentlest possible simmer for 3 hours, skimming as necessary.

3. If using a pot with a built-in colander, lift out the colander, discarding the solids. If not using a built-in colander, line a fine-mesh sieve with dampened cheesecloth and set over a large bowl. Ladle – do not pour – the liquid into the bowl. (Do not pour, for all the impurities remain at the bottom and make for a cloudy stock.) Measure. If it exceeds 3 litres (5 pints), return to moderate heat and reduce.

Bouquet garni is an essential ingredient in the Provençal kitchen.

MAKES ABOUT 2 LITRES (3½ PINTS) LIGHT STOCK

TIPS FOR FINER STOCK ᴔ A few tips on how to make a clear full-flavoured stock:

- Do not cover the stock pot. Impurities will continue to rise to the surface as it cooks and should be skimmed off regularly.
- Once the stock is cooked, strain before cooling. Allowing to cool with vegetables and herbs may darken and cloud the stock.

STRAINING TIP ᴔ I always make my stocks in a large stainless pasta cooking pot with a built-in colander. When it comes time to strain the stock, you simply need to lift out the strainer and much of the straining has been done for you. I then pass this liquid through cheesecloth and allow the stock to cool overnight so it can be fully defatted.

THOUGHTS ON BLANCHING ᴔ When preparing any poultry stock, I always blanch the chicken parts first in boiling water. This rids the chicken of excess fat, and, more importantly, helps you begin with very clean ingredients.

RAS AL HANOUT

Ras al Hanout, which translates as 'best in the shop,' is a popular Middle Eastern blend of spices traditionally used to flavour soups, couscous, and stewlike *tagines.* In France, the spice is usually found ready ground. But one Sunday while visiting the food and flea market in the nearby village of Jonquières, I found a marvellous whole-spice mix at a colourful Moroccan food stand, ready for grinding at home. It's a heady, deliciously perfumed mix, one that I use readily to season rabbit stews, sprinkle on couscous, or add a dash to olives tossed with spicy *Harissa* (page 320).

EQUIPMENT: A spice grinder

½ cinnamon stick
Small piece dried ginger, about the size of a fingernail
1 teaspoon ground turmeric
1 teaspoon coriander seeds
1 teaspoon allspice
1 teaspoon cumin seeds
1 teaspoon caraway seeds
1 teaspoon fennel seeds
1 teaspoon whole black peppercorns
1 teaspoon whole white peppercorns
1 teaspoon whole cloves

Combine the ingredients in a spice grinder and grind to a fine powder. (This may have to be done in batches.) Transfer the ground spices to an airtight spice jar. Store in a cool, dry, dark spot for up to six months.

ABOUT 3 TABLESPOONS

TOMATO SAUCE

This is my idea of what a homemade tomato sauce should be: rich, elegant, smooth and tasting of fresh herbs. I sometimes double the recipe, so there's always some in my freezer for those days I don't have time to cook.

2 tablespoons extra-virgin olive oil

1 small onion, finely chopped

3 plump fresh garlic cloves, finely chopped

Sea salt to taste

One 765-g (28-oz) can of peeled plum tomatoes in juice, or one 765 g (28-oz) can of crushed tomatoes in a purée

Bouquet garni: several sprigs of fresh parsley, bay leaves, and celery leaves, tied in a bundle with string

1. In a large unheated saucepan, combine the oil, onion, garlic and salt, and stir to coat with oil. Cook over moderate heat, just until the garlic turns golden but does not brown, 2 to 3 minutes.

2. If using whole canned tomatoes, place a food mill over the frying pan and purée the tomatoes directly into it. Crushed tomatoes can be added directly from the can. Add the bouquet garni, stir to blend and simmer, uncovered, until the sauce begins to thicken, about 15 minutes. For a thicker sauce, for pizzas and toppings, cook for 5 minutes more. Taste for seasoning. Remove and discard the bouquet garni.

3. The sauce may used immediately, stored in the refrigerator (well sealed) for up to 2 days, or frozen up to 2 months. If small quantities of sauce will be needed for pizzas or other toppings, freeze in ice cube trays. To serve, bring to room temperature and stir once again.

MAKES ABOUT 750 ML (27 FL OZ)

SALT-CURED BLACK OLIVES

In Provence, salt-cured olives are known as *olives piquées* because the cure consists of pricking the olives with a small fork to allow the salt to penetrate the fruit quickly and rid it of its natural bitterness. We pick our ripe wrinkled black olives – of the tanche variety – at Christmas time, which usually coincides with the first freeze.

I never quite understood the necessity of the 'first freeze' until one farmer suggested that I place the olives in the freezer so they would cure more quickly. Only then did I realize that the freezing actually managed to speed up the ripening process of the fruit (the opposite being true of days of sunshine), which would thus speed up the curing of the olive. That year we had newly cured olives within just 3 or 4 days! The first year that I prepared these I was told by everyone: 'These don't keep long.' But no one would tell me how long was long. After preparing them, I soon discovered that salt-cured olives don't spoil: their fresh vibrant olive flavour simply fades in about 6 months.

Not coincidentally, this coincides with the time that the brine-cured olives are just about ready for eating. Smart, clever folks those farmers of days past! Now I generally store a portion of my uncured crop in the freezer, and pull the olives out whenever my salt-cured stock runs out.

Geographically, our olive trees lie in the Government-defined zone for *Olives de Nyons*. Nyons olives were recently awarded an Appellation d'Origine Contrôlée, the only olive in France to boast that honour. The AOC – much like the regulations concerning wine – serves as a standard of excellence for French agriculture.

> 1 kg (2 lb) ripe uncured black olives
> 100 g (3½ oz) coarse sea salt
> 6 branches of fresh thyme
> 6 branches of fresh rosemary
> 6 fresh or dried bay leaves
> Several teaspoons extra-virgin olive oil
>
> OPTIONAL FLAVOURINGS
> Fresh thyme
> Fresh rosemary
> Fresh bay leaves
> Extra-virgin olive oil
> Whole black peppercorns
> Red wine vinegar
> Fresh finely chopped garlic
> Grated zest of a lemon
> Grated zest of an orange
> Hot red chilli peppers

1. Do not wash the olives. If there are any leaves or stems still attached, remove and discard them. With a small seafood fork or a toothpick, prick the olives three or four times all over, piercing all the way to the centre. (The pricking allows the fruit quickly to absorb the salt all the way to the stone.)

2. Place in a large shallow bowl and add the salt. Toss with your hands to coat with salt. Add the thyme, rosemary and bay leaves and toss again. Leave the olives uncovered, at room temperature, tossing them once or twice a day. After 3 or 4 days, sample one. If it tastes bitter, cure for several more days. By this time the olives should have absorbed much of the salt. A small bit of clear brine may form at the bottom of the bowl. Leave it there, for the olives will eventually absorb the brine.

3. Transfer the olives and any brine to small glass jars. Sprinkle with a teaspoon or so of olive oil, just enough to moisten the olives. Seal. (Do not add additional flavourings at this time. These will mask the olives' fresh vibrant flavour.) Cover the jars and store in a dark place, at room temperature, for up to 6 months.

4. At serving time, season to taste with any of the optional flavourings. Toss to distribute the flavours and serve.

MAKES ABOUT 1 KG (2 LB) OLIVES

THE MASON'S BRINE-CURED BLACK OLIVES

A huge jar of brine-cured black olives sits on the counter in my kitchen in Provence year round, curing away in a inky brine that is filled with history. Our mason, Jean-Claude Tricart and his wife, Colette, were the first of our friends to serve us their own cured olives. When it came time to cure my own ripe olives, the Tricarts kindly gave me a wine bottle filled with brine that had been in their family for years. I now proudly pass a bit of my brine on – much like a 'mother' of vinegar – to any-one who asks. Actually, you can begin with a simple brine of water and 10 per cent salt, which is the standard Provençal recipe for curing the olives we harvest in December.

The ripe olives are simply placed in brine until they are edible, a curing process that takes several weeks to several months, depending upon the ripeness and size of the olives. Unlike salt-cured olives, which are pricked with a fork to allow the salt to penetrate the meat of the olive, brine-cured olives are cured submerged in brine. Once cured, the olives can be kept for about one year. Longer than that, they begin to lose flavour and vitality. This is similar to the curing process used in the tiny Niçoise olives from Nice.

> About 1 kg (2 lb) ripe uncured black olives
> About 100 g (3½ oz) fine sea salt
> 1 litre (1¾ pints) water
>
> OPTIONAL FLAVOURINGS
> Fresh thyme
> Fresh rosemary
> Fresh bay leaves
> Extra-virgin olive oil
> Whole black peppercorns
> Red wine vinegar
> Fresh finely chopped garlic
> Grated zest of a lemon
> Grated zest of an orange
> Hot red chilli peppers

1. Do not wash the olives. If there are any leaves or stems still attached, remove and discard them.
2. In a large crock, combine the salt and the water and stir to dissolve. Add the olives, cover and set aside in a cool spot for several months, stirring from time to time. They can be covered with a small plate, to keep them all immersed in the brine. A scum will form on top, but it is harmless and can be discarded as the olives are used. When starting with a fresh brine, the olives will take 3 to 4 months of curing before they are edible. Once

cured, they can be kept indefinitely. Never discard the salt brine, which will become black and inky. It can be used indefinitely, year after year. Do not add any seasonings other than salt and water to the brine. For specific flavourings, add those at serving time.
3. To serve, remove the olives from the brine with a slotted spoon or a specially designed perforated wooden ladle. Taste the olives. If they are excessively salty, they can be rinsed or soaked in cold water to remove some of the saltiness. Serve as they are, or season with any of the optional seasonings noted above.

MAKES ABOUT 1 KG (2 LB) OLIVES

Petite olives à piquer, *tiny fresh ripe olives, ready for curing in salt.*

SALT-CURED ANCHOVIES

Pungent, with the rich salty flavours of the sea, salt-cured anchovies are essential to my family's larder. Anchovies deepen the flavour of pasta sauces, provide an essential taste to *La Broufade*: Beef & White Wine Daube from Arles (page 256), and are delicious all on their own, on top of a slice of freshly grilled bread.

1 kg (2 lb) very fresh anchovies
1 kg (2 lb) coarse sea salt
Several sprigs of fresh thyme
Several bay leaves, preferably fresh

1. Quickly rinse (do not wash or soak) the anchovies. Individually head and gut the fish by holding each fish firmly just beneath the head. Discard the head and entrails.
2. Place a thick layer of salt on the bottom of a large preserving jar. Place a layer of anchovies – side by side – on top the salt. Sprinkle a thin layer of salt on top. Continue until all the anchovies and salt have been used. Every layer or so, add several sprigs of fresh thyme and bay leaf. Cover securely. A brine will form as the anchovies absorb the salt and are cured.
3. The anchovies are ready to eat in about 2 weeks and can be stored, indefinitely, in a cool dark spot. Properly cured anchovies are a deep mahogany colour, much like ham. To eat, simply fillet the anchovies and use in any dish calling for cured anchovies.

MAKES ABOUT 2 LITRES (3½ PINTS)

Beekeeper and honey maker Christine Poquet at her stand outside the post office at the Vaison market.

❧ **A TASTE OF HONEY** ❧ I grew up on thin, runny supermarket honey, often a not-too-fragrant blend of clover, lemon, orange and wild flowers. So the sweet spread never intrigued me – until I discovered the thick, creamy raw honey of Provence. I use distinctly flavoured single-flower honeys such as lavender, rosemary, orange blossom, clover and acacia honey for flavouring teas, on toast with butter, or simply eaten from the spoon by themselves. For cooking, I reach for the stronger varieties, such as buckwheat and chestnut. Thyme and rosemary honeys are also excellent for recipes that rely heavily on the juxtaposition of sweet and salty, for example, with pork or ham.

To restore creamy honey to its liquid state for easier measuring and cooking, simply place the jar in tepid water. Avoid hot water because the exposure to extreme temperature can ruin the composition and flavour. Like most fine food, honey does not remain at its peak forever. Buy it in small jars and use within a year, for best flavour and fragrance.

I feel a recipe is only a theme,
which an intelligent cook can play each time with a variation.
MADAME BENOIT

BAKED FRUIT *&* HONEY WITH BEAUMES DE VENISE

This is a favourite summer dessert at Chanteduc. When I fire up my wood-burning oven to make dinner, I frequently slip in some fresh fruits to bake in the residual heat while I serve the main course. Sometimes, I use only fresh purple figs, other times I use a combination of stoned summer fruits, such as sliced peaches, apricots, nectarines and plums, with a few raspberries and blueberries added for colour and texture. Here, the sweet, honey-like flavour of Muscat de Beaumes-de-Venise – a rich fortified wine – is the perfect foil for summer fruits and honey.

EQUIPMENT: One 27-cm (10½-in) round porcelain baking dish

1 tablespoon unsalted butter, at room temperature
1.5 kg (3 lb) mixed fresh fruits, such as figs, peaches, nectarines, apricots, plums,
blueberries and raspberries
2 tablespoons raw honey, heated gently to soften
4 tablespoons Muscat de Beaumes-de-Venise (or see Wine Suggestions for variations)

1. Preheat the oven to 190°C/375°F/gas mark 5.
2. Generously butter the baking dish. If using a mixture of stoned fruits, halve them and layer them, slightly overlapping and cut side up, in the dish. Scatter the mixed berries on top. Drizzle with the honey and the Muscat de Beaumes-de-Venise. Place in the centre of the oven and bake until the fruits are soft, plump, and tender, about 30 minutes. Remove from the oven, drizzle with the remaining Muscat de Beaumes-de-Venise, and serve, accompanied by Lavender Honey Ice Cream (page 279).

SERVES 4-6

WINE SUGGESTIONS: My favourite muscats come from the vineyards of Domaine de Coyeaux and Domaine Durban in the nearby village of Beaumes-de-Venise. Varied sweet fortified wines could be served here, including a French Banuyls, an Italian moscato, or a dark Spanish sherry such as a Gonzalez Byass Oloroso Dulce, Soldera 1847.

CHUNKY PEACH ICE CREAM

Peach trees are plentiful in Provence, but difficult to grow on our land. We have a single wild peach, called *pêche de vigne* since it traditionally sprouted up between the vines. Every peach tree at Chanteduc has been short-lived but dearly loved. One September a friend staying at the house faxed me daily 'peach reports' to Paris. She spoke lovingly to the ripening fruit on the beautiful white-fleshed *pêche blanche* tree, begging it not to fall until I arrived. That year, we had a bumper crop! When peaches are in season, this is a sublime way to enjoy them. This ice cream is light and makes best use of the fragile, fleeting peach flavour by using chunks of the fruit rather than turning it into a purée.

EQUIPMENT: One 1-litre (1¾-pint) capacity ice cream maker

1 kg (2 lb) ripe peaches (6 to 8)
2 tablespoons fresh lemon juice
60 g (2 oz) sugar
250 ml (8 fl oz) double cream

1. In a large pot of boiling water, blanch the peaches for several seconds. Transfer to a colander to drain. Rinse quickly with cold water to stop the cooking and make the fruit easier to peel. Peel, halve and stone the peaches. Place the peach halves in a bowl and crush them with your hands until no large clumps remain; do not purée. You should have about 1 litre (1¾ pints) of pulp.
2. Add the lemon juice and sugar and stir to blend and to dissolve the sugar. Taste for sweetness. Cover with plastic wrap and refrigerate until well chilled, for several hours, or overnight.
3. When the peach mixture is thoroughly chilled, stir in the double cream. Transfer to an ice cream maker and freeze according to manufacturer's instructions.

MAKES ABOUT 1 LITRE (1¾ PINTS) ICE CREAM

⌁ **A PEACHY STORY** ↝ My favourite peach story involves Madame Récamier, a renowned beauty who hosted one of Paris's most fashionable salons. She was depicted by the likes of such celebrated painters as Jacques Louis David and Ingres, at the beginning of the nineteenth century. She fell sick and refused to eat anything. Anything? When she was offered peaches drizzled with syrup and cream, she apparently ate every last bite and regained her strength and appetite soon after.

*Chanteduc's 'sunset terrace' was designed to capture the cool of the day
and the glorious evening sunsets to the west.*

MOSTARDA: FIG & PRUNE CHUTNEY

Mostarda is an Italian fruit chutney, often pickled fruit spiced with hot mustard oil, thus the name. Traditionally, it is served as an accompaniment to soft cheese, such as a Mascarpone. One of the best versions I ever sampled was at Pina Bongiovanni's Osteria dell'Unione in the Piedmont, where she served a thick slice of firm Toma cheese (made from a blend of goats' and sheep's milk), with her puckery, sweet-and-sour fruit mostarda. This is my version, one I serve with roast pork, goose or duck, or with a tray of oatmeal biscuits (page 173) and Roquefort cheese.

500 g (1 lb) stoned prunes
500 g (1 lb) stoned and stemmed dried figs or stoned dried apricots, quartered
500 ml (16 fl oz) best-quality red wine vinegar
2 tablespoons creamy rosemary or thyme honey, or to taste
2 whole cinnamon sticks

1. In a large saucepan, combine all the ingredients. Stir to blend, cover and cook over lowest possible heat until most of the liquid has been absorbed and the fruit is soft and almost falling apart, with a thin veil of liquid still remaining, 45 minutes to 1 hour. Do not allow the mixture to reduce to a thick purée. Stir frequently to blend and break down the fruits and to avoid scorching the pan. Remove and discard the cinnamon stick. Cool thoroughly.
2. Store in a covered container in the refrigerator for up to 1 month. Remove from the refrigerator about 30 minutes before serving.

MAKES ABOUT 1 LITRE (1¾ PINTS) MOSTARDA

CHANTAL'S BACHELOR'S CONFITURE

This *confiture de garçon* or batchelor's preserve is a blend of fruits that ripen over time in a mixture of sugar, alcohol, and water, and is sampled either as dessert itself or, much like a liqueur, after a meal. Our winemaker's wife, Chantal Combe, makes one of the best versions I've ever tasted. She limits her choice of fruits to those with stones, which tend to be a bit firmer and break down less than softer fruits like strawberries or raspberries. The stones also impart a wonderful nutty flavour. You can make the preserve all at once, or add fruits as they come into season. While most recipes are made with sugar and alcohol, Chantal prepares hers with sugar syrup, producing a clear, unclouded liquid and an even distribution of sugar.

1 kg (2 lb) combination of mixed fresh fruits with stones, preferably a colourful
   mixture of cherries, plums, peaches, nectarines, apricots and grapes
About 1 litre (1¾ pints) sugar syrup (see below), cooled
About 1 litre (1¾ pints) clear eau-de-vie or vodka

1. In a large wide-mouthed jar, begin layering the fruit in a colourful pattern. Leave cherries and grapes whole, and halve or quarter the other fruits. Do not peel the fruits and do not discard the stones. If, in halving or quartering the fruit, the stone detaches from the fruit, simply arrange the stones along with the fruit in the jar. Pour equal portions of the cooled sugar syrup and alcohol over the fruit.
2. Cover securely with plastic wrap and weight so the fruit is totally immersed in liquid. Set aside in a cool, dry place for at least 2 months. As the confiture ripens, the liquid will change from a clear to rose colour. Additional fruit can be, if you wish, added as they come into season.
3. To serve, ladle a few fruits into a small bowl along with a little bit of liquid, as an after-dinner drink. Or, serve over ice cream, sorbet or cake.

MAKES ABOUT 1 KG (2 LB)

CLASSIC SUGAR SYRUP

1 kg (2 lb) sugar
1 litre (1¾ pints) water

In a large saucepan combine the sugar and water. Bring to a boil over high heat, stirring with a wooden spoon until all the sugar is dissolved. Set aside to cool. The sugar syrup can be stored, carefully sealed and refrigerated, for up to two weeks.

FRESH CHERRY WINE

Come May, our five cherry trees produce more cherries than we know what to do with. So I spend hours turning the fresh plump vermilion fruit into cherry wine or pickled cherries, a few batches for the freezer, and of course cherry jam.

This is an easy homemade liqueur, filled with the vibrant dense flavour of cherries. Serve it in tiny glasses at the end of a meal, ideally with a cherry dessert alongside.

> 1 kg (2 lb) ripe sweet cherries
> 1 plump moist vanilla bean, halved
> 200 g (7 oz) sugar
> Clear eau-de-vie or vodka
> Red wine, such as a simple Côtes-du-Rhône

1. Stone the cherries, reserving the stones. Combine the cherries, stones, vanilla bean and sugar in a 3-litre (5-pint) heavy-bottomed saucepan. Simmer over moderate heat, stirring from time to time, for 30 minutes. The mixture will be dark and syrupy.

2. Meanwhile, place a large sieve over a bowl and line the sieve with dampened cheese-cloth. Pour the cherries and syrup into the sieve to strain the juice. Press down on the cherries to extract every bit of the juice you can. (The quantity of juice will vary according to the size and ripeness of the cherries.) Discard the cherries and vanilla. Measure the strained liquid into a dry sterilized bottle.

3. For each 125 ml (4 fl oz) of juice, add 125 ml (4 fl oz) of eau-de-vie or vodka. Cork and set aside to macerate for 1 week.

4. For each 125 ml (4 fl oz) of liquid, add 250 ml (8 fl oz) of red wine. Cork and allow to age for 2 months before sampling.

5. Use within 1 year. After that time, the delicate cherry flavour will fade.

MAKES ABOUT 1 LITRE (1¾ PINTS) CHERRY WINE

FACING PHOTOGRAPH: *A variation of Chantal's Bachelor's Confiture, prepared with wild cherry plums.*

Local pears, ready for preserving or for eating out of hand.

᭲ **PLANT PEARS FOR YOUR HEIRS** ᭳ The expression refers to the fact that it can take a pear tree up to 9 years to bear fruit. Patience, patience!

᭲ **ON APPLES AND PEARS** ᭳ Once you come to know the different varieties of apples and pears, you will have a sense of how they behave when cooked. Golden Delicious, Granny Smith and Discovery are firm-fleshed varieties that offer an intense apple flavour and a pleasant tang. They also hold their shape when cooked. McIntosh tend to fall apart, but a few can be tossed into a mixture of firm-fleshed varieties to add dimension to the flavour. For pears, the Bartlett and Bosc are the most versatile: they not only hold their shape during cooking, they impart a distinctive flavour. The Anjou, though less firm, provides plenty of sweet juice for pies and tarts.

᭲ **A TEST FOR RIPENESS** ᭳ What's the best way to tell if a pear is ripe? We tend to poke at the fruit, seeking in the flesh a tender spot, a softness. This softness, however, can most often mean that it's already too late. Instead, pull on the stem of the pear. When ripe, the stem should provide little resistance to pressure.

ELI'S APPLE CRISP

Early one November my friend Eli Zabar brought over a crate full of different varieties of apples from his orchard in Provence. The sky that day was a brilliant blue, a few golden leaves were still clinging to the vines in our vineyards and the scent of a warming apple dessert wafting through my kitchen seemed like an ideal way to end a perfect autumn Saturday.

Prepare this with a good tangy cooking apple, and if possible, combine several varieties – such as Granny Smith, McIntosh and Fuji – for a more complex depth of flavour and texture. This is a quick easy appealing and inexpensive dessert, and you don't have to make pastry!

EQUIPMENT: One 27-cm (10½-in) baking dish

> Unsalted butter for preparing the baking dish
> 45 g (1½ oz) unsalted butter
> 1 kg (2 lb) cooking apples, peeled, cored and cut lengthwise into 8 even wedges
> 2 tablespoons freshly squeezed lemon juice
> ½ teaspoon ground cinnamon
> 1½ teaspoons pure vanilla extract
> 2 large eggs, at room temperature
> 75 g (2½ oz) sugar
> 250 ml (8 fl oz) crème fraîche or double cream

1. Preheat the oven to 200°C/400°F/gas mark 6.
2. Generously butter the bottom and sides of the baking dish. Set aside.
3. In a large frying pan, combine the butter, apples, lemon juice and ¼ teaspoon cinnamon and cook just until soft, about 7 minutes. Stir in ½ teaspoon of vanilla extract.
4. Transfer the apples to the baking dish, evening them into a single layer with a spatula.
5. In a large bowl, combine the eggs and sugar and whisk until well blended. Add the cream, the remaining vanilla extract and cinnamon. Whisk to blend and pour over the apples in the baking dish.
6. Place the baking dish in the centre of the oven and bake until the top is a deep golden-brown, 30 to 45 minutes. Do not underbake, or the results will be soggy, rather than crisp.
7. Serve cut into wedges, accompanied by a dollop of crème fraîche. The dessert is best served the day it is made, as the delicate flavours will fade.

SERVES 8

*A gap in the hedge gave a view into the gardens: a border of jasmine, pansies,
and verbena which ran along the wide path was interplanted with fragrant wallflowers
the faded rose of old Cordoba leather. A long green hole snaking across the gravel drive
sent up every few yards a vertical, prismatic fan, and the multicoloured drops
showered over the flowers in a perfumed cloud.*

MARCEL PROUST

*I doubt the world holds for anyone a more soul-stirring surprise
than the first adventure with ice cream.*

HEYWOOD BROUN

FRESH LEMON VERBENA ICE CREAM

One of the earliest signs of spring at Chanteduc is the sight of the first bright green shoots of lemon verbena – or verveine – sprouting from this hearty perennial's stalky frame. Within weeks they grow into long pointed rough-textured leaves with an intense, lemony perfume. Throughout the spring and summer, I use lemon verbena leaves liberally, preparing refreshing and lightly sedative herbal teas, or infusions, as well as this popular summer ice cream. The dessert is also delicious prepared with fresh mint, or with less traditional 'sweet' herbs, such as thyme or rosemary.

500 ml (16 fl oz) double cream
250 ml (8 fl oz) whole milk
125 g (4 oz) sugar
60 fresh lemon verbena leaves

1. In a large saucepan, combine the cream, milk, sugar and verbena leaves and place over moderate heat just until tiny bubbles form around the edges of the pan. Remove from the heat, cover and let steep for 1 hour.
2. Strain through a fine-mesh sieve, discarding the verbena. Refrigerate until thoroughly chilled.
3. Transfer to an ice cream maker and freeze according to manufacturer's instructions.
4. Serve with *Croquettes*: Provençal Almond Cookies (page 284).

SERVES 4

FRESH CHEESE WITH PINE NUTS & HONEY

Soft fresh cheese drizzled with honey and sprinkled with pine nuts make a popular Mediterranean dessert. The sweet honey counters the saltiness of cheese and the meaty flavour and crunch of pine nuts add depth and texture.

At Chanteduc, I always have a variety of honeys on hand, and the market provides fresh goats'- and sheep's-milk cheese all year round. While our giant umbrella pines could supply us with tiny meaty pine nuts, I gave up after one laborious attempt to extract the tiny nuts from the cones. I decided it was a lot less bothersome simply to purchase pine nuts in town! If you don't have time to make the cheese, buy a fresh ricotta or a fresh mild goats' cheese.

EQUIPMENT: One 1.5-litre (2½-pint) perforated mould, such as a porcelain *coeur à la crème* mould, or large sieve

THE CHEESE
500 ml (16 fl oz) small-curd whole milk cottage cheese
500 ml (16 fl oz) whole-milk yogurt

GARNISH
About 125 ml (4 fl oz) strong-flavoured raw honey, such as chestnut or buckwheat
4 tablespoons pine nuts, lightly toasted and cooled

1. The day before, or early in the morning of the day you plan to serve the dessert, combine the cottage cheese and yogurt in the bowl of a food processor. Purée until completely smooth. Scoop the mixture into a the cheesecloth-lined mould or sieve set over a bowl. Cover loosely with a cloth. Set aside to drain at room temperature, until the cheese becomes dry and firm, about 12 hours. (Do not be surprised at the quantity of liquid the cheese will release.) It is ready when no more liquid drips from it. With the back of a spoon, carefully smooth out the top of the cheese. Cover and refrigerate until ready to use. (The cheese will benefit from a day's curing, to allow the flavours to develop and mellow.)

2. To serve: If you made the cheese in a perforated mould, unmould it on a chilled serving platter. If you prepared it in a cheesecloth-lined sieve, spoon the cheese into a decorative bowl. Pass honey and pine nuts, letting your guests drizzle their own toppings.

SERVES 6-8

'44'—HOMEMADE ORANGE LIQUEUR

Orange liqueur, or '44,' is one of the most traditional European homemade aperitifs. You'll find versions in Spain, Italy, and France, some made with cloves and cinnamon, some with a mix of oranges, bitter oranges, and lemons, some flavoured with coffee beans, and those sweetened with honey. The original recipe given to me called for a single orange studded with 44 coffee beans, mixed with 44 sugar cubes and a bottle of clear eau-de-vie. The mixture is then set aside for 44 days. The result is a fragrant, fruity drink, which can mixed with a bit of white wine as an aperitif or served 'as is' with dessert or as an after-meal liqueur. I found the original version too sweet for my taste, so have cut the amount of sugar in half.

EQUIPMENT: 1½-quart preserving jar with lid, thoroughly washed and dried

1 large orange, preferably organic
44 coffee beans
22 sugar cubes (or 6 tablespoons granulated sugar)
1 litre (1¾ pints) clear eau-de-vie or vodka

Thoroughly scrub and dry the orange. With the end of a sharp knife, pierce the orange all over, and insert the 44 coffee beans into the skin, embedding each bean in the orange. Place the orange in a preserving jar. Add the sugar cubes and the eau-de-vie. Cover securely. Turn the jar upside down and shake to help dissolve the sugar. Place in a cool, dry, dark spot. Shake the jar daily, until the sugar is completely dissolved. Set aside for 44 days. During this time, the liquid will turn from clear to a pale orange and will take on a lovely coffee-orange fragrance. The '44' can be stored indefinitely as is, or the liquid can be filtered and transferred to an attractive liqueur bottle. The orange and coffee beans are not consumed, and should be discarded once they lose their vigour. The '44' can be served chilled or at room temperature, added to white wine or served in tiny liqueur glasses as an accompaniment to fruit desserts or as an after-dinner drink.

MAKES ABOUT 1 LITRE (1¾ PINTS) LIQUEUR

VARIATION: In Provence, many cooks prepare their orange liqueur by piercing the orange with cloves, tying the fruit with string, then suspending it in clear glass jar partially filled with clear eau-de-vie. (The orange should never touch the alcohol.) The jar is sealed, and the aromatic oils of the orange infuse the alcohol with their fruity essence, turning the eau-de-vie a pale, glistening orange. After about one month, the orange is discarded, the aperitif is sweetened to taste and transferred to a sealed bottle.

FACING PHOTOGRAPH: *The makings of '44' – Homemade Orange Liquor, and a suspended orange variation prepared with cloves and eau-de-vie.*

GRAPES IN EAU-DE-VIE

In Provence, people preserve all manner of fruits in eau-de-vie, the powerful colourless alcohol obtained by distilling the grape skins, seeds and stems that are left over from winemaking. In the past, almost every winemaker made his own alcohol, but now the Government strictly controls its distillation. So now I preserve my fruits in good quality marc, grappa or a clear flavourless alcohol such as vodka. The fruits are served at the end of the meal as dessert or after it. The infused eau-de-vie is then served as an after dinner *digestif.* The best fruits for preserving in alcohol are cherries and grapes.

> 500 g (1 lb) Muscat grapes (or use fresh stemmed cherries)
> 1 litre (1¾ pints) marc, grappa or vodka

Rinse and pat dry the fruit. Place in a sterilized 1.5-litre (2½-pint) jar. Pour the alcohol over it. Seal the jar and allow the fruit to macerate in the liquid at least 6 weeks. During this time, turn the jar upside down from time to time to redistribute the alcohol and the natural sugars in the fruit. To serve, place several pieces of fruit in a small stemmed glass and add a few tablespoons of the fruity liquid. (Use within 1 year. After that time, the fruity flavours will fade.)

MAKES ABOUT 1.5 LITRES (2½ PINTS)

RASPBERRIES IN EAU-DE-VIE

Raspberries are one of the world's most sumptuous fruits. Nothing is more luxurious than your own raspberries floating about in a raspberry eau-de-vie, a way to double the flavour and pleasure of a fruit liqueur.

> 500 g (1 lb) fresh raspberries
> 2 raspberry leaves, if available
> 250 g (8 oz) sugar
> 500 ml (16 fl oz) raspberry eau-de-vie

Rinse and dry the raspberries. Layer the fruit and sugar in a sterilized 1.5-litre (2½-pint) jar. Pour the alcohol over the fruit. Seal the jar and allow the fruit to macerate at least 1 month in a dark, cool spot. During this time, turn the jar upside down from time to time to redistribute the alcohol and the sugars in the fruit. To serve, place several pieces of fruit in a small stemmed glass and add a few tablespoons of alcohol. Or dribble the liquid over fresh raspberry sorbet or homemade Vanilla-Bean Ice Cream (page 289), then spoon a few preserved berries over it all.

MAKES ABOUT 1.5 LITRES (2½ PINTS)

INDEX

(Page numbers in *italic* refer to illustrations.)

ABOUT THE AUTHOR

PATRICIA WELLS began her journalistic career at the *Washington Post* in the 1970s, where she worked as a copy editor and art critic. She moved to the *New York Times* in 1976, where she became a food reporter on the newly created 'Living Section'. In 1980, she moved to Paris with her journalist husband, Walter, for what they thought would be a two-year stint at the *International Herald Tribune.* Their love of France grew, and soon they knew they had come to the point of no return. Patricia went to Paris without a word of French but a hope of writing the sort of food guide that did not exist. After years of trying to convince publishers that the idea would sell, her *Food Lover's Guide to Paris* was published to rave reviews in 1984. Soon Patricia was packing her bags for points north, south, east, and west, exploring the food, vineyards, markets, artisans, and restaurateurs of France. When *The Food Lover's Guide to France* was published in 1987, the French decided to call Patricia their own, and made her restaurant critic of the newsweekly *L'Express.* She became the only female and only foreigner to have ever held that post. Recipes gathered on her tour de France became the inspiration for the classic *Bistro Cooking,* published in 1989 and translated into seven languages. The same year, the French government honoured her for contributions to French culture, awarding her the coveted Chevalier de l'Ordre des Arts et des Lettres. Her respect and admiration for French chef Joël Robuchon turned into a four-year project, out of which came *Simply French,* a book that is still among France's top-selling cookbooks. An assignment in Italy and a series of inspirational meals at casual eateries led to a two-year quest for the best of modern-day Italian trattoria fare, and became her best-selling *Patricia Wells' Trattoria,* published in 1993 and now available in six languages. During all this, Patricia nurtured another passion—Chanteduc—the farmhouse in Provence she and Walter acquired in 1984. Chanteduc soon became a refuge, a haven for the couple and their friends, as well as a dream to be pampered. Year in and year out, they have restored, rebuilt, and refurbished the old farmhouse, bringing in their own winemaker and establishing their own vineyard. *Patricia Wells at Home in Provence* is the culmination of more than a decade of life in Provence, where neighbours, merchants, friends, and family have inspired a cuisine that is rich with the textures, flavours, colour, and aroma of their adopted land.